A2 3

ARIZONA AT SEVENTY-FIVE

ARIZONA
AT SEVENTY-FIVE

THE NEXT TWENTY-FIVE YEARS

Edited by Beth Luey and Noel J. Stowe

Arizona State University Public History Program
and the
Arizona Historical Society
1987

ISBN 0-910037-24-8

Distributed by the
University of Arizona Press
1230 North Park, #102
Tucson, Arizona 85719

Library of Congress Catalog
Card Number 87-72583

CONTENTS

PREFACE AND ACKNOWLEDGMENTS

This book began as a conference commemorating the seventy-fifth anniversary of Arizona's statehood. The contributors were asked to write essays, present talks based on those essays, and then revise the essays for publication. They were to examine Arizona's history in the period of statehood, to speculate about the future of the state, and to suggest topics for historical study that have been neglected and appear promising—to set a historical agenda for the next twenty-five years.

The editors selected contributors—except those writing on historical resources—on the basis of their knowledge of western, rather than Arizona, history. Our hope was that such historians would bring a broader perspective to these issues, avoiding the parochialism that often springs up when you gather together people who work in the same field, in the same state, and who talk together frequently. The strategy was successful: the essayists have looked at Arizona in its regional and national settings and have raised new, interesting, and important questions.

Since historical study relies on the existence of historical resources—documents, artifacts, oral histories, and buildings—the editors also invited Arizona historians actively involved in the collection, preservation, and use of these resources to contribute. The final essay in this volume assesses the state's historical resources, emphasizing an evaluation of their adequacy to meet the historical agenda set by the first five writers.

The panel discussions at the conference and subsequent evaluations of the papers raised a number of topics that could not be covered in a single day—or within the page limitations we imposed. Our headnotes mention some of these topics in the hope that they will inspire future writers and conference organizers. The notes or suggestions for further reading at the end of each essay direct readers to sources of additional information.

We are greatly indebted to the contributors to this volume, who have performed a difficult job in a short time. We must also thank Jim Moss, Executive Director of the Arizona Historical Society, for his assistance in fundraising, publicity, and publication. Sharon Brockus, the Secretary of the History Department's Graduate Program, has provided countless hours of assistance and good cheer. Budge Ruffner kindly provided introductions to Arizona's former governors. Robert A. Trennert, Chair of the History Department, assisted in numerous ways.

Much of the project's success is due to the panelists who reviewed the essays and discussed them at the February 28 conference. We are most grateful to Shirley Agnos, Gerald Anton, James Ballinger, George Britton, Katherin Chase, Kathleen Ferris, Alfredo Gutiérrez, Joy Hanley, Bradford J. Luckingham, Phylis C. Martinelli, Myra Millinger, James Officer, Clinton Pattea, Gertrude Hodges Randall, Alberto Ríos, F. Arturo Rosales, Katherine Stevens, Lee S. Stith, Stewart Udall, and David Wilkins. We are also grateful to former governors Paul J. Fannin, Samuel P. Goddard, Jr., J. Howard Pyle, and Jack Williams for a lively discussion after lunch.

Finally, it is a pleasure to thank the financial contributors who made the conference and the book possible. Jack Pfister and the Salt River Project, Jack Whiteman and Empire Southwest, and John Driggs and Western Savings made the initial generous contributions that permitted us to go forward with the project. The Arizona Humanities Council awarded us both a planning grant and a general grant, and its Executive Director, Lorraine Frank, made helpful program suggestions. Additional substantial contributions came from the Arizona Department of Education, Arizona Public Service Company, Dorothy Chafin, the Flinn Foundation, Talley Industries, and United Bank. We are grateful to all of them.

ARIZONA AT SEVENTY-FIVE

INTRODUCTION

Beth Luey
Noel J. Stowe

On February 14, 1987, Arizona celebrated the seventy-fifth anniversary of its statehood. This anniversary offered an opportunity not only to look back on seventy-five years of history, but also to look forward to twenty-five years of future history. Unlike a centennial, which seems to round off an era, this anniversary appeared as an appropriate moment to look in three directions—backward, around, and ahead.

Of course, any official anniversary is an artificial point. The year 1912 was the beginning only of Arizona's present official, political incarnation. The land has been here far longer, and many of Arizona's citizens are descended from people who lived here thousands of years ago. Many have ancestors who lived on the same land when it was Spanish or Mexican, rather than U.S., territory. For some Arizonans, entering the Union was an event to be regretted; for many, it undoubtedly seemed unimportant. In fact, in 1912,

1

the parents and grandparents of most present-day Arizonans probably did not even know where Arizona was, let alone contemplate the possibility of living here.

The Meaning of Statehood

Despite its artificiality, however, the period of statehood warrants historical examination. The circumstance of statehood, simply put, is one step in a state's maturing process. In fact, in the case of Arizona, statehood came long after the maturation process got underway. In general, political acts of statehood probably represent a reality that a majority of local citizens recognized and accepted in their hearts and minds years before.

What was the consequence of becoming a state in 1912? Did it mean anything? We know it was officially celebrated at the time as big-event history with parades, speeches, bell ringing, pan clanging, and the like. Yet it was hard to perceive immediate concrete differences between 1911, 1912, and 1913. Those differences took years to manifest themselves. Demographically, the population continued to grow slowly until after World War II, when fast-paced growth began. Socially and economically, statehood had little significance. The basic social arrangements (with attendant tensions) among the primary ethnic groups had fallen into place in the 1880s and 1890s. Economic characteristics, trends, and overtones were also well ensconced before the twentieth century's second decade. Politically, though, statehood was an important threshold. It had profound meaning for Arizona in its long-term process of becoming. Statehood marks another milestone in the political bearing of outside influences.

Arizona's political history began with the Native American populations—with their efforts to cope successfully with the environment and to shape a home for themselves politically and spiritually in various niches of what is now the state. The ebb and flow of Native American arrangements on the landscape was interrupted in the sixteenth century by European invaders, such as Marcos de Niza and Francisco Vásquez de Coronado. The systematic work of

Jesuit and Franciscan clergy and a few soldiers and settlers in the following two centuries pulled Arizona into Spain's overseas empire, albeit as a tiny, remote, peripheral outpost. Mexican independence in 1821 brought no remarkable changes. This frontier remained neglected as the political events in Mexico's heartland consumed the country's primary energy and interests.

Yet despite Arizona's status as a distant outpost, Spanish and Mexican political governance had far-reaching consequences, bringing this area into a new political realm and attaching it to a European pool of ideas. Arizona operated now within a European context that balanced precariously on a north-south axis. Politically, religiously, socially, and culturally, Spanish and Mexican rule had important consequences in Arizona. U.S. acquisition of Arizona in 1848 and 1854 disrupted this north-south arrangement, superimposing an east-west orientation and introducing new values, political ideas, population, and cultural patterns that profoundly expressed non-Hispanic themes and exuded definite anti-Hispanic prejudices.

For Arizona after 1848, political development meant territorial status in combination with New Mexico, organized under a fresh set of principles neither Native American nor Hispanic. The east-west axis of the Union introduced new events and struggles, such as the Civil War, into Arizona. The prevalent, somewhat monolithic, patterns of the past were swept aside or submerged.

As an event, statehood culminated the Anglo trends introduced into the territory following the Treaty of Guadalupe Hidalgo. Being a state, even more than being a territory, responded significantly to fundamental Anglo values of governance—the goals of a society and political structure imposed in the face of Mexico's defeat in the late 1840s. Statehood confirmed these values and systematically solidified them more concretely than is possible in a territory. While territorial status introduced Arizona to the Union, statehood drew Arizona into the political mainstream of U.S. institutions. For example, Arizona participated actively in the workings of Congress, was compelled to codify laws for itself more thoroughly as a state than as a territory, and in general was forced into greater conformity with norms emanating from the Anglo dominance that extended from the East throughout the West.

This eastern dominance overlay ancient Native American traditions and the two-and-a-half-century-old Hispanic culture. Statehood culminated the process begun with the conquest imposed by the 1848 treaty with Mexico, and already affirmed in nearby states such as California in 1850, Nevada in 1864, and Utah in 1896.

On the one hand, statehood is a nondramatic event. It lacks the richness of other topics, such as older Native American dwelling arrangements and development, irrigation systems, craft skills, and the ability to interrelate land, resources, and water. Similarly, it lacks the vision, adventurousness, and energy bound up in the work of a Vásquez de Coronado or Kino. Yet it marks an important moment in the maturing of Arizona, in the Angloization process initially hinted at in the 1820s, when the first Anglo interlopers encroached on Mexican territory as fur trappers and traders. It confirms that coming of Anglo culture in a more systematized way.

Arizona has come to mean a cultural mix resulting from interesting strata of cultures. Indigenous Native American cultures are overlain with a Hispanic one thrust from the south and reinforced through time by familial ties to Sonora. The Hispanic influence gradually Europeanized Arizona—religiously, ethnically, intellectually, politically, and technologically. The Anglo impact was more startling. Territorial status capped by statehood compelled a more organized, sustained, efficient drive to prevent Arizona from remaining the isolated, outlier territory divorced from the impact of the Eastern Seaboard's westward thrust. Conceptually statehood meant much in Arizona's emergence: it reaffirmed the values and cultural overtones inherent in the background of the 1848 conqueror.

Although it can be argued that the 1880s, 1890s, and early 1900s witnessed the expansion of Anglo interests and the intersection of these aggressive influences with older ones, statehood affirmed that these newer trends would be sustained, nurtured, and institutionalized. Statehood meant that Arizona had to conform politically to eastern values, that it needed new codes to implement those values, that it had to organize to do what other states normally did within the Union.

In spite of this Angloization, Arizona's older cultural patterns live on and influence us today. Our thinking about certain problems or opportunities is constrained or enhanced by the multicultural dimensions of the state's heritage. Our concepts about the value of land and its proper use or about water distribution are established on a varied base of ideas. Native American, Hispanic, and Anglo concepts of land use intersect and contrast. Is vacant land undeveloped? The answer to that question reflects cultural values about space relationships, notions of what good use is, and ideas about what constitutes "development." Water distribution reflects eastern restrictions imposed in the form of 160-acre limits but modified by previous Hispanic rules about prior use. The value of urban living extends through time in the state's history. Arizona's history can be read in its urban development, whether in an ancient urban project such as Tuzigoot, Spanish outposts such as Tubac or Tucson, or territorial-period towns such as Tombstone, Tempe, Phoenix, or Prescott. In significant respects, long-standing urban patterns and relationships characterize Arizona more than rural ones.

In examining Arizona's history since 1912 and looking to the future, we must give extraordinary consideration to the prevalence of the past. Our preference for urban living means we must continually look at how to maintain urban areas and manage growth. We are not the first to face these problems. Previous residents who have since disappeared, such as the Anasazi and Hohokam, had a similar reckoning with an especially fragile environment. Our future pressing problems include managing water and improving air quality. Our development threatens to overwhelm the environment we cherish.

Demographic forecasters project a growing Hispanic population. Many of the state's areas will have Hispanic populations of significant size. The school-age population in most areas is likely to have a majority of minority groups. The Hispanic population of the twenty-first century will be ready to assume new roles as an ever-growing, well-educated citizenry. That role for Hispanics has lain dormant since an Anglo population thrust aside Hispanic influences in the late nineteenth century. Areas until now traditionally Anglo in orientation, such as Phoenix, will see larger numbers of Hispanics (and other groups such as Blacks) in positions of political and economic importance as the twenty-first century unfolds. Hispanic values, in some respects submerged under decades of Anglo control, may well rise in the state and in the Phoenix area to a position of importance not seen in Arizona since the third quarter of the nineteenth century.

What the future holds for Arizona is a confrontation with its past. In many respects we worship that past at historical sites such as Montezuma Well or Tubac. Yet the peoples whose heritage stems from that past remain citizens of Arizona and are reemerging as important decision makers for Arizona's future. Statehood in 1912 may represent that unique moment in Arizona's history when the Anglo population predominated politically, then and in the succeeding seventy-five years. Capturing Arizona at 75 means examining and appreciating that moment and understanding it within the total fabric of Arizona history. Imagining Arizona at 100 means anticipating a revitalization of residual patterns and themes. J. Russell Nelson, president of Arizona State University, in his opening remarks for the February 28 conference suggested that Arizona's statehood was at its post-adolescent stage. He predicted that as its statehood phases evolve, increasing importance will come to the role of Hispanics. Statehood ultimately may mean a melding of diverse multiethnic values and cultural patterns in arrangements heretofore unseen.

Continuing Themes

The essays in this volume cover a range of topics and issues that have been important since 1912 and will continue to be significant through 2012. Despite their variety, they express the continuity of certain overriding themes. This continuity was underscored by a discussion among Arizona's former governors during the conference from which this book stems. Former governors Paul Fannin, Sam Goddard, Howard Pyle, and Jack Williams uniformly agreed that the availability of water, the maintenance of environmental quality, properly managed growth, a high-quality education system, and the international link to Mexico had long been important to

Arizona development and would continue to occupy the attention of Arizonans. Although the specific aspect of the problem under discussion might vary—for example, the creation of an adequate water storage system as opposed to a need for conservation and management of established water resources—the key issue (in this case, water) would remain a vital topic of public discussion. Although these issues cannot be settled for once and for all, they must be studied and discussed, and alternative solutions must be debated.

The first of these recurring themes is the importance of the environment—the land, the climate, the natural resources. Much of Arizona is desert, and this geographic fact has affected its development in dramatic ways. An entire essay in this book is devoted to water—because of its scarcity and the difficulties of distributing and allocating it. Differences between Indian and Anglo attitudes toward the land are a major source of disagreements between Indian tribes and Anglo governments. The maintenance of large tracts of land as federal property, particularly in national parks, has helped the tourist industry to flourish and occasionally maddened developers. Arizona has not been spared the conflicts between those who would conserve and those who would exploit. The beauty of the land has moved writers and artists to portray—and defend—it. Whether as a stark yet beautiful reality, or as a religious and aesthetic concept, the land has shaped Arizona's economy, politics, and society.

Anglo settlements in some parts of Arizona were originally opened because the climate was beneficial to those suffering from respiratory and other ailments; today, the deterioration of air quality is a source of political and economic unease, as well as physical discomfort. Tourism has flourished because of the dramatic landscapes and warm winters. The aircraft industry developed here in part because of the great number of days of good flying weather available. The outstanding facilities for astronomical studies were built because of Arizona's location and clear skies, which remain ideal despite fears of encroaching light pollution from urban sprawl.

The state's natural resources—especially copper, silver, gold, and land for farming and ranching—have shaped its growth. As some of the writers in this volume point out, Arizona was for decades an economic colony, contributing raw materials to industries that prospered in other states. Genuine integration into the nation's economy awaited the development of infrastructure by outside, national forces, such as railroad companies and, in the case of highways, the federal government.

Colonial status continues to be reflected in other areas as well, as some of our writers note. Arizona's Indian citizens who live on reservations are in a position that is not quite colonial, yet not entirely independent. Even those who live outside the reservation have a different relationship with the federal government than that of other citizens. Many of them, in fact, feel that they have yet to be granted full citizenship. A lingering sense of colonial status may also underlie Arizona's frequent resistance to federal authority on issues ranging from speed limits to criminal procedure. Finally, Arizona artists sometimes find themselves looking over their shoulders, fearful of the empires of Los Angeles, San Francisco, Santa Fe, and Taos.

A third recurring theme is the growth of Arizona's cities. Despite its image as a state of farmers and ranchers, Arizona houses more than 80 percent of its citizens in urban areas. We have long been overwhelmingly a state of city dwellers. This concentration of population affects the way we use land and water and influences the blend of economic enterprises that we require. The growth of cities permits the centralization of financial resources and interest that allows the arts and education to flourish. Cities also act as a magnet for Hispanic and Indian young people who want to participate in mainstream society—whether temporarily, as students, or permanently, as urban workers. This shift in population inevitably brings a challenge to the maintenance of tradition. At the same time, it exposes Anglo society to new views and ways of life. Whether the result is cultural conflict, cultural amalgamation, or cultural suicide, it will certainly bring change.

A fourth recurring theme is the variety of Arizona's people. Arizona's heritage is multiracial. We are Anglo, Hispanic, Indian, Black, and Asian. To a large extent, each group has maintained its identity and separateness, sometimes by choice. Anglo society has incorporated ethnic cultures in superficial ways—in street names and restaurants, for example—but except in its southernmost areas, Arizona is far less culturally integrated than New Mexico. The causes of this separation, and the extent to which it will be maintained, are important issues.

Similarly, Arizona is a state of varied religions. Roman Catholics, Mormons, and other Christians are dominant, but Phoenix and Tucson have significant Jewish communities as well. The number of Muslim students at the state's universities, some of whom settle here permanently, along with other immigrants from the Middle East and Pakistan, is large enough that Tempe boasts a new mosque.

As extractive industries and agriculture have become less dominant, the importance of Arizona's human resources has grown. The high technology, information, and financial industries require well-educated personnel, and Arizona's schools and universities are being challenged to meet their demands. Similarly, the educated, sophisticated workforce that these industries hope to attract and retain demand good schools for their children and cultural and artistic amenities for themselves. The setting that such groups envision is a far cry from the primitive frontier image that the state continues to project.

And that is perhaps the most pervasive theme of this volume: the gap between image and reality, especially in historical investigation. To prospective tourists, readers of popular history and fiction, and the general public, Arizona is still a frontier state. Historians themselves concentrate largely on the frontier period. Our view of Hispanics and Indians is romanticized and anachronistic. We retain the image of land untouched by highways and developers and climate unaffected by paving and swimming pools. We view the cultural scene as a desert, with occasional oases irrigated by outside influences.

The reality is far different. Although much of Arizona's land is still wide open spaces, cities, highways, and economic development are rapidly encroaching. Few Arizonans—less than 20 percent, in fact—live in rural areas. Many Indians live on reservations, but many are nevertheless active in urban, Anglo economies and societies. Still others are city dwellers. Many Hispanics live in barrios, but many others are well integrated into Anglo urban life. Arizona poets appear in the most exclusive anthologies, and in 1987 one of them, Rita Dove, won a Pulitzer Prize. Arizonans may drive pickup trucks and wear cowboy boots, but our daily business is far more likely to involve computer chips and traffic jams than horses and lonesome trails. One goal of this book is to bring Arizonans, and Arizona historians, face to face with the late twentieth century, to bridge that gap between image and reality. Studying the past is an essential element in mastering the future.

CONTOURS OF CULTURE
IN ARIZONA
AND THE MODERN WEST

Richard W. Etulain

Is Arizona's cultural landscape as much of a desert as its physical landscape? Is there a distinct Arizona literature? Is Arizona art purely the product of visitors? In this essay, Richard Etulain discusses the history and present state of Arizona literature and art, its links to the larger region and the nation, and its promise. He also describes changes and growth in the state's educational and religious institutions. In Etulain's view, the future of Arizona culture is bright, and the future of Arizona's cultural history lies in a view or definition that is expanded to include urban culture, popular culture, and regional culture.

Conference panelists and the audience raised a number of topics that Etulain was unable to touch on, including crafts, poetry, music, and film. Literature in Spanish or in Indian languages is another field largely unstudied. It is reassuring to know that Arizona's cultural life is sufficiently rich that it cannot be covered in a single essay. Certainly Etulain's recommendation that historians take a broader view of culture will be productive when applied to these topics as well.

11

When John Steinbeck swung his camper across the Southwest in the early 1960s collecting information and reflections for his *Travels with Charley*, he zipped through Arizona and New Mexico, paying scant attention to the history and culture of the two states in his dash from California to Texas. It was as though his itinerary led from one behemoth to another, leaving space for one paragraph on Arizona and a handful more on New Mexico. At much the same time that Steinbeck sped from one southern corner of the West to the other, well-known western historian W. Eugene Hollon concluded in his regional history *The Southwest: Old and New* that Arizona "lagged behind the other sections of the Southwest in cultural interest and achievement."[1]

These two views reflect much of what has been concluded about cultural developments in modern Arizona. Most often the state's cultural endeavors have been overlooked or undervalued as not worthy of much attention. Neither of these contentions, though perhaps widely accepted among historians, journalists, and other observers, helps specialists or newcomers to understand cultural activities in the state. Yet these conclusions are understandable. As we shall see, traditional approaches to western history have generally blinded scholars and students to cultural movements in the modern West, and until recently definitions of "culture" have been so restrictive that much of the richness and variety of cultural achievement in the United States has been missed.[2]

Things need to change in western history—in the topics covered and in the approaches utilized. As a modest move in these directions, the following pages briefly summarize the contributions of historians, authors, artists, churches, and schools to the cultural history of Arizona. After this survey I will suggest a few perspectives from which contemporary and future cultural activities might be interpreted. But in launching these worthy studies to mark out the hazy paths from the past and present into the future, we need fewer coroners and more investigators of culture, analysts whose research probes more deeply and expansively into the intellectual endeavors of the state without falling victim to blinding filiopietism or numbing chauvinism.

Historians and Arizona

Like most historians writing about the American West, chroniclers of Arizona's past have betrayed an inordinate fascination with the early years of the state's history. At the same time these historians have shown little interest in analyzing what many consider the less lively and romantic decades of the twentieth century. Nor have most western historians been intrigued with cultural history, devoting most of their attention instead to economic developments, political struggles, and, more recently, social complexities. Clearly, devotees of Clio interested in the cultural history of modern Arizona and the West must swim upstream against contemporary currents in the study of western history.[3]

By the 1920s a clear tradition had been established in the scholarly and popular study of the American West. Following one of the emphases of the brilliant scholar Frederick Jackson Turner, academic and popular historians concluded that the frontier did more than any other experience to shape American history. But in putting such extraordinary emphasis on Turner's frontier thesis, these writers overlooked Turner's other thesis concerning the development of sections (or regions) in America and his concomitant stress on the evolution of social institutions on the frontier. In limiting their adherence to Turnerian doctrines to his discussions of movement to the frontier, his students and other true believers severely restricted the possibilities of understanding the frontier and the American West. Not only did they fail to notice his growing interest in postfrontier periods—those generations that followed the successful settling of new frontiers and that helped to establish sections to replace frontiers—they also overlooked his concern with the growth of institutions that led from frontier to section. Unfortunately, present emphases in the study of the American West con-

tinue to betray these narrowed views of Turner's important historio-
graphic legacies.[4]

While professional historians limited the full force of Turner's
views, writers of popular western history, although giving lip service
to Turner's frontier emphasis, capitalized on the fascination of many
Americans—and of people around the world. They have produced
thousands of books and essays celebrating an Old West that owe
more to nostalgia and escape than to research and analysis. Similar
to the emotional attachment of many readers to a bugle-and-bullets
view of the Civil War, followers of the Wild West interpretation of
the frontier are drawn to the dashing escapades of mountain men,
cowboys, outlaws, and "bad" women but show little interest in studies
of the culture of either the frontier or the twentieth-century West.[5]

If limited understanding of Turner's pathbreaking interpretations of the frontier and section and overemphasis on the Wild West
have characterized many interpretations of the American West, they
have also dominated the historical treatments of Arizona. From the
early accounts in H. H. Bancroft's *History of Arizona and New Mexico
1530–1888* (1889) to the publication of the first substantial professional history, *Arizona: The History of a Frontier State* (1950) by Rufus
K. Wyllys, historians of the state have focused on the prestatehood
period, devoting most of their chapters to such topics as exploration,
conflicts with the Indians, frontier military activities, outbreaks of
violence, and narratives of outlaws. Discussions of cultural activities
and institutions and treatments of the period after 1912 are as
scarce as sheepherders at a fall roundup.

Several one-volume histories of Arizona completed after 1970
dutifully follow these historiographical traditions. For example,
Odie B. Faulk's *Arizona: A Short History* (1970) places major stress
on the prestatehood era, with extraordinary emphasis on political
and economic history, some discussion of social configurations, and
almost nothing on cultural happenings. For Faulk, although his
book was written in the 1960s, Arizona was a frontier experience,
neither replicating earlier cultural legacies of its immigrants nor
formulating a culture of its own in the twentieth century. The final
sections of his compact and smoothly written volume treat politics,
mining developments, competition for sources of water, new modes
of transportation, and the impact of World War II on the state, but

Faulk eschews comment on cultural developments of the nearly sixty years after statehood.

The same emphases are evident in Marshall Trimble's *Arizona: A Panoramic History of a Frontier State* (1977). Narrative and anecdotal in approach, this volume devotes nearly all of its 320 pages to the pre-1912 period and contains very little on cultural history. The author seems convinced that an account of the pioneer period, when "the material accentuates the character and the style of the times about which one is writing," is preferable to the historical work of "the purist [who] will use only that information which he can document or footnote" (p. vii). Unfortunately, Trimble's volume, while well written and clear, too severely truncates the length and breadth of the state's history and leaves one with a colorful but unanalytical account of Arizona.

Better researched and more scholarly than Trimble's work, *Arizona: Historic Land* (1982) by Bert M. Fireman also provides more extensive treatment of recent Arizona. At the same time, the author, nearly a lifelong resident, argues that "not enough time has elapsed to give the first seven decades of statehood the mellowing patina that adds to historical perspective and understanding" (p. 258). This reservation notwithstanding, Fireman treats twentieth-century Arizona politics, economic developments, and social adjustments— but not cultural activities. It is as though modern Arizona contained no literature, art, churches, or schools.[6]

Not all historians of Arizona have placed inordinate stress on the nineteenth century or have overlooked cultural history, however. *Arizona: A Bicentennial History* (1976), by noted bookman Lawrence Clark Powell, avoids most of the preoccupations of recent western historiography. From the opening section of his book—"Great Dry and Wrinkled Land"—to the penultimate chapter on "A Look at the Arts," Powell, more than most historians, comprehends the mutual relationships between people and environment. Similar to cultural geographers, Powell's interest in cultural landscape allows him to depict the shaping power of setting on the growth of human institutions. In addition to noting the molding influence of urbanization in modern Arizona, the author sketches briefly the development of the arts in the state, particularly its prose, poetry, and art.

Had Powell expanded his overview another fifty pages—which

the format of the bicentennial series of state histories allowed—he might also have added commentaries on schools and churches in Arizona. Although he touches on the universities at Tucson and Tempe and mentions the establishment of public schools, Powell— like nearly all western historians—seems little interested in showing how schools and schooling are notable reflections of a state or region's cultural development. The same gap is evident in the writer's discussion of religion. While he mentions Spanish missionary efforts to Indians and the Mormon settlements in northeastern Arizona, the religious involvements of a majority of Arizonans—those of the last seventy years—are overlooked. It is as though religion has been an unimportant part of the lives of recent residents of the state.

Nevertheless, Powell's brief account does more to examine the cultural heritage of Arizona than any other book-length study of the state. More than most historians, Powell is attuned to the importance of Arizona's recent past, its urban nature, and its literary heritage. And Powell himself is a gifted writer, sensing and weighing the metaphorical and symbolic power of the words he employs to evoke landscape and the changes humankind brings to that setting. With expansion of the topics Powell already covers and the addition of subjects he has overlooked, his book might serve as a model for the needed emphasis on cultural developments in Arizona's history.

If most historians producing book-length studies of Arizona have been reluctant to deal with the recent past or with cultural topics,[7] a small group of journalists and specialists in modern American and western history and geography have been more willing to treat one or both of these subjects. Beginning with Neil Morgan's stimulating *Westward Tilt* (1963) through Neal Peirce's well-written volumes on the Plains, Rockies, and Pacific states (1972–73), and on to Peter Wiley and Robert Gottlieb's provocative *Empires in the Sun* (1982), several journalists have provided readable accounts of the modern West that include sections on Arizona and place particular stress on the West since World War II. Most of these writers focus on political and economic history with some notice of varied ethnic experiences, but none has been much interested in cultural developments.

In addition to treating the modern period of the Southwest, several regional historians such as Lynn Perrigo and W. Eugene

Hollon provide useful if brief sections on southwestern culture. More than any other historian, Gerald D. Nash has laid out a thought-provoking interpretative framework as well as profiled cultural activities in the post-1900 West. Another writer, geographer D. W. Meinig, has challenged readers to understand the shaping power of land forms, transportation grids, and shifting tides of immigrants and other demographic transitions upon the cultural landscape of the Southwest. Finally, urban historian Bradford Luckingham and several of his students have produced notable monographs and essays on the rise of cities in the Southwest and within those studies have included useful comments on urban culture.[8]

Clearly, then, although most book-length histories treating Arizona have betrayed a familiar fixation on the frontier, have deemphasized the period after 1900, and have downplayed cultural history, changes are in the air. Not only have writers like Lawrence Clark Powell and Gerald Nash dealt with modern Arizona and the recent West, but they have also pinpointed specific cultural activities. Should other historians follow their trailblazing efforts or imitate the first-rate cultural histories of Franklin Walker or Kevin Starr on modern California, the patterns of Arizona culture will become much clearer.

Literature

Literature written in English about Arizona has not differed much from that which arose in other parts of the West. Commencing with the nineteenth-century accounts of exploration and travel, through the works of the local color writers, on to the increasingly perceptive works of literary regionalists, and finally to the works of contemporary authors, the literary history of Arizona—for the most part—has moved through periods of development characterizing those of other sections of the literary West.[9]

The early historical narratives of discovery, travel, military conquest, or topographical report, such as those by James Ohio Pattie, Philip St. George Cooke, William H. Emory, and many other writers, emphasized the rugged terrain, the isolation, and the unique characteristics of Indian and Spanish peoples in Arizona. Intended as documentary accounts of what these explorers and visitors had seen and experienced, these works of "literature" were not primarily imaginative reshapings of the travelers' activities but rather straightforward attempts to chronicle their journeys into this new and strange country. As one might expect, these writers often highlighted the differences they perceived between what they had known in Europe and the American East and the novel settings and peoples they encountered in the new West. These historical narratives defined the first genre of Anglo literature about the West.

In the next stage of literary development in Arizona, between the 1890s and World War I, authors who visited the territory or state and others who lived there for some time ushered in a new era of local color writing. The first of these authors, Alfred Henry Lewis, an eastern lawyer and newspaperman, traveled through and worked for a spell in Arizona and New Mexico in the 1880s and '90s, gathering materials for his Wolfville series, ostensibly set in Tombstone. Beginning with *Wolfville* (1897), Lewis produced several volumes of fictional sketches peopled with pungent frontier types including his garrulous narrator, the Old Cattleman; Doc Peets, the town's pundit; Sam Enright, *alcalde;* and two remarkable women, Faro Nell and Tucson Jennie. Owing much to the earlier humor and caricatures of Bret Harte and Mark Twain, Lewis moved beyond them in creating and sustaining a western fictional community with its remuda of lively vernacular characters.[10]

At much the same time, another eastern journalist, Charles Fletcher Lummis, traversed Arizona on his famous cross-country walk from Cleveland to Los Angeles. Later, Lummis returned to Arizona, collecting information on Indians and Hispanics, the Grand Canyon, and numerous other settings. Exploiting these accumulated materials, he wrote a steady stream of enthusiastic essays, poems, and books saluting the colorful history of the Southwest. Some of these works first appeared in two journals he edited—*Land of Sunshine* and *Out West*—significant regional magazines that promoted far western and southwestern literature and culture. Like Lewis, Lummis was an outsider, but also like Lewis, he did much to call attention to the possibilities for local color writing about Arizona.[11]

Although less bombastic than Lummis in his reactions to the Southwest, Stewart Edward White likewise came to embrace the land and peoples of Arizona and California. Drawing in his writings upon his hunting and camping trips through the region, White illustrated his position as both a local color and regional writer in his best works on Arizona—*Arizona Nights* (1907) and *The Killer* ˋ (1919). While employing the anecdotal and mock-heroic form and tone of many local color writers, he also centered on the shaping power of the southwestern environment on character so notable in the works of western regionalists. In White's classic story "Rawhide" (in *Arizona Nights*), for instance, he revealed his understanding of western types such as settlers and cowboys and their varied and shifting reactions to landscape and setting.[12]

One of the frequent contributors to Lummis's magazines was Sharlot Hall, whom Lawrence Clark Powell calls "the first indigenous voice of Arizona literature." Similar to Lummis, who published many of her essays and poems and remained her most influential literary friend, Hall staunchly defended the Old West, praising its sturdy men and women in her lyric and epic poems and lauding pioneer Arizonans in her essays and histories. In the final decades of her life she restored the territorial governor's mansion in Prescott and crisscrossed the state gathering artifacts and records documenting and memorializing the region's history.[13]

The least-known of the authors who dominated the Arizona literary scene in the early twentieth century was Dick Wick Hall. Trained as a mining engineer, he immigrated as a young man to Wickenburg, where he took up writing and owned a newspaper for several years. A humorist who utilized hyperbole, understatement, and malapropisms to undercut western pretensions and to create such monsters as a giant seven-pound bullfrog that could not swim and a "high horse and low bridge . . . giraft" who wins a controversial race—by a neck, Hall won a place with his hilarious yarns directly in the frontier tradition of Mark Twain, Wyoming's Bill Nye, and other ring-tail roarers.[14]

These local color writers served as a bridge between the earlier narratives of discovery and exploration and the works of literary regionalists who emerged during the 1920s and '30s and who held sway even after World War II. What Lewis, Lummis, White, Sharlot Hall, and Dick Wick Hall did for Arizona, Harte and Twain did for California and Nevada, Mary Hallock Foote for Colorado and Idaho, and Joaquin Miller for the Pacific Northwest and California. Not so much intrigued as the later regionalists with depicting the molding force of landscape on character development, the local colorists emphasized dialect, dress, and social customs of the West. Their central characters are picturesque miners, gamblers, outlaws, cowpunchers, and a host of other frontier rubes and recruits—people with no histories who are often adroitly vernacular in gulling eastern provincials and in harpooning western boasters. Within their limits, local color writers in Arizona and other parts of the West demonstrated some of the area's early literary possibilities.

Although in the first half of the twentieth century Arizona lacked a Hamlin Garland, Jack London, Frank Norris, Mary Austin, or Willa Cather to whom one could point as a founder of its modern literary traditions, it did play host to a number of authors who wrote on a variety of topics. Arizona did not experience a rich outpouring of regional literature, as did California, New Mexico, and the Pacific Northwest between the two world wars, but several writers dealing with Arizona made significant contributions to its literary history.[15]

A number of authors—after either brief visits or longer stays in Arizona—produced novels about Indians of the area. General Charles King, who had served earlier with George Crook on the Arizona frontier, drew on his cavalry experiences in *An Apache Princess* (1903), which depicts a young Apache woman falling in love with a cavalry lieutenant. Racial attitudes of the time—with which King agreed—forbade any such union, so the lieutenant persuades her to marry a man of her own race. More romantic are the images of Indians in the writings of Marah Ellis Ryan, whose novels *Indian Love Letters* (1907) and *The Flute of the Gods* (1909) deal with southwestern Indians. The former, which C. L. Sonnichsen declares a "hopelessly . . . sentimentalized" portrait, consists of a series of love letters from a Hopi young man to a white woman. Before she had met an Indian, Ryan also wrote *The Flute of the Gods,* which indicts the Spaniards as callous overlords and destroyers of Indian life and culture. To some reviewers, Ryan's style is lyrical and appealing; for most readers, however, her writing and attitudes smack of excessive romanticism and mysticism.

Perhaps the best of the fiction dealing with Indians was Oliver La Farge's *Laughing Boy* (1929), his first novel, which won a Pulitzer Prize. An easterner who came west, La Farge drew upon his anthropological field work among the Navajo for his memorable depiction of a romance between Laughing Boy, a traditionalist, and Slim Girl, also a Navajo but one whose associations with missionaries and other Anglos had loosened her ties to Indian traditions. Enlarging the meaning of his tragic story through the careful use of Indian history and lore, La Farge produced a notable novel, still appealing for its thorough understanding of Indian sociocultural life. As historian Robert Berkhofer has written, "With the publication of Oliver La Farge's *Laughing Boy*, the genre of the Indian novel reached full maturity."[16] Equally revealing was the author's later work *The Enemy Gods* (1937), which portrayed the difficulties Indians faced from an assimilating white world.

The figure of the cowboy, so noticeable in fiction, film, and art about the Old West, likewise attracted Arizona writers. In addition to varied images of the cowboy and cattle country in the hundreds of popular Westerns produced by such writers as Zane Grey, Louis L'Amour, Nelson Nye, and Brian Garfield—which will be noted later—Ross Santee produced his notable novel, *Cowboy* (1928), which J. Frank Dobie termed "the best story of the making of a cowboy yet written."[17] In this story of initiation, Santee's hero, a runaway from East Texas who "lites" out for Arizona, gradually matures to become a working cowboy who experiences all the pressures of becoming a man among men. Like the good regionalist that he was, Santee showed the forming influence of physical, psychological, and human environments on Shorty, whose story reads like the autobiography of a cowboy in the making. A working cowboy himself, an artist as well as an editor, Santee produced in *Cowboy* and in an earlier collection of stories, *Men and Heroes* (1926), realistic regional portraits of the cowman's life in Arizona.

World War II affected literary life as it did so much of the West's economic, social, and cultural life, helping to usher in a more diverse literary scene in Arizona. While J. P. S. Brown duplicated the earlier realism of Santee in his well-plotted and persuasively set cattleman novels *Jim Kane* (1970) and *The Outfit* (1971), and while Elliott Arnold and Edwin Corle continued the strong interest of westerners in treating Indians in a white man's world in their novels *Blood Brother* (1947) and *In Winter Light* (1949), other authors turned to different subjects. Several writers revived Tombstone and its gallery of outlaws and lawmen, while others dealt with contemporary themes. In his novel *Hail Hero* (1968), John Weston portrayed a student from an Arizona ranch sent off to Vietnam, and Edward Abbey treated futuristic clashes over wilderness and individual rights in *Good News* (1980). Meanwhile, experiences along the border interested novelist Glendon Swarthout, and C. F. Kippler chronicled the dilemmas of a psychiatrist in southern Arizona suffering from treatment at the hands of one of his own patients in *The Otter* (1964).

Perhaps the best-known of recent Arizona writers is Edward Abbey (1927–). Like many historians and novelists writing about the state, Abbey's roots are both eastern and western. Born and reared in Pennsylvania, he first came west in 1944 and then returned to the Southwest for undergraduate and master's work at the University of New Mexico. Strongly attached to the out-of-doors and the desert settings of the Southwest, Abbey has lived, by turn, in New Mexico, Utah, and Arizona, where he currently resides. Like the hero in his first novel, *Jonathan Troy* (1954), Abbey fled an urban-industrial East for a regenerating West.[18]

Beginning with his second and third novels, *The Brave Cowboy* (1956) and *Fire on the Mountain* (1962), and in his notable nonfictional *Desert Solitaire* (1968), Abbey celebrates individualists attempting to confront mindless and faceless bureaucracies, but he also champions those trying to save western wilderness from myriad two-legged predators. Like Wallace Stegner (with whom Abbey studied for a short time at Stanford University), Ken Kesey, and Larry McMurtry, Abbey has been attracted to unspoiled stretches of the West, drawn to what he considers the greater freedoms of the rural West, and repulsed by land developers, inane government officials, and sprawling suburbs. Abbey's later works, while sometimes humorous like *The Monkey Wrench Gang* (1975), are unfortunately too often preachy and strident—for example, *The Journey Home* (1977) and *Good News* (1980). Although frequently entertaining and provocative, Abbey too often drops his pen to step into his pulpit.

At the same time that Abbey has become a leading literary spokesman for wilderness preservation and the confronting of numbing legalisms, his career also reflects the increasing difficulties one encounters in trying to locate a regional perspective in western writing. As less a regionalist and more an ecologist and social critic, Abbey may well epitomize the contention of several recent critics that a unique regional voice is no longer possible in Arizona. Or one might conclude that regional literature is not likely to appear in Arizona—or in most parts of the Sunbelt—where dramatic and constant socioeconomic changes of the last generation or two preclude the establishment of a clear, stable regional identity. At any rate, the strong sense of place, so recognizable in the earlier works of Willa Cather, John Steinbeck, and Wallace Stegner, is missing in much recent writing about Arizona. Indeed, that sense of rootedness may be impossible in a region of the West invaded and flooded by so many waves of rapid change since World War II.

Yet there are other promising signs. The 1987 Pulitzer Prize for poetry went to Arizona poet Rita Dove, and such well-known western writers as Frank Waters and William Eastlake reside at least part-time in Arizona and have dealt in the past with the state in their writings. Even more promising is the recent move of three distinguished Native American authors, Vine Deloria, N. Scott Momaday, and Leslie Silko, to Tucson, making that area the unrivaled capital of Indian literary endeavors. If these and other writers turn to their immediate surroundings in their fiction, or if Arizona plays host to an additional crop of authors, it could experience a rich harvest of new and notable literature.

Art

Art in nineteenth-century Arizona, like the literature written about the territory, was the product of outsiders who usually came to see the Grand Canyon or to visit Indian settlements or reservations.

Travelers continued to be the best-known artists of Arizona in the first decades of the twentieth century. While interest in indigenous artistic efforts grew between the world wars, not until after World War II did attention to art in the state expand considerably, reflecting some of the diversity of styles and approaches apparent in contemporary American art.

Many of the first artists who traversed Arizona served as illustrators for private or government-sponsored expeditions. Before the perfection of the camera, artists were the pictorial historians of westering voyagers, providing sponsors with artistic records of what travelers had seen and experienced. Yet these artists were not modern copy machines, going about their work like robots devoid of individual and diverse talents and interests. Moreover, the first depictions of Arizona landscapes and peoples were as much products of artists' preconceptions of the frontier as they were of settings and natives the artists encountered. Nor can one avoid noting that just as preconceptions of the frontier changed over time, so did currently popular artistic styles and points of view. In truth, in the nineteenth and early twentieth centuries, Arizona, like most of the West, was a colonial culture, in which artistic expression and subject matter owed more to alien than native influences.[19]

Commencing with John Mix Stanley's drawings as a draughtsman with the Corps of Topographic Engineers accompanying General Stephen Watts Kearny's march to California in the Mexican-American War, artists were expected to provide exact details of the terrain through which explorers and soldiers traveled. Some of Stanley's works, later used as lithographs for government reports, were indeed useful renderings of Arizona scenes. Yet he sometimes changed details and romanticized his settings, as he did in his oil painting *Chain of Spires Along the Gila River* (1855). This juxtaposition of accurate, detailed images with romanticized scenery typified much of the early art by visitors to Arizona.

A quarter of a century later, noted landscapist Thomas Moran attended John Wesley Powell on his return trip to the Grand Canyon, from which came Moran's massive (roughly 7' by 12') *Chasm of the Colorado* (1874). Illustrating the strong ties of Moran and his contemporary, artist Albert Bierstadt, to American and European romantic traditions, Moran's works likewise reflect an artist's willingness to switch details and colors of scenes to create not an exact replication of a scene but an impression of its reality. Moran's picturesque view of the Colorado—so "awful, sublime, and glorious," to quote Powell's use of popular nineteenth-century landscape terms—attracted many imitators and patrons to Moran and Bierstadt and, in turn, helped foster popular images of Arizona and the West as pristine and wild wilderness that later artists tried to emulate.

If Moran and his contemporary artists like Samuel Colman and William Henry Holmes pictured the Grand Canyon and other Arizona scenes in grandiloquent terms, in the sublime and picturesque traditions of romantic artists like the Hudson River painters, other well-known artists such as Frederic Remington and Charles Russell provided another vista of Arizona in their lively illustrations *A Dash for the Timber* (1889) and *They Left Him Thar' in the Trail* (1897) by Remington and *Navajo Trackers* by Russell. Still other artists were fascinated with Indians, particularly the Hopis living on their isolated mesas in the northeastern part of the territory. *Ceremonial Dance, Oraibi* (1900) by Frank Paul Sauerwein, *Snake Dance at Walpi, Arizona* (1925) by Swedish-born artist Carl Oscar Borg, and *Snake Dance (Walpi* [n.d.]) illustrate this enduring attachment of visiting artists to Arizona Indians. A few artists, notably William Robinson Leigh, produced both large landscapes and picturesque depictions of Indian life.

Overall, these artists painted a pleasant, friendly Arizona, a region devoid of threatening wilderness and fearsome "savages." Like the artists of the Taos-Santa Fe colony in New Mexico (some of whom also visited and painted Arizona early in the twentieth century), those who treated Arizona were not interested in presenting city life, advances in technology, or documents of social criticism. They were in love with an Old West of expansive and open scenery and independent and self-sufficient Indians, the emphases in most of their artistic depictions of Arizona. Since several of these artists were also under contract to the Atchison, Topeka and Santa Fe Railroad to produce paintings for depots and for other kinds of illustrations, they felt additional pressure to turn out works attractive to the railroad and tourists alike.

The most notable of the artistic visitors during the first decades of the twentieth century was Maynard Dixon, a California native who ventured into Arizona at the turn of the century. Following the advice of Charles F. Lummis to visit the desert Southwest, Dixon roamed throughout Arizona, particularly drawn to its scenery and Indians. Several of his later impressive cloud scenes and depictions of climate owed much to these early experiences. Other trips to Lorenzo Hubbell's Ganado Trading Post led to sketches of Hopi and Navajo life. In 1907, the Southern Pacific Railroad commissioned Dixon to do a series of four murals for its depot in Tucson—*The Cattleman, The Apache, The Prospector,* and *Irrigation.*

Always a nervous, aloof, and independent sort—Dixon once told a person he must live so that he could "look every damn man in the eye and tell him to go to hell"—Dixon especially identified with the separate existence of Arizona Indians. Convinced that their lifestyles were heroic and noble, he saw Indian society as a healthy alternative to "the social sickness of hyper-self-conscious modernism." Concurrently drawn to the striking coloration of Arizona deserts, Dixon tried to incorporate these rich reds and other bright hues into his desert paintings. His murals for the Biltmore in Phoenix, *Legend of the Earth and Sun* (1929), won critical acclaim, as did many of his other paintings, for their "clarity and crispness." In the late 1930s Dixon returned to Tucson and traveled throughout southern Arizona, sketching landscapes and Indian scenes. In the first four decades of the twentieth century, no well-known artist was more acquainted than Dixon with the varied terrains and native groups of Arizona. In his numerous sketches, paintings, and murals, he provided memorable portraits of many facets of Arizona landscape and social life.[20]

During the 1930s and early '40s the New Deal programs of Franklin D. Roosevelt's administration were further encouragements to artists in Arizona. Although some historians mistakenly argue that such agencies as the Public Works of Art Project, the Works Progress Administration's Federal Art Project, and the WPA Art Program fathered regionalism in the West, they did build on and expand regional movements of art and literature already in place in the 1920s. In addition to providing monthly wages for a number of needy painters, these organizations encouraged artists (as parallel organizations urged writers) to utilize local and regional materials in their paintings.

More painters in New Mexico than in Arizona took part in these New Deal groups (largely because of the sizable group of artists living in Taos and Santa Fe), but such Arizona painters as Lucy Drake Marlow, Kate Cory, Creston Baumgartner, David Swing, and Theodore Van Soelen participated in the early programs with their murals and oil paintings. Even more significant was the impact of the Federal Art Project of the WPA. Nationally more than five thousand artists produced in excess of a hundred thousand paintings in this program, usually at an average weekly salary of $23.00. In Arizona, the WPA/FAP offered classes in art education and established the Phoenix Federal Art Center (later Phoenix Art Center), which influenced art in Arizona well beyond the 1930s. Artists, including several Hispanic and Indian painters, involved in these and other New Deal organizations executed dozens of murals for county, state, and local buildings. Of course, not all of these artists enjoyed being tied to government agencies for support and direction, but their work is nonetheless an illuminating window onto artistic activities in Arizona during the 1930s and '40s.[21]

As it was for so many other aspects of culture in the West, World War II was a turning point for art in Arizona. If the war redirected regional experiences in the Southwest, it also brought thousands of immigrants to the region as travelers, government workers, and new residents. These newcomers arrived with more varied artistic backgrounds, which helped to diversify artistic traditions in Arizona.

Several artists visiting or working in Arizona adapted the nascent methods of Abstract Expressionist and Surrealist artists, but others followed less novel approaches. For example, George L. K. Morris, a lifelong advocate of abstract art, became fascinated with Indian art in Arizona as a compelling form of abstractionism. His *Indian Compositions* series and *Arizona Altar* (1949) reflected his innovative uses of Indian artifacts and other Arizona materials. Adolph Gottlieb also found Indian art and the brilliant light and color of Arizona to be shaping influences on his still-life and pictographic

compositions such as *Arizona Still Life* (1938). Following the drip
techniques of Jackson Pollack, another noted expressionist, Helen
Frankenthaler, utilized Arizona settings for *Sedona* (1977), *Into the
West* (1977), and *Indian Redscape* (1977). Not so much interested
in painting specific scenes, Frankenthaler employed a soak-stain
method to provide her personal impressions of land forms, colors,
and desert settings. As a result of his trips through Arizona, a short
stay in Sedona, and earlier influences of Dada and Surrealism, Max
Ernst combined these experiences in his works *Colline Inspirée* (*The
Inspired Hill,* 1950) and *Arizona Landscape* (1959).[22]

Wilfred Midgette, another visitor to Arizona, was much less
interested in expressionistic techniques in his series of paintings
treating Navajo and Hopi subjects. In his gigantic *Powwow* (1975;
9′ × 26′), a mural of modern spectators at an Indian war dance,
Midgette dramatizes the conflicts of traditional and contemporary
cultures impinging on Anglos and Indians. David Hockney, born
and reared in England, also broke from Abstract Expressionism
to join a generation of more realistic, representational artists. For
Hockney, California and the Southwest are best seen in works of
Pop Art, in which tourist, postcard images are juxtaposed against
the colorful, flat background of the Southwest in a work like *Arizona*
(1964). Still another group of the nonabstractionists, the Photo-
Realists, have not been attracted to Arizona as a setting for their
works.

Although Peter Iverson discusses sociocultural aspects of Arizona Indians elsewhere in this book, the emergence of a number
of well-known Indian artists in the last two generations deserves
mention here. If Indian artists before the 1930s were part of a rich
native artistic tradition, since that time they have often combined
native traditions with training in government-sponsored Indian
schools or in other public schools to produce new kinds of artistic
works. And the summer sessions sponsored by the Rockefeller
Foundation in 1961 and 1962 at the University of Arizona and the
later Institute of American Indian Arts in Santa Fe have encouraged
many young Indian artists to use their cultural and artistic traditions
as, at the same time, they utilize modern trends in American and
international art. Several Arizona Indians, including Hopi artist

Fred Kabotie and Navajo R. C. Gorman, and an Indian from outside Arizona, Fritz Scholder, have used southwestern traditions and settings in their numerous works.[23]

Recent developments in painting in Arizona, then, have been so multifaceted that James K. Ballinger, an authority on the state's art, could conclude: "Hardly a movement has run its course which could not find one of its aficionados traveling or living in the state of Arizona." Visitors' varied artistic backgrounds have combined with their experiences in Arizona to bring about a clear result: "Given this special flavor, subjects resultant from Arizona's landscape and experiences with its inhabitants make up a microcosm of American art and will continue to do so in the future."[24]

One suspects that in the next two or three decades, painters are likely to follow these trends of postwar generations. That is, numerous visitors are likely to make generous use of the scenery and native peoples of the state, but also to apply a wide variety of artistic forms and techniques in treating these topics. At the same time, Indian and other resident painters, sensing increasing aesthetic and financial support for their works, are likely to continue adding to the diversity and richness of painting in recent Arizona. In this regard, the future may be more promising for painters in the state than for historians and novelists.

Churches

By the time of the first notable religious census in 1906 that included reliable figures for the American far West, most of those church groups dominating the history of Arizona were already in place. Roman Catholics made up about two-thirds of the church population in 1906; the Church of Jesus Christ of Latter-day Saints (Mormons) ranked second with between 10 and 15 percent of the churchgoers; and Presbyterians and Methodists each had about half as many members as the Mormons. These rankings remained fairly stable until the close of World War II, but since then other notable trends have emerged.[25]

From the seventeenth until well into the nineteenth century,

Roman Catholics directed major missionary efforts toward Indian groups in what is now Arizona, as well as providing spiritual instruction and guidance for Spanish and Mexican newcomers hoping to remain in the area. First under the indefatigable leadership of Jesuit Eusebio Francisco Kino (from the 1680s to 1711) and later following the dynamic generalship of Franciscan Francisco Garcés in the late eighteenth century, the Catholics established and maintained missionaries among the Pima, Yuma, Papago, Navajo, and Hopi tribes. Before the 1860s these efforts and other church work were administered from Santa Fe, but from 1866 to 1868 new parishes were begun in Tucson and Yuma, and a separate jurisdiction for Arizona was established under Father Jean Baptiste Salpointe. In the closing decades of the nineteenth century and the early years of the twentieth, evangelization of the Indians continued, separate schools for boys and girls were established, and other churches were planted throughout the state, especially under the leadership of European-trained priests. By 1926, of the 153,086 churchgoing Arizonans, about 63 percent (96,471) were Roman Catholics, a majority of whom were Indians and Spanish- and English-speaking Mexicans.

Meanwhile Mormons had settled in northeastern Arizona as early as the 1860s and expanded to farms and towns on the Little Colorado, Gila, and Salt rivers within a generation. At first the Mormons kept to themselves as they carved out and began to irrigate farms in these regions. Gradually, especially in the twentieth century, they too began concentrated efforts to evangelize Indians and incoming Mexican groups. So marked was LDS expansion in Arizona and the Southwest that the ninth Mormon temple was completed in Mesa in 1927 to serve Arizona, New Mexico, and southern California. One year earlier a religious census had revealed that the Mormons were the second largest church group in Arizona, with 16,891 (11 percent) of the religiously affiliated in the state.

At much the same time, Protestant groups began establishing preaching points and church congregations in Arizona. By the late 1860s Presbyterians had opened mission stations among the territory's Indians, and Methodists sent ministers in the 1870s. Before 1881 ended, Baptist, Congregational, and Episcopal pastors were also shepherding small flocks in the territory. One year later there were about twenty-five Protestant congregations throughout the state. Probably most of these groups were similar in beliefs to many Protestants in the West: evangelical (stressing biblical literalism and the necessity of a "born-again" experience), advocates of a "stern moralism," and—as a result of isolation and distance—less high church than their coreligionists in eastern America and Europe.[26]

This separation can be overemphasized, however, for national religious controversies likewise buffeted Arizona. If churchgoers in the East were split by disagreements between fundamentalists and liberals, "drys" and "wets," and between Ku Klux Klan and Catholic and Jewish groups, so were believers in Arizona. For example, Dr. R. S. Beal, notable pastor of the First Baptist Church in Tucson, led thirty churches out of the Northern Baptist alignment (which he considered too liberal and insufficiently sound on fundamentals) to found the Conservative Baptists. Fervent Protestants in Arizona also backed prohibition and denounced others who supported its repeal. Anti-Catholic feelings, while not so militant or well organized as in Texas or Oregon, were nonetheless central to growing KKK membership in the 1920s.

In the half-century between 1930 and 1980, shifts in religious affiliation began to take place and new patterns emerged. Catholics and Mormons remained the two largest denominations in 1950, for example, but Baptists were growing rapidly, with more churches than any other combined denomination in the state. While nine of the state's fourteen counties were more than 50 percent Catholic— three others above 25 percent—Coconino (more than 50 percent) and Mohave (25 percent plus) counties were Methodist. The LDS population in Arizona, meanwhile, ranked fourth in the country, outnumbered only by Mormon members in Utah, Idaho, and California.[27]

By 1980, these trends were taking on new meaning. Although the Catholics were still the largest denomination, they now made up roughly 45 percent of the religious adherents in the state, down from 60 to 70 percent earlier in the century. Mormons remained at about 13 percent of the total, but Southern Baptists—the fastest growing of the newer denominations—had surpassed the Methodists and Presbyterians. Growing more rapidly than the Catholics and Mormons, the Southern Baptists, along with other Baptist groups, made up 13 to 14 percent of the church-affiliated population. Indeed, if one combined the fundamental/evangelical Baptists, the Holiness churches (such as the Nazarenes and the Church of God), and the Pentecostals (Assembly of God), these groups included more than 16 percent of the state's religious population. As further evidence of this trend, the evangelical magazine *Christianity Today* announced that the First Assembly of God Church of Phoenix was the fastest-growing church in the United States during 1985, adding 2,307 new members in one year for a total of 7,688.[28]

These new patterns in Arizona religious history echoed changes taking place elsewhere in the United States. The Catholics continue to be by far the largest church in the nation, but their percentage of growth and leadership is shrinking. That decrease will likely be smaller in Arizona, however, because most of the Mexican immigrants who continue to cross the border are Catholic. The Mormons are now the dominant religious group in northeastern Arizona, and they also have large numbers in the Phoenix (especially Mesa) and Tucson areas. Finally, the new evangelical groups of Southern Baptists, Holiness, and Protestant groups seem to have assumed the evangelical thrust of such groups as the Presbyterians and Methodists of nearly a century earlier. Barring a dramatic, unpredictable shift in immigration, these trends are likely to continue in the next quarter-century.

Schools

Although historians dealing with pioneer Arizona point out the paucity of private and public schools and the backwardness of these first institutions, Arizona was not far behind other areas in the American West in setting up systems of schooling. Nor were these schools as primitive as romantic historians would have one believe. Since the most popular views of the West emphasize a rough, wide-open, rural region with little regard for sociocultural institutions, these interpreters have been reluctant to believe that early Arizonans were interested in schools. But these Wild West contentions are misleading, as is the emphasis on differences between eastern and western schools; continuities from East to West have bulked larger than the differences.[29]

Educational activities in Arizona in the half-century between 1863 and World War I mirrored several developments nationwide. Within a year after establishment of territorial Arizona, its legislature appropriated nearly 10 percent of its meager budget of $16,137 to education and even authorized a university, which was not established until 1885. A low tax base and the lack of ready cash (problems that plagued nearly all frontier schools) made it difficult to establish a territory-wide system of schools; but within a generation such an organization was underway, with a particularly rapid growth of elementary schools in the 1880s. Meanwhile parochial schools for boys and girls were established. When the need for more trained teachers became apparent, Arizona Territorial Normal School in Tempe (now Arizona State University) was opened in 1886, followed in 1899 by Northern Arizona Normal School (Northern Arizona University) in Flagstaff. In 1885 the University of Arizona, a land-grant institution, was established, but it did not begin formal instruction until 1891. Like nearly all western state institutions of higher education, it had few students in its early years and experienced many financial difficulties.

If Arizona followed eastern and western precedents in establishing its state public school system and teachers colleges, it also imitated previous patterns in professionalizing its educational organizations and in opening high schools late in the nineteenth and early in the twentieth century. In 1889 a separate school superintendency was set up, and funds were raised for uniform school textbooks. High schools came to Arizona a decade or two later than in other parts of the nation, but they were in place by 1920.

The Depression played havoc with educational systems in Arizona, and not until World War II were schools once again on a solid basis. Then the waves of new immigrants brought numerous, rapid changes to Arizona schools. Surging urban populations called for the reorganization of school districts in city areas and forced the closing or consolidation of numerous rural one-teacher schools, a movement widespread throughout the West.

In other respects, Arizona matched or exceeded national averages in several categories. In 1950, Arizona had more students between the ages of five and twenty-nine (50.7 percent) than did the nation (49.4). And twenty-five-year-olds in the state averaged more years of schooling (10.0 years) than the national average (9.3). Ten years later Arizona had even widened the gap in the latter category. At much the same time, Arizona, like New Mexico and California, was spending more per pupil than other states to educate its young people.[30]

In the last generation, continuity and change have marked educational developments in Arizona. Continued waves of newcomers have swelled public school systems to the bursting point, forcing the construction of dozens of new elementary, middle, and high schools. Concurrently, the University of Arizona spiraled from 13,000 students in 1960 to more than 32,000 by 1980, only to be surpassed by Arizona State University, which more than tripled in those two decades from 11,000 to nearly 38,000. Northern Arizona University also grew rapidly, as did junior or community colleges set up to take care of entering college students as well as vocational, community, and adult educational needs. Incoming populations were sufficiently large to encourage the opening of Grand Canyon College, which the Southern Baptists established in Prescott in 1949 and transferred to Phoenix in 1951, and the founding of Prescott College by the Congregationalists in 1966. The three state universities, and to a lesser extent the junior colleges and private schools, took advantage of the science-related industries that relocated to Arizona after the war to build new combinations of higher education and science- and war-related industries that still characterize the Sunbelt and far western regions of the country.

If educationists in Arizona and elsewhere in the nation were convinced of the necessity of "Americanizing" minority populations in the first half of the twentieth century, that conviction has rapidly changed since 1950. In fact, although controversial, programs of bilingual education are available in the state, and courses in the history and culture of Indian and Hispanic groups are part of the curriculum of many public schools. And the federal government, while still aiding in the cost of educating Indian children, is now encouraging those students to attend nearby public schools rather than being placed in separate schools for Indian young people.

Educational change in Arizona has progressed fairly smoothly from the 1960s to the present. The campus disruptions, hot politcal debates, and statewide controversies often evident in Texas and California, for example, have been largely absent from Arizona. One suspects that this relative placidity will reign into the next generation. Obviously additional numbers of students will continue to stretch the public school system and necessitate the establishment of institutions like Arizona State University West, but this growth is unlikely to carry with it disquieting change. Like nearly all aspects of Arizona culture, education has shown remarkable growth while following well-established national and regional patterns.

Toward a Wider View of Culture

For those interested in tracing cultural developments in Arizona, the topics discussed thus far—historiography, literature, art, churches, and schools—are a rich, little-tapped archive beckoning the curious and ambitious. Indeed, a whole generation of lay historians, graduate students, and seasoned scholars could plunder these subjects without exhausting the research possibilities of the frontier era, the early twentieth century, or the near-present. Without moving beyond these traditional chronological boundaries of cultural history, beginners and veterans alike will find more than enough projects to keep them occupied for several years.

But a wider view of culture in Arizona and the modern West must be brought into focus if historians are to comprehend more of the contours of the state and region's cultural terrain. For two or three generations, anthropologists, geographers, and social science–minded historians have argued for a more inclusive definition of culture, something akin to German *Kultur.* For these scholars, culture denotes a combination of setting, people, ideas, and value systems. If pushed far enough, historians advocating this spread-eagle definition of culture are forced to write "total history"—a panoramic view of the past dealing with "the sum total of a way of life" without respect to class, gender, or racial lines. If one had pages enough and time, this broad-based perspective would lead to a book-length study of culture in modern Arizona. On the other hand, by focusing briefly on three topics—urban, popular, and regional cultures—one can concentrate on facets of this broader view of culture and, at the same time, suggest several topics significant to Arizona's culture that merit additional study.[31]

Urban Culture

No characterstic of recent Arizona is more notable, or apparent, than its increasingly urban nature. As historians Bradford Luckingham (and his students) and C. L. Sonnichsen have noted, Arizona has moved dramatically from a rural to an urban state since 1940. In that year approximately one-third of the state's population lived in urban areas (then defined as incorporated areas of at least 2,500 residents). Twenty years later, three-quarters of the people of the state resided in cities. By 1980, more than eight of ten Arizonans lived in cities.

Meanwhile Tucson had sprung from 35,752 in 1940 to 212,892 in 1960, and to 331,506 in 1980. The changes in Phoenix were even more meteoric: 56,414 in 1940; 439,170 in 1960; and up to 789,749 in 1980. And when population figures include the metropolitan areas clustered around Tucson and Phoenix, one realizes how urban Arizona has become. If seven out of ten Arizonans lived in either greater Tucson or Phoenix in 1970, nearly 80 percent resided in the two metropolitan areas ten years later. By 1980, about 55 percent of the state's population lived in Phoenix, the fastest growing of the thirty leading Standard Metropolitan Statistical Areas in the United States. While only 74 percent of all Americans were urbanites, 84 percent of Arizona's population lived in metropolitan areas. Clearly, the culture of modern Arizona is heavily urban and is likely to remain so in the near future.[32]

Although recently completed studies of urban Arizona have emphasized economic and political changes and touched on social developments, they have not stressed cultural activities. We have heard a great deal, for example, about how economic forces and political divisions influence planning, subdivisions, and annexations, but the human dimensions of these decisions—the specific people involved—remain obscure. We ought to know more about the Del Webbs and about the persons and ideas that shaped their thinking. Since developers, suburbs, and annexations have played dominant parts in the Arizona drama, and will continue to do so in the next twenty-five years, we should have a plethora of probing studies of these topics.[33]

A parallel subject meriting much more attention is urban, and especially suburban, family life. Not a few sociologists, psychologists, and historians have centered on the manifold difficulties that poor Anglo, Hispanic, Black, and Indian families face in inner cities or decaying neighborhoods of western urban areas, yet we understand little about the social and cultural experiences of middle-class suburban families. Since families constitute one of the two or three most significant ingredients of American life, we ought to devote much more attention to families and their components.

How little has been written, for example, about women's experiences in the modern West. The lifestyles and daily activities of pioneer women are just now coming into focus in recent historical studies, and we have but a handful or two of monographs focusing on women in the twentieth-century West. One would like to comprehend, for instance, more about the pressures women in Arizona experienced in trying to cope with the devastating Depression, difficulties that many women faced as they worked outside their homes for the first time during World War II, and the ongoing dilemmas increasing numbers of women share in trying to fulfill the dual roles of homemaker and working woman. If the experiences of women in modern Arizona—mostly in urban settings—remain obscure, we know even less about children as segments of families, as outside families, as students, or as workers. And the facts we have about men, not so much as leaders, voters, or workers, but as husbands, fathers, as culture makers, are as plentiful as icebergs along the Gila. Few subjects remain so little studied and so open to research and reflection as the diverse roles of families in Arizona and the modern West.[34]

If we can shift some of the current fixation of journalists and historians away from additional studies of dams, water policy, and the bureaucratic maneuverings involved in these topics toward additional work on transitions in recent civilization in Arizona, we are likely to come to a larger understanding of the state. What have been the valuable contributions of volunteer associations like women's clubs, literary societies, and other broad-based groups that sponsor musical, theatrical, and museum organizations? Just now we are beginning to understand the impact of women's groups, for example, in helping shape attitudes toward political issues, literary and artistic norms, and the moral stances of western communities. These intriguing topics stand as notable possibilities for ambitious historical researchers of the present and future.

Finally, each year thousands of outsiders become part-time or full-fledged residents of Arizona. As Carey McWilliams has demonstrated in his brilliant re-creation of sociocultural life in modern California, these newcomers often force moving changes upon the cultural landscape of their new host society. In the early decades of the twentieth century, new kinds of churches, eating establishments, pet parlors, and cemeteries sprang up to satisfy the desires of these newly arrived immigrants.[35] What sorts of parallel changes have "snowbird" residents brought to Arizona? Has the state become an Iowa Southwest, as some writers have suggested in interpreting aspects of modern California? One might likewise isolate and study a new generation of intellectuals who have moved recently to the state. Students of history and literature like C. L. Sonnichsen and Lawrence Clark Powell have fled Texas and California, novelists N. Scott Momaday and Leslie Silko have left New Mexico, and writers like Vine Deloria and Edward Abbey have abandoned other points to the east to settle in Arizona. Has this new influx of "outside-in" writers brought changes to the Arizona intellectual terrain, or is this new movement nothing more than a series of literary London bridges, *on* but not *of* Arizona culture?

If future historians of cultural Arizona can move away from their fascination with a rural, romantic Old West and commence a series of essays and longer studies of recent Arizona culture, especially its urban nature, they will have achieved the most-needed reorientation of Arizona and western history. This refocusing of historical endeavors will become even more necessary in the next quarter of a century.

Popular Culture

Histories written about the tumultuous sociocultural changes in the United States during the 1960s and '70s and centering on such topics as ethnic conflict, new roles for women and families, and other newly recognized social groups often illustrate what has been called the "new social history." Historians interested in these subjects have worked with history "from the bottom up"—that is, with ordinary citizens such as blue-collar workers, clerical and department store employees, housewives, and children, as well as with slaves, hoboes, and a variety of social deviants. However much recent historians have been aware of and participated in these methodological and thematic shifts in social history, they seem much less cognizant of the newly formulated interpretative approaches to cultural history.

At the same time that social historians have located or rediscovered segments of society omitted from earlier historical works, cultural historians have constructed new pegs on which to hang pathbreaking interpretations of varied facets of American culture. These cultural specialists have begun to treat such previously neglected topics as popular histories, fiction, films and documentaries, and popular cultural activities such as circuses, festivals, rodeos, and dude ranching; they have also emphasized the importance of unlimited study of popular views and entertainments so as to obtain a more wholistic view of our culture.

Less attention has been paid to the necessity and methods of studying popular culture than social historians have devoted to examining the approaches to their field, but what the study of non-elites has meant to social historians the new scrutiny of popular culture has meant to cultural historians. Obviously this new interest in popular culture in the United States owes much to social science and humanities scholars such as Clifford Geertz, Robert Darnton, Henry Nash Smith, and John Cawelti. Advocating a new and broader study of popular experiences, ideologies, and writings, these thinkers have helped make the study of mass culture a major new ingredient in the expanding interest in cultural history in the United States.[36]

An enlarged interest in the study of popular culture in Arizona
could add much to an understanding of the state's history—and its
future. Consider, for example, the value of evaluating popular histories, biographies, and fiction written about Indian groups and
individuals, Tombstone, and such Wild West worthies as Wyatt Earp,
Billy the Kid, and Johnny Ringo. Examining the shifting points of
view presented over time in these writings, popular cultural specialists argue, often tells one as much about changing currents of opinion in America as about the subject being treated. Why, for example,
was Billy the Kid treated as something of a buck-toothed, satanic
figure in writings that appeared in the half-century after his death
in 1881 but as a saintly Robin Hood during most of the 1920s and
'30s?[37] On a related subject, someone ought to undertake a careful
study of the popular writings of Walter Noble Burns (his papers
are on file at the University of Arizona Library) to test the conclusions of several scholars who argue that his histories and biographies
did more than most other sources to shape the present-day images
of Billy the Kid and Wyatt Earp.

Other students should scrutinize the numerous formulaic Westerns written about Arizona or by Arizona writers. Although most
of these works by such writers as Zane Grey, Louis L'Amour, Nelson
Nye, and Brian Garfield are dismissed as mindless horse opera, a
second look could reveal a good deal about shifting popular attitudes in America. Grey, for example, incorporated numerous comments about Mormons, World War I, and sociocultural mores of
the 1920s in his Westerns, and L'Amour's attitudes toward Indians
and women in an early novel like *Hondo* (1953), which is set in
Arizona, are much different from those he displays in *Comstock Lode*
(1981) and *The Cherokee Trail* (1982). In limiting nearly all their
comments to what they consider the literary inadequacies of these
novels, critics have missed their importance as useful barometers
of shifting popular attitudes.[38]

In another medium, sales figures for and the impact of *Arizona
Highways,* the leading popular magazine of the state, perhaps rival
those of the novels of Grey and L'Amour. Established in the mid-
1920s, *Arizona Highways* has blended a steady diet of colorful visual
images by notable painters and photographers, smoothly written if
conservative editorials and essays, and appealing layout and forceful

marketing. As Gary Topping has shown in his revealing history of the magazine, it has undergone change in its six decades but has avoided being out of step with its steadily growing readership. By the middle of the 1950s—and up to the 1980s—sales have ranged between five hundred thousand and one million per issue. Interestingly, more than 95 percent of the subscribers live outside the state, with more purchasers in Los Angeles than in Arizona. Still, *Arizona Highways* has been a powerful magnet for Arizona, as a recent poll indicated: one in three immigrants replied that "it was the magazine that had brought them." Here is another revelation of how much the study of popular culture may reveal about Arizona and the modern West.[39]

The same can be said for the importance of treating such popular artists as Ted De Grazia and many of those painters taking part in the annual cowboy art roundups in Phoenix. Established in 1965, the Cowboy Artists of America perpetuate "the memory and culture of the Old West as typified by the late Frederic Remington, Charles Russell and others; [hoping to ensure] authentic representation of the life of the West, as it was and is." Rather than merely ridiculing these painters as purveyors of romantic, nostalgic nonsense, historians and critics ought to ask why these yearly roundups draw as many as thirty thousand viewers and command increasingly higher prices for the paintings on display. What does such enthusiasm tell us about popular attitudes toward the West?

Perhaps the best-known of all Arizona artists was Ettorino (Ted) De Grazia. Born and reared in the small mining town of Morenci in the Gila Mountains of southeastern Arizona, De Grazia also spent five years in Italy and other stints wandering through northern Mexico. Drawn to Indian, Hispanic, and Mexican cultural traditions and self-taught as an artist, he enjoyed pursuing a maverick, nose-thumbing career, particularly after he began selling his paintings to *Arizona Highways* and greeting card markets. In fact, by the 1950s and '60s, the American Cancer Society had used his *Navajo Madonna* to market more than a quarter-million cards, and *Los Niños*, appearing on a UNICEF card, sold more than "five million boxes of greeting cards." Marching to no artistic creed or form, De Grazia produced hundreds of colorful, large-eyed angels, Indian and Hispanic children, and impressions of animals and religious artifacts. Often overlooked or dismissed by art critics (whom he referred to as "miserable bastards, feeding off someone else's talent"), De Grazia deserves more attention as a popular regional artist who may be the most widely reprinted American painter around the world.[40]

Two or three other aspects of mass culture in Arizona merit at least brief mention. Since churches and schools are important agents of social and moral order, historians of the modern West need to take note of the powerful shaping forces of these institutions. Historians in other regions have studied such facets of churches as Sunday schools, youth groups, and the social action arms of several denominations, but interpreters of the West—whether dealing with the pioneer or modern period—have yet to discover the significance of these organizations. Nor have they paid much attention to the popular ideologies and value systems that have done so much to shape school policies and standards in Arizona and the modern West. We have learned much recently about nineteenth-century frontier schools through a study of the textbooks used in these institutions, but we lack such systematic analyses of modern school books and other teaching tools. Because churches and schools will continue to be central institutions in Arizona to the end of the century and beyond, historians ought to take a closer look at their pivotal influences in the mass culture of the state.

Finally, think of how much sports and other recreational activities mean to Americans—and even more to Arizonans, whose climate so invites out-of-doors events. Indeed, one wonders how many Nobel or Pulitzer Prize winners it would take to elicit the hoopla and headlines surrounding the 1987 Arizona State Rose Bowl victory, or to raise as much money as was donated to sponsor the 1987 national collegiate football championship in Tempe's Fiesta Bowl. (Interestingly, when Rita Dove, a professor of English at Arizona State University, won a Pulitzer Prize, J. Russell Nelson, president of the university, declared the event "as exciting as the Rose Bowl, and it's more significant.") Truth to tell, sports—whether at the public school, collegiate, community, or professional levels—are important to Arizonans. They support these programs with their taxes and at box offices, but western historians have yet to discover this important dimension of popular culture in Arizona. One hopes they soon will.

Reflections on Regional Cultures

Many students of American cultural history flee from regional subjects much as if they were disease-infested predators whose bites might bring on blindness and shriveled minds. For these writers regional topics are by nature inferior and unworthy of study. Nearly a century ago, however, the historian and philosopher Josiah Royce argued persuasively that a healthy provincialism—the balanced adherence to and study of the sociocultural life of a region—provided a needed bulwark against excessive nationalizing tendencies at work in the United States. Royce's argument is still valid; one of the most illuminating means by which to examine a national culture is through its regions. Artificial though state boundaries are at times in studying aspects of national and regional culture, on other occasions these political divisions aid in illuminating obscure corners of national trends.[41]

In examining the present and future contours of Arizona culture, a few questions are in order. What major interpretations have been advanced thus far concerning regionalism in the West, and how useful are they for understanding culture in Arizona and the modern West? Are some of these views more handy than others for scrutinizing aspects of Arizona's cultural life? Finally, since economic and social developments are undergoing such marked and rapid change in Arizona, are similar dramatic changes likely to occur in the state's culture, and, if so, are interpretations useful for the present likely to be outdated twenty-five years hence?

A number of essays and books utilizing a regionalistic interpretation of the West are useful to a discussion of culture in Arizona and the modern West. In the first place, Frederick Jackson Turner's frontier thesis (1893), except in a metaphorical sense, is less applicable than his sectional hypothesis (1925), in which he dealt with the significance of postfrontier sections in interpreting American history. Like Walter Prescott Webb in *The Great Plains* (1931), Turner asserted that sections (regions) were noteworthy, unique segments of national society and culture. More recently in his essay "New West, True West" (1987), Donald Worster argues that western historiography must abandon its stress on frontier themes and portray the West as a region if we are to understand its modern era.[42]

Meanwhile Bernard DeVoto, sharing the regional defensiveness permeating Webb's writings, concluded that the West had been a plundered province, a colony of the Northeast, to which it supplied raw materials and from which it purchased manufactured goods. Several journalists, social scientists, and other historians agreed with the Webb-DeVoto position and declared that until the West asserted itself it would remain under the thumb of eastern interests and not an independent region controlling its future.[43]

While Turner and Webb stressed the innovating, novel qualities of the frontier and regional Wests, Earl Pomeroy, in the most provocative of the recent views of the West, called for a "Reorientation of Western History" (1955), for more attention to be paid to continuities between East and West. After examining political and constitutional, economic, social, and cultural developments in the West, Pomeroy was convinced that eastern legacies bulked as large as new experiences in the region. Contrary to what some observers have written, Pomeroy was not anti-Turnerian but challenged the master's followers to be less tied to radical environmental determinist views of the West.[44]

Although he follows some of the propositions of Webb and Pomeroy, Gerald Nash in *The West in the Twentieth Century* (1973) has added a new twist to their views. He sees the West marching through colonial and regional stages by the end of World War II and, after that watershed experience, emerging as a pacesetting region, particularly in its economic and sociocultural influences on the remainder of the nation. In the most recent gloss on these perspectives, William G. Robbins (1986) perceives a more complicated story, in which some parts of the West (California and the Southwest) have been pace-setting but with other subregions (notably the Pacific Northwest and the Rockies) remaining "plundered provinces," still under the thrall of outside interests.[45]

Finally, other journalists and historians have pictured Arizona as part of a Sunbelt America that represents a new power shift toward the South and West, a southward and westward tilt away from the Northeast. Such writers as Neil Morgan, Kirkpatrick Sale, Peter Wiley, Robert Gottlieb, and Carl Abbott tie Arizona to larger regions stretching from Florida to California and up to the Pacific

Northwest, or from Texas to California, while social scientists Donald Meinig and Raymond Gastil marry Arizona to an interior Southwest. In the most sweeping reading of modern North America, journalist Joel Garreau assigns Arizona to MexAmerica, a region stretching from Mexico north nearly to Denver, west to Los Angeles and San Francisco, and east to Houston.[46]

Future writers are liable to produce other regional interpretations that see Arizona in new lights and different contexts, but existing views contain material enough for a few brief conclusions on the state's culture. At the end of seventy-five years of statehood, culture in Arizona is best described as an extension of regional and national patterns, with little evidence that the state's culture differs from these outside traditions. Although this tentative deduction may not please cheerleaders for a greater Arizona, it is a conclusion describing the cultural status of most western states, with California, Texas, and perhaps Oregon as exceptions.

Most historians treating Arizona's past are locked into its frontier traditions and exhibit little interest in dealing with post–World War II events or cultural history. Moreover, chroniclers of the state's history are not much attuned to the new social history that has occupied many national historians in the last generation. Nor can one speak of a coterie of pathbreaking authors pioneering new literary traditions in Arizona. For the most part, writers have followed trails blazed elsewhere. Even Edward Abbey, who grabs more headlines than any other contemporary writer in the state, is a charter member of the well-known "alarmist" school of western letters apparent in California and Texas. The recent arrival of a new group of Indian writers near Tucson may be the harbinger of an outpouring of rich writings about American Indians, however.

The future of artistic activities in Arizona is more difficult to predict. Visitors and outside influences from other regions and other parts of the West have dominated the artistic scene thus far, but perhaps the next generation of painters will be less beholden to these foreign trends and more inclined toward an open marriage of Arizona scenes and subjects and individualistic philosophies and techniques. Developments in churches and schools in Arizona have not broken new ground either. While denominations and schools have experienced unprecedented growth and expansion, most of these changes have followed fairly closely those in other mushrooming Sunbelt areas.

There are, however, a few signs of difference between Arizona and the West and the nation. Not only is Arizona an urban society, but it is urbanizing more rapidly than elsewhere, a fact that a few urban historians are noting. In addition, Indian cultural traditions run stronger and deeper in the state than in most other parts of the United States. And one can only conclude that Hispanic culture, with periodic infusions from the south, will retain much of its character, even if in partially assimilated form. Generally, then, to invoke a metaphor popular in current social science circles, the periphery (Arizona) has been more similar to than different from its cores (the nation and the West). Still, Arizona watchers must keep this relationship between the national and local in the forefront of their thinking; for, like our governmental system that calls for dual allegiances to nation and state, culture in the United States often unites the national and the local.

In other repsects, one might argue that Arizona is more a "border" culture than a regional one, that it has fronted—and will front—on several cultural systems without developing its own. Throughout the first half or so of the nineteenth century, the area served as the northern boundary for the Spanish Empire and Mexico, blocked somewhat the southern expansion of the Mormons, and lay next to burgeoning California. These social and cultural boundaries, already apparent in 1900, have continued into the present and are likely to persist in the future. Similar to Idaho in the northern West, perched between the Pacific Coast states and the expanding Mormons of Utah, Arizona lies among California, Nevada, Utah, New Mexico, Mexico, and Colorado—without replicating exactly any of their cultures.

In some respects, cultural contours in Arizona are different from those of these surrounding areas. Nothing in Arizona closely resembles the gambling, ranching, Sagebrush Rebellion matrix of Nevada or the Mormon hegemony in Utah. Nor do the cultural explosions of Mexico dramatically alter civilization in Arizona. And the state differs from New Mexico, its oldest neighbor and former parent. Hispanic influences are more predominant in New Mexico, which is less urban and more tied to oil than its friend to the west. And, to Arizona's relief, it does not border on Texas.

But Arizona has its own behemoth to the west. For Arizonans, living next to California is like sleeping next to an elephant: when the beast twitches or stretches, its neighbor is thrown out of bed. During the next few years, Arizona is liable to continue its love/hate relationship with Calfornia. While Arizona seems inclined to follow what it considers the prosperity and progress of California, to join its athletic conferences (and thereby to cut its ties with the Rockies), and to compete with its western neighbor for water, government largesse, and football coaches, it seems also ambivalent about its associations with the Golden State, feeling as if it is treated as a poor country cousin and sensing that it may be repeating mistakes California has begun to recognize. But having bordered on California for so long, Arizona may have become stuck to its tarbaby, where it may remain for the next decade or two. If so, the "next-to" or border image is likely to be the most useful metaphor in defining Arizona's immediate cultural future.

In the long run, attempting to guess the cultural contours of Arizona in the fourth quarter of its statehood centennial is like trying to gift wrap a cartload of watermelons. Even though at this point cultural continuities from outside the state bulk larger than local innovations, growth and its twin, change, complicate the future. Thus, to invoke another comparison, predicting the future of cultural Arizona is reminiscent of the man who tries to trap the reflection of the moon: just as he thinks he has caught his quarry, it escapes and saunters off. Finally, the continuing numbers of newcomers to Arizona are as pebbles tossed in a pond, forming new patterns that ripple into earlier currents, creating a disarray of the old and new but never solidifying into a recognizable, stable design. Clearly, continuity and change, at the same time, will continue to characterize the culture of Arizona.

If John Steinbeck were alive to swing his camper once more through Arizona, a quarter of a century after his earlier headlong dash, he would encounter a state more urban, more bound to government funding and high tech, more tied to California, and more

conscious of trying to define itself culturally. And, if an insightful
and curious historian, Steinbeck would want to examine the cultural
relationship between Arizona, the West, and the rest of the nation.

What one would hope from a resurrected Steinbeck is what
one wishes from historians chronicling the history of Arizona. If
they do their job well, they will discover the appropriateness of
artist Georgia O'Keeffe's apt phrase, the "faraway nearby."[47] Arizona
will undoubtedly remain associated with the "faraway" (national
and regional cultural traditions) while it endeavors to nourish its
"nearby" (novel local happenings). But in treating this confluence
of the faraway nearby, disciples of Clio will have to elude the major
pitfall of regional history: the frequently excessive emphasis on the
local to the detriment of surrounding, shaping contexts. In other
words, they will have to avoid hydroponic history, romantic narratives rooted in nothing but the hot air of chauvinism and boosterism,
sustained by the too-strong attachment to the local, and fertilized
by the blindly provincial that worships the next-door and dismisses
the rich possibilities for regional comparisons and contrasts. If historians depicting Arizona can avoid these traps and instead discover
the fertile field of modern cultural history, they can illuminate the
present and future of Arizona's cultural development as they add
to it.

Notes

1. John Steinbeck, *Travels with Charley in Search of America* (New York: Viking
Press, 1962); W. Eugene Hollon, *The Southwest: Old and New* (New York: Alfred A.
Knopf, 1961), 435.

2. Two handy collections of western historiographical essays are available in
Michael P. Malone, ed., *Historians and the American West* (Lincoln: University of Ne-
braska Press, 1983); and Roger L. Nichols, ed., *American Frontier and Western Issues:
A Historiographical Review* (Westport, Conn.: Greenwood Press, 1986). For a provoca-
tive discussion of broader definitions of cultural history, see Robert Berkhofer, Jr.,
"Clio and the Culture Concept: Some Impressions of a Changing Relationship in
American Historiography," *Social Science Quarterly* 53 (September 1972): 297–320.
The best of the recent discussions of cultural-intellectual history in the West is
Howard R. Lamar, "Much to Celebrate: The Western History Association's Twenty-
Fifth Birthday," *Western Historical Quarterly* 17 (October 1986): 397–416. For an in-
teresting overview of Arizona cultural life, see *Culture and Values in Arizona Life*
(Tempe: Arizona State University, School of Public Affairs, Morrison Institute for
Public Policy, 1987).

3. Richard W. Etulain, "Shifting Interpretations of Western American Cultural History," *Historians and the American West*, ed. Malone, 414–32.

4. These points are argued at greater length in Richard W. Etulain, "A New Historiographical Frontier: The Twentieth-Century West," in a forthcoming volume of original essays edited by Gerald D. Nash and Richard W. Etulain (Albuquerque: University of New Mexico Press, 1988).

5. Henry Nash Smith, *Virgin Land: The American West as Symbol and Myth* (Cambridge: Harvard University Press, 1950); Ray Allen Billington, *Land of Savagery/Land of Promise: The European Image of the American Frontier in the Nineteenth Century* (New York: W. W. Norton and Company, 1981); William H. Goetzmann, *The West of the Imagination* (New York: W. W. Norton and Company, 1986).

6. Bert M. Fireman, *Arizona: Historic Land* (New York: Alfred A. Knopf, 1982), contains a brief but useful treatment of previous histories of Arizona, pp. 243–50.

7. Three helpful historiographical essays dealing with Arizona contain little or no mention of cultural history: Ray Brandes, "Opportunities for Research in Arizona History," *The Historian* 22 (August 1960): 414–24; Richard O. Davies, "Arizona's Recent Past: Opportunities for Research," *Arizona and the West* 9 (Autumn 1967): 243–58; James T. Stensvaag, "Seeking the Impossible: The State Histories of New Mexico, Arizona, and Nevada—An Assessment," *Pacific Historical Review* 50 (November 1981): 499–525.

8. Gerald D. Nash, *The American West in the Twentieth Century: A Short History of an Urban Oasis* (Englewood Cliffs, N. J.: Prentice-Hall, 1973; Albuquerque: University of New Mexico Press, 1977); D. W. Meinig, *Southwest: Three Peoples in Geographical Change, 1600–1970* (New York: Oxford University Press, 1971); Bradford Luckingham, *The Urban Southwest: A Profile History of Albuquerque, El Paso, Phoenix, and Tucson* (El Paso: Texas Western Press, 1983). Luckingham's helpful book and two of his essays list most of the recent works on southwestern urbanization: "The Southwestern Urban Frontier, 1880–1930," *Journal of the West* 18 (July 1979): 40–50; "The American Southwest: An Urban View," *Western Historical Quarterly* 15 (July 1984): 261–80.

9. For a 1,400-page reference guide to western literature, see J. Golden Taylor and Thomas J. Lyon, et al., eds., *A Literary History of the American West* (Fort Worth: Texas Christian University Press, 1987). A much briefer guide to the subject is available in Richard W. Etulain, ed., *The American Literary West* (Manhattan, Kans.: Sunflower University Press, 1980).

10. Abe C. Ravitz, *Alfred Henry Lewis*, Western Writers Series, no. 32 (Boise: Boise State University, 1978), is a handy introduction to Lewis.

11. Edwin R. Bingham, *Charles F. Lummis: Editor of the Southwest* (San Marino, Calif.: Huntington Library, 1955); Robert E. Fleming, *Charles F. Lummis*, Western Writers Series, no. 50 (Boise: Boise State University, 1981).

12. Judy Alter, *Stewart Edward White*, Western Writers Series, no. 18 (Boise: Boise State University, 1975).

13. Margaret F. Maxwell, *A Passion for Freedom: The Life of Sharlot Hall* (Tucson: University of Arizona Press, 1982).

14. Samuel L. Myers, "Dick Wick Hall: Humorist with a Serious Purpose," *Journal of Arizona History* 11 (Winter 1970): 255–78. Selections from many of the early Arizona writers are included in Mary G. Boyer, ed., *Arizona in Literature* (Glendale, Calif.: Arthur H. Clark, 1935). There is no modern anthology of Arizona literature; one is needed. For additional listings of books and essays about these and other Arizona writers, see Richard W. Etulain, *A Bibliographical Guide to the Study of*

Western American Literature (Lincoln: University of Nebraska Press, 1982). Also consult Jon Tuska and Vicki Piekarski, eds., *Encyclopedia of Frontier and Western Fiction* (New York: McGraw-Hill Book Company, 1983); and James Vinson and D. L. Kirkpatrick, eds., *Twentieth-Century Western Writers* (London: Macmillan Publishers, 1982).

15. Fred Erisman has provided two very helpful overviews of western regional literature in "Western Regional Writers and the Uses of Place," *Journal of the West* 19 (January 1980): 36–44, and "The Changing Face of Western Literary Regionalism," in Nash and Etulain. The best recent discussion of American regionalism is Richard Maxwell Brown, "The New Regionalism in America, 1970–81," in *Regionalism and the Pacific Northwest*, ed. William G. Robbins et al. (Corvallis: Oregon State University Press, 1983), 37–96.

16. Robert Berkhofer, Jr., *The White Man's Indian: Images of the American Indian from Columbus to the Present* (New York: Alfred A. Knopf, 1978), 107.

17. Quoted in Sam H. Henderson, "Ross Santee," in *Twentieth-Century Western Writers*, ed. Vinson and Kirkpatrick, 684; also see C. L. Sonnichsen, *From Hopalong to Hud: Thoughts on Western Fiction* (College Station: Texas A&M University Press, 1978).

18. Ann Ronald, *The New West of Edward Abbey* (Albuquerque: University of New Mexico Press, 1982); Ronald, "Edward Abbey, (1927–)," in *Fifty Western Writers: A Bio-Bibliographical Sourcebook*, ed. Fred Erisman and Richard W. Etulain (Westport, Conn.: Greenwood Press, 1982), 3–12; Garth McCann, *Edward Abbey*, Western Writers Series, no. 29 (Boise: Boise State University, 1977).

19. This section on art is heavily indebted to James K. Ballinger and Andrea D. Rubinstein, *Visitors to Arizona 1846 to 1980* (Phoenix: Phoenix Art Museum, 1980). See also Doris DuBose, "Art and Artists in Arizona 1847–1912" (master's thesis, Arizona State University, 1974); and Saralie E. Martin Neal, "Romance and Realism— The Grand Canyon Painters Between 1874–1920: Thomas Moran, William Robinson Leigh, and Fernand H. Lungren" (master's thesis, University of Arizona, 1977). The best overview of this topic is H. Wayne Morgan, "Main Trends in Twentieth-Century Western Art," in Nash and Etulain.

20. Wesley M. Burnside, *Maynard Dixon: Artist of the West* (Provo: Brigham Young University Press, 1974).

21. Peter Bermingham, *The New Deal in the Southwest: Arizona and New Mexico* (Tucson: University of Arizona Museum of Art, 1980); Daniel E. Hall, "Federal Patronage of Art in Arizona from 1933 to 1943" (master's thesis, Arizona State University, 1974).

22. Patricia Janis Broder, *The American West: The Modern Vision* (Boston: Little, Brown and Company, A New York Graphic Society Book, 1984).

23. Dorothy Dunn, *American Indian Painting of the Southwest and Plains Areas* (Albuquerque: University of New Mexico Press, 1968); Clara Lee Tanner, *Southwest Indian Painting: A Changing Art* (Tucson: University of Arizona, 1973); *Fred Kabotie: Hopi Indian Artist,* an autobiography told with Bill Belnap (Flagstaff: Museum of Northern Arizona with Northland Press, 1977).

24. Ballinger and Rubinstein, *Visitors to Arizona*, 35.

25. No thorough study is available on religious developments in the modern West, but see Gary Topping, "Religion in the West," *Journal of American Culture* 3 (Summer 1980): 330–50, for a general survey of the nineteenth and twentieth centuries. Other useful generalizations and statistics are available in *Arizona: A State*

Guide (New York: Hastings House, 1941), 120–22; Robert M. Bretall, ed., "Religion," in *Arizona's People and Resources*, rev. ed. (Tucson: University of Arizona Press, 1972), 343–54; Edward H. Peplow, Jr., *History of Arizona*, vol. 3 (New York: Lewis Historical Publishing Company, 1958), 413-26.

26. Ferenc Szasz of the University of New Mexico is completing a study of Protestantism in the West up to about 1920; some of the generalizations here are based on his observations. The best study of Mormons in Arizona is Charles S. Peterson, *Take Up Your Mission: Mormon Colonizing Along the Little Colorado River, 1870–1900* (Tucson: University of Arizona Press, 1973).

27. Edwin R. Gaustad, *Historical Atlas of Religion in America* (New York: Harper and Row, 1962); and Bernard Quinn et al., *Churches and Church Membership in the United States 1980* . . . (Atlanta: Glenmary Research Center, 1982) provide many useful statistics.

28. *Christianity Today,* October 17, 1986, p. 53.

29. Ronald E. Butchart, "Education and Culture in the Trans-Mississippi West: An Interpretation," *Journal of American Culture* 3 (Summer 1980): 351–73; Butchart, "The Growth of an American School System: The Coconino County, Arizona Experience, 1875–1925" (master's thesis, Northern Arizona University, 1973); Roy M. Claridge, "Education," in *Arizona's People and Resources*, 329–41; *Arizona: A State Guide*, 117–20.

30. Lynn Perrigo, *The American Southwest: Its Peoples and Cultures* (New York: Holt, Rinehart and Winston, 1971), 401; *Arizona Statistical Review* 41 (September 1985): 58; Neal R. Peirce, *The Mountain States of America: People, Politics, and Power in the Eight Rocky Mountain States* (New York: W. W. Norton and Company, 1972), 227 *ff.*

31. Several essays in John Higham and Paul K. Conkin, eds., *New Directions in American Intellectual History* (Baltimore: Johns Hopkins University Press, 1979), utilize these broader definitions of culture; see also Berkhofer, "Clio and the Culture Concept."

32. In addition to the essays by Luckingham mentioned in note 8, see his "The Urban Dimension of Western History," in *Historians and the American West*, ed. Malone, 323–43; and "Phoenix: The Desert Metropolis," in *Sunbelt Cities: Politics and Growth Since World War II*, ed. Richard M. Bernard and Bradley R. Rice (Austin: University of Texas Press, 1983), 309–27; Michael Kotlanger, "Phoenix, Arizona: 1920–1940" (Ph.D. dissertation, Arizona State University, 1983); Michael Konig, "Toward Metropolis Status: Phoenix, 1945–1960" (Ph.D. dissertation, Arizona State University, 1983); C. L. Sonnichsen, *Tucson: The Life and Times of an American City* (Norman: University of Oklahoma Press, 1982); and Don Bufkin, "From Mud Village to Modern Metropolis: The Urbanization of Tucson," *Journal of Arizona History* 22 (Spring 1981): 63–98.

33. Kenneth T. Jackson, *Crabgrass Frontier: The Suburbanization of the United States* (New York: Oxford University Press, 1985).

34. Karen Anderson provides a beginning place for the study of women in the modern West by touching on several important themes in her "Western Women: The Twentieth-Century Experience," in Nash and Etulain.

35. Carey McWilliams, *Southern California Country: An Island on the Land* (New York: Duell, Sloan & Pearce, 1946), and *California: The Great Exception* (New York: A. A. Wyn, 1949). Other first-rate models for sociocultural history include Franklin Walker, *A Literary History of Southern California* (Berkeley: University of California

Press, 1950), and two volumes by Kevin Starr: *Americans and the California Dream 1850–1915* (1973) and *Inventing the Dream: California Through the Progressive Era* (1985), both published by Oxford University Press.

36. For helpful discussions of recent trends in social and cultural history, see the essays by Peter N. Stearns—"Toward a Wider Vision: Trends in Social History"—and Robert Darnton—"Intellectual and Cultural History"—in *The Past Before Us: Contemporary Historical Writing in the United States*, ed. Michael Kammen (Ithaca: Cornell University Press, 1980), 205–30, 327–54; also consult the collected essays in Higham and Conkin, *New Directions in American Intellectual History.* The important roles of Henry Nash Smith and John C. Cawelti in western cultural-intellectual history are discussed in Richard W. Etulain, "The American Literary West and Its Interpreters: The Rise of a New Historiography," *Pacific Historical Review* 45 (August 1976): 311–48.

37. Stephen Tatum, *Inventing Billy the Kid: Visions of the Outlaw in America, 1881– 1981* (Albuquerque: University of New Mexico Press, 1982), and Jon Tuska, *Billy the Kid: A Bio-Bibliography* (Westport, Conn.: Greenwood Press, 1983), treat the images of Billy the Kid in American popular culture.

38. Candace C. Kent deals with one aspect of Grey's career in *Zane Grey's Arizona* (Flagstaff: Northland Press, 1984). Robert Gale has written the only full-length published study of L'Amour in his *Louis L'Amour* (Boston: Twayne, 1985).

39. Gary Topping treats the rise of *Arizona Highways* in "A History of *Arizona Highways* Magazine, 1925–1970" (master's thesis, Northern Arizona University, 1970), and "*Arizona Highways:* A Half-Century of Southwestern Journalism," *Journal of the West* 19 (April 1980): 71–79; Lawrence Clark Powell, *Arizona,* 136.

40. *Cowboy Artists of America 1985* (Flagstaff: Northland Press, 1985); Nancy Gottesman, "Cowboy Art Roundup in Phoenix," *Western's World* (October 1986), 14, 17; *De Grazia* (Tucson: University of Arizona Museum of Art, 1973); William Reed, *De Grazia: The Irreverent Angel* (San Diego: Frontier Heritage Press, 1971).

41. Earl Pomeroy, "Josiah Royce: Historian in Quest of Community," *Pacific Historical Review* 40 (February 1971): 1–20; Etulain, "Frontier, Region, and Myth: Changing Interpretations of Western American Culture," *Journal of American Culture* 3 (Summer 1980): 268–84.

42. Turner's essays on the frontier and on sections are reprinted in Ray Allen Billington, ed., *Frontier and Section: Selected Essays of Frederick Jackson Turner* (Englewood Cliffs, N.J.: Prentice-Hall, 1961); Worster, "New West, True West: Interpreting the Region's History," *Western Historical Quarterly* 18 (April 1987). Several of the titles mentioned in this and following paragraphs are discussed in Gerald D. Nash, *The American West Transformed: The Impact of the Second World War* (Bloomington: Indiana University Press, 1985), 208–13; Gene M. Gressley, *The Twentieth-Century West: A Potpourri* (Columbia: University of Missouri Press, 1977), 31–47; Gressley, "Whither Western American History? Speculations on a Direction," *Pacific Historical Review* 53 (November 1984): 493–501; and Etulain, "A New Historiographical Frontier."

43. Bernard DeVoto, "The West: A Plundered Province," *Harper's Magazine* 169 (August 1934): 355–64.

44. Pomeroy, "Toward a Reorientation of Western History: Continuity and Environment," *Mississippi Valley Historical Review* 41 (March 1955): 579–600; Jack L. August, Jr., summarizes and evaluates the notable works of Pomeroy, Nash, and Gressley in his "The Future of Western History: The Third Wave," *Journal of Arizona History* 27 (Summer 1986): 229–44.

45. Robbins, "The 'Plundered Province' Thesis and Recent Historiography of the American West," *Pacific Historical Review* 55 (November 1986): 577–97.

46. Morgan, *Westward Tilt: The American West Today* (New York: Random House, 1963); Sale, *Power Shift: The Rise of the Southern Rim and Its Challenge to the Eastern Establishment* (New York: Random House, 1975); Wiley and Gottlieb, *Empires in the Sun: The Rise of the New American West* (New York: G. P. Putnam's Sons, 1982); Abbott, *The New Urban America: Growth and Politics in Sunbelt Cities* (Chapel Hill: University of North Carolina Press, 1981); Abbott, "The Metropolitan Region: Western Cities in the New Urban Era," in Nash and Etulain; Meinig, *Southwest;* Raymond D. Gastil, *Cultural Regions of the United States* (Seattle: University of Washington Press, 1975); and Joel Garreau, *The Nine Nations of North America* (Boston: Houghton Mifflin Company, 1981), especially 207–44.

47. Georgia O'Keeffe's painting *From the Faraway Nearby* (1937) depicts a gigantic set of bleached antlers in the foreground ("nearby") against a broad-canvas background of desert, mountains, and sky ("faraway").

THE INDIANS
OF ARIZONA

Peter Iverson

Descendants of Arizona's first residents, the Indians of our state bring a tradition that is at once fascinating to outsiders and difficult of access. They have been separated from Anglo society not only by language and culture but by physical distance and political and military conflict. The relationships between Indians and Anglos in the period of statehood have been complex and changing; they will continue to be so over the next quarter-century.

In his essay, Peter Iverson focuses on five topics likely to be crucial in the coming years: economics, urbanization, government, education, and identity. He urges that the historian's perspective be broad enough to go beyond studies of a single community or institution. Others may disagree, seeing each tribe as unique, necessitating narrower studies. No matter what approach is taken, it is clear that the field of Indian history is rich with opportunities for the economic, political, social, or cultural historian.

It is lovely, indeed, it is lovely indeed.
I, I am the spirit within the earth . . .
The feet of the earth are my feet . . .
The legs of the earth are my legs . . .
The bodily strength of the earth is my bodily strength . . .
The thoughts of the earth are my thoughts . . .
The voice of earth is my voice . . .
The feather of the earth belongs to me . . .
All that surrounds the earth surrounds me . . .
I, I am the sacred words of the earth . . .
It is lovely indeed, it is lovely indeed.

—Navajo Origin Legend

These words from the origin story of the Navajos remind us that the land is at the heart of the Indian experience in Arizona. And while it is useful to recall and commemorate in this seventy-fifth year of statehood the people who ushered in that transition from territorial status, it is important to realize that such movers and shakers were not truly pioneers or founding fathers and mothers. Long before the Anglos migrated here, the Spaniards came in search of gold and silver and in the service of God. And long before those first Spanish adventurers and emissaries ventured northward into what would one day become Arizona, Indian peoples began that slow process of coming to terms with the land.

The Indians, then, were the true pioneers of Arizona. They tilled the first fields, built the first communities, constructed the first irrigation canals. They named the flora and fauna and came to know their character and quality. They climbed the mountains and crossed the deserts. As with later generations, theirs is a chronicle both of failure and of success. We would do well to remember that they did not always win. In any calendar year we are reminded of the power of winter and summer in this region. In the days before air conditioners or backyard pools, nature could exact remorse for the temerity of people willing to brave the Colorado plateau or the Sonoran desert. Drought and famine, blizzard and starvation could mark those days. And as elsewhere within the Americas, conflict with neighboring peoples could arise over one matter or another. Life tended to be short and to offer little respite from the strenuous demands of a variety of forces. It is not surprising that the people's songs, teachings, and prayers from time immemorial speak to the fragile environment in which we find ourselves and to the rapidity with which one person's actions may disturb that elusive harmony we seek as individuals and as a society.

It is not the purpose of this essay to rehearse in depth the long history of Indian adaptation and change from earliest times. Other works have done that well, and there is little reason to mimic anemically those accounts. But for the span of centuries leading up to the incursion of the Spaniards, several significant aspects of early Indian life seem especially worthy of attention. They illustrate but do not describe fully Indian existence and its components before the white man came.

They were builders. The Anasazi of the north and the surrounding high country, for example, erected buildings in the most extraordinary sites. Anyone who has journeyed to Mesa Verde, Betatakin, or Canyon de Chelly understands and appreciates that fact. But the Anasazi were also builders of communities, of which the dozen cities in the Chaco Canyon area of northwestern New Mexico are collectively the most overwhelming. The crown jewel of Chaco Canyon was Pueblo Bonito, which alone housed perhaps a thousand people within its walls. As Donald Pike has observed, its more than eight hundred rooms qualified it as the largest apartment building in the world until a more sizable one arose in New York City in 1882.[1] Today a luxurious new condominium apartment development stands in north Phoenix with walls the color of western Oklahoma dirt; this contemporary community has been christened Anasazi and has advertised widely with the obligatory accompanying flute music that is supposed to conjure up the spirit of the distant past. Although this is somewhat less dismal a fate than being honored by a freeway or a recreational vehicle, as the Hohokam or the Winnebago would attest, it is more in the tradition of a later and lesser emulation, such as Cairo, Illinois, or Paris, Texas.

Given the technology with which they had to labor, one is equally amazed by the success of the ancient people as builders of irrigation canals. Here the Hohokam emerge as preeminent for their feats in engineering. They were the first to demonstrate how the southwestern desert could sustain human life in a settled, agricultural community. Their early mastery of water diversion would be acknowledged even by the Anglo-American promoters of another day who actually extended some of the canals of the Hohokam to bring water to modern farms of Maricopa County. For the Hohokam water management was, of course, not designed to add a decorative and soothing element to suburban residential life; it was life itself and they never took it for granted or used it extravagantly. What they would think of Big Surf or artificial lakes can only be imagined.

The Indians of ancient Arizona were also farmers. They struggled at it, no doubt, despite their ability to irrigate many of their fields. Like farmers of all generations, they contended against uncertain weather and other inhospitable elements. Still, on a relatively small scale, they often were productive. They grew corn, beans, squash, and other vegetables. As in other sedentary Indian communities, such as the great village tribes of the upper Missouri River country, successful agriculture yielded protection against the most feared of all enemies: hunger. Except for periods of extended drought, they could store crops from season to season and rest somewhat more assured. One cannot control the skies, nonetheless, and these peoples developed a progressively more elaborate ritual life that included prayers and songs for good harvests.

They were people for whom form mattered. One sees that priority expressed through not only architecture but also the art they created. The pictographs and petroglyphs that we may still view within our state testify to a well-developed aesthetic sense. Even a crowded metropolitan area such as Phoenix offers examples at South Mountain or Adobe Dam. In the more rural reaches of Arizona, only the birds and the wind may join you. I believe there is no more magnificent a place in Arizona than Three Turkey Ruins between Spider Rock and Nazlini Wash in Navajo country. Or look at jewelry and the pottery from Snaketown or from the Mimbres branch of the Mogollon culture or at the O'otam bowls with their star designs. Their striking geometric patterns and bold use of black and white are, of course, familiar to us from the inspiration they provided artists of another day.

Finally, they did not always succeed. The disappearance of the Anasazi is still shrouded in mystery, but all the explanations point to one kind of failure or another. Perhaps they could not combat migrants to the area who proved more powerful militarily. Perhaps they succumbed to disease to which they had no immunity. Perhaps their food supplies could not last through a period of particularly prolonged drought. Perhaps their numbers grew too rapidly and their resources were inadequate for survival. Perhaps soil depletion, erosion, salinity, and other environmental results of increasing pressure upon resources led to their downfall. Even though we may see obvious linkages between the Anasazi and Puebloan communities of later eras, or between other pre-Columbian cultures and contemporary Indian societies, one must recognize that decline and failure joined rise and success within the historical record of the ancient ones.

There is general agreement that the Hohokam can be connected with the Pima and Papago, even if we lack a good deal of direct evidence about that murky period before the Spaniards pushed their way into Arizona. Equally, there is consensus that by the time the Spaniards intruded, the Apaches and the Navajos not only were in the region, but were becoming a growing presence within it. Old Oraibi predated the Spaniards by hundreds of years, and other villages had joined that Hopi community when the Spaniards began to move north of the Gila River. The Havasupai had made their homes in Cataract Canyon, with use of the Coconino Plateau in winter for hunting and gathering. In the northern Arizona country, the Walapai and Yavapai also ranged over a wide amount of territory. Other Yuman language speakers, including the Mohave, Quechan, and Cocopa, had come to the Colorado River country in what is today southwestern Arizona, while the related Maricopa people occupied land immediately to the east, near the Gila River. Thus, by the point of European contact, Indian tribes that we know today were a part of Arizona.[2] Moreover, while the Spanish presence often proved debilitating to the Indians of New Mexico, given such stalwart foes of cultural pluralism as the intrepid Vásquez de Coronado, the Spaniards did not eradicate the Indians from Arizona. When one stops and thinks about it, it is striking how high the percentage is today of recognizable Indian communities that could be clearly identified four centuries ago.[3] That should tell us something.

The Spanish presence nonetheless altered the course of all Indian cultures in Arizona. As many scholars have observed, some of the peoples least directly affected by the Spaniards changed the most. The obvious cases in point would be the Navajos and the Apaches. Though they were not baptized in large numbers or converted to other elements within the Spanish culture, they were fundamentally changed by what the Spaniards brought with them to the Americas, for example, sheep and horses. This leads us to consider on what terms new dimensions were added to various Indian cultural systems and to realize how elusive the impact of cultural change may be for us to assess. With the Spaniards primarily concentrated in settlements to the east along the Río Grande and to the far south, below the Gila and the Salt rivers, this model of indirect cultural change is especially relevant for many Arizona Indians. More fixed residential communities in the south, while more directly affected, were not affected uniformly in the same way. While there were missionary efforts among the Tohono O'odham, for example, not all settlements were near a mission or reached by the missionary message.[4]

The nineteenth century provided an era of exceptionally rapid change and upheaval within a great many Indian communities in Arizona. Increased Mexican migration within the first years of the 1800s, followed by Mexican independence in 1821 from Spain, often led to greater contact with a wider range of Arizona Indians and resultant friction between different sides. Misunderstanding and hostility proved generally limited, however, in comparison to what would follow the acquisition of the region by the United States through the Treaty of Guadalupe Hidalgo and the subsequent Gadsden Purchase from Mexico in 1854. Within a generation the Anglo-Americans moved forcibly into different parts of Arizona to exert their dominance over the native inhabitants. The events of this traumatic transitional period are remembered still through the stories told from one generation to the next.[5] Whether we speak of the Long Walk of the Navajos or the Camp Grant massacre, or the persisting resistance of the legendary Geronimo, one centennial or another during the past few decades has commemorated well-publicized episodes in nineteenth-century Arizona history.

Until recently within courses on American Indian history, this thirty-year era from 1860 to 1890 would indeed be the major focal point for both students and teachers. The fascination with the military aspects of this time surely continues, as well it should, for those confrontations did matter, and people of varying character and courage were centrally involved. We are now, however, devoting more attention than we used to, to an overlapping period that some have labeled the Americanization era. With the gradual defeat and confinement of Indians, with the establishment of reservations and the conclusion of treaty making, federal policy entered a new and significant phase. I am fond of quoting a commissioner of Indian affairs who commented with unconscious irony that it was time, after all, to make the Indians feel at home in America.[6]

The Americanization program included several crucial features that had profound and lasting effects upon Indian individuals, communities, and entire tribes. Given the relatively small Anglo-American population in Arizona during territorial days and the first decade of statehood, this era actually was less devastating for Indians here than in other locales, such as the northern plains. For example, settlers, land speculators, and would-be "friends of the Indian" (as they called themselves) lobbied for their own reasons for wholesale reductions of the Indian land base. The allotment of Indian reservation land into individually held parcels, with the consequent reduction of the tribal estate, had relatively little effect in Arizona. The congressionally mandated General Allotment Act of 1887 (or the Dawes Act as it is sometimes called, after its sponsor) and other pieces of federal legislation left a deeper imprint elsewhere.

Still, the gradual ending of the American frontier together with growing commercial interests in Arizona would leave their mark. While the "big reservation" of the Tohono O'odham would be large, its dimensions were reduced by the demands of cattlemen who vied for what they deemed their fair share of the Sonoran desert range. Though the Hopis were not relocated from their ancestral homelands, they were enclosed by an invisible line drawn in the administration of Chester Alan Arthur that later and inevitably would bring controversy and tragedy. No sooner had the same reservation of Fort McDowell been created by executive order in 1903 than efforts began to remove the Yavapais from this enclave on the Verde River; fortunately for that community, Carlos Montezuma and other leaders lobbied effectively to ensure its survival.[7]

While land bases could be maintained (or even expanded in the case of tribes such as the Navajos, who resided in areas more removed from Anglo demographic pressure), the continuation of a reservation did not guarantee either its autonomy or its prosperity. Other inroads were made during this time. The classic example is the Pimas and their water supply. Renowned as productive farmers who utilized irrigation from the Gila River with great effectiveness, the Pimas plunged to poverty by the early twentieth century when Anglo-American farmers appropriated most of the Indian water supply. Economic decline promoted social instability, with long-term consequences for Pima society.[8] Another kind of inroad occurred with the beginnings of required school attendance. Though not all Arizona Indians in fact were compelled to go to school or necessarily went to school for many years, those who did go had to confront values and perspectives frequently foreign to them. Establishment of off-reservation schools, including one in the embryonic city of Phoenix, brought students from many different tribes together in a common setting. And while the schools featured military discipline and a harsh environment, students who endured sometimes did not see their experience in entirely negative terms. They could gain in some instances a sense of themselves as Indians as well as members of a tribe, and they might obtain a more thorough knowledge of that outside world which increasingly impinged upon a once more insular one. On-reservation schools also could meet with fierce resistance. Indian individuals and families confronted difficult choices about how cooperative they should be with the efforts to promote departures from tradition—through school attendance, division of tribal or community lands, and other such matters.

At the Hopi village of Oraibi these issues indeed inspired factionalism during the final years of the nineteenth century and the first of the twentieth. It was not simply a contest of old versus new,

for internal religious considerations figured prominently in the disagreements. But a contest did finally decide which side would leave
Oraibi and start a new community. The "friendlies" vanquished the
"hostiles" in a struggle to shove the "hostiles'" leader, Yokioma,
across a line; Hotevilla then was constructed by the losers after they
left Oraibi. Ironically, the "friendly" leader, Tewaquaptewa, was
forced by the federal government to attend the Bureau boarding
school at Riverside, California. He returned with anti-Christian sentiments, and his subsequent vigilance caused two more villages to
be built—first at Bakabi by Hotevilla residents denied a return to
Oraibi, and then New Oraibi, below Third Mesa, which soon housed
a day school, a mission, trading post, and a growing populace that
dwarfed the remnant that remained in Old Oraibi.[9]

With the waning of the 1920s, the Americanization era began
to draw to a close. The prevailing policy had come under increasing
criticism, culminating in a special study commissioned by the secretary of the interior and carried out under the aegis of the Institute
for Government Research. *The Problem of Indian Administration*,
known also as the Meriam Report after its principal investigator,
Lewis Meriam, paved the way for far-reaching reform movements
during the following decade. Newly elected President Franklin D.
Roosevelt appointed as commissioner of Indian affairs one of the
most strident opponents of the old order.

John Collier's "Indian New Deal" had wide-ranging consequences for the Indians of Arizona. Efforts to halt soil erosion, for
example, led to an imposed plan to reduce the numbers of livestock
grazing on reservation lands. While the analyses may have been
correct—the cattle, sheep, horses, and goats were damaging the
soil—the manner in which the scheme was carried out prompted
resentment and resistance. Navajos today still speak of the horrors
of stock reduction, and their memory of John Collier is not a happy
one.[10] Sheep for the Navajos represented more than an economic
resource. Symbolically and actually, sheep were at the core of Navajo
culture, and their loss hit hard at the poorest, least acculturated
members of the tribe. The Navajos angrily lashed out at Collier and
his colleagues, including Superintendent E. R. Fryer. Under the
terms of the Indian Reorganization Act, or Wheeler-Howard Act,

of 1934, the congressional mandate which partially endorsed some of Collier's initiatives, Indian tribes had the opportunity to accept or reject its provisions. The Navajos voted to reject. And they balked at other programs, including day schools which, though imposed, anticipated many elements of Indian-controlled schools of the 1960s.

While it has become more fashionable in recent examinations of this era to castigate Collier, it is worth remembering that his commissionership did mark a clear move away from the Americanization era. Many of his instincts were right on target: the cessation of land allotment and consolidation of tribal landholdings, the need for local schools that included the use of tribal cultures in the curriculum, the support of Indian arts and crafts, the defense of freedom of religion, the development of responsive governments that would be sensitive to the duties and demands of a modern day, and the promotion of tribal economies that would allow individuals to remain as reservation residents if they so chose. Even though his efforts often proved heavy-handed, he believed in the Indian future and worked to ensure it. And some of his people in the field worked anonymously to move things in potentially fruitful directions. At San Carlos, for example, Superintendent James B. Kitch aided in the strengthening of Apache livestock associations and the reducing of incursions upon Apache lands by non-Indian ranchers.

The onset of World War II limited the reforming tendencies of the Collier administration and ushered in yet another phase of Arizona Indian history. Like the New Deal generally, the Indian New Deal became subsumed under the war effort. For many Arizona Indians, the war provided their first extended experience with the world beyond the reservation. One Pima man symbolized commitment to the war. Ira Hayes gained fame overnight by being photographed as one of the soldiers raising the flag at Iwo Jima. Hailed as a national hero, he returned to the United States to sell war bonds. His story had a tragic ending, for he struggled with the world he found upon return and as an alcoholic died while still a relatively young man. For others who fought and survived, the years that followed brought more lasting recognition. The Navajos who served as codetalkers in the Pacific campaign continue to be honored by their tribe and their country. Whether they were in the armed services or working in war-related industries, Arizona Indians returned home with a growing recognition that their reservation homes would become progressively less insular and that new approaches to education, economic development, and other matters would be needed within their communities.

Students of American Indian history refer to the period from the close of World War II until the early 1960s as the termination era. They do so because of a federal policy during this time that emphasized something akin to the earlier phases of Americanization. Again reflecting the national mood, this policy promoted individualism, industrialization, urbanization, and more thorough incorporation of Indian reservations under state rather than federal jurisdiction. Western congressmen and Bureau of Indian Affairs personnel advocated terminating federal services for and protection of Indian communities. Indians within the state did not feel the full brunt of the harsher actions of this time—no Arizona tribes lost their reservations, and the state did not take over general civil and criminal jurisdiction on reservations—but the impact could not be denied. Just the threat of termination and the specter of state jurisdiction stimulated tribal leaders to consider alternatives, including a greater role by Indian people themselves in controlling different aspects of their lives. The 1960s and the 1970s would resound with cries for self-determination, but we may perceive the origins of this movement in the somewhat quieter period that immediately preceded it.[11]

The past two decades have witnessed many developments which appear to be of lasting consequence. As Arizona's population has grown rapidly, the state has had to confront new and renewed questions about its priorities, its quality of life, and the demands its people place upon local and state governments, upon land and water resources, upon rural and urban economies, and upon educational systems. We have had to face continuing issues in regard to our relationship with the federal government, with neighboring states, and with Mexico and other nations. Our group portrait seems to reflect varying admixtures of self-congratulation, self-criticism, self-confusion, and even self-contradiction. Legislation and leaders of the 1980s appear at once to be propelling us toward the twenty-first century and pushing us back toward the nineteenth.

Indian lives have been, are, and will be caught up in the maelstrom of modern Arizona. As this state celebrates its seventy-fifth anniversary and looks forward to the centennial of 2012, descendants of its first residents are attempting to deal with equally pressing questions and issues. Situations may be quite different for Indian people within different parts of the state, within different communities, and within different families. It may be more dangerous than useful for the outside observer to generalize, given the complexity of the contemporary scene and the pace of change. But one may at least try to identify crucial overlapping issues of the recent past, the present, and the immediate future. Although any such listing is by definition arbitrary and limited, the following discussion is divided into five topics: economics, urbanization, government, education, and identity. Attention is paid to how each subject could be examined more fully and fruitfully in the years to come.

Economics

Indian reservations occupy approximately one-fourth of Arizona acreage, but when that land was being parceled out it was not being reserved for Indians because of its quality. Indian reservations tended to be located on what was left—land of little value to non-Indians. Actually, Indians in Arizona received somewhat more land than their counterparts in most of the western states. This hardly represented a victory for the forces of cultural pluralism; rather, it testified to the small non-Indian population in Arizona at the time reservations were created and in some instances its distance from those lands.

Of course the great irony of the twentieth century is that reservation lands often became desirable to outsiders. Unanticipated mineral wealth spurred interest; livestock was grazed on some lands. Scenic terrain was wanted for inclusion in national monuments or parks; water resources were diverted. Throughout the first seventy-five years of Arizona statehood, then, Indians have struggled both with attempts by others to exploit their resources without proper compensation and with the dilemma of invigorating their economies in the face of significant obstacles.

As Arizona has changed and with fluctuations in the regional and national economy, outside interest in various Indian resources has also shifted. In the 1950s, the Navajos and Hopis were cajoled by federal officials devoted to economic development, and by corporate representatives who knew a bargain when they saw one, into signing long-term leases for some of their richest coal reserves. The financial returns to the tribes proved less than they had anticipated, particularly since inflation was not calculated into the flat rate per ton offered over a long-term lease. Tribal officials also hoped that mining companies and other related enterprises would provide significant numbers of jobs. Yet both in number and in duration these positions were disappointing.

Within the American West generally and in Arizona particularly, land resources have figured prominently in plans for reservation economic development. Because Arizona's Indian reservations emerged from the era of land allotment more unscathed than their counterparts in such areas as the northern plains, tribally held land could be devoted to large-scale efforts. In addition, Indian values generally stress sharing and reciprocity, so that communally oriented enterprises have often been seen as appropriate. The Navajo Forest Products Industries and the livestock associations at San Carlos represent examples of such an approach.

Given the prevailing aridity of Arizona, water is an especially critical resource. Indian water rights within the state have been the subject of considerable controversy, with major confrontations occurring within the judicial system. While changes in the marketplace have altered the prospects for some forms of irrigated farming, sufficient water from irrigation remains a compelling need for the Indian present and future. Writers such as Charles Bowden (*Killing the Hidden Waters*) remind us that aggressive non-Indian exploitation of water in the Southwest has altered the lives of Indian people and endangers life for all beings in a land of little rain.

Unemployment remains a vexing problem for tribal leaders and for all who seek to live on reservations, regardless of size. Some support small business development in theory, but it is a goal difficult to translate into reality. Where kinship ties are strong, corresponding obligations may imperil an individual who seeks profit in the marketplace. Where border town merchants are nearby, the volume of their sales may make it impossible to establish a competitive alternative within the reservation community. The Navajos have enjoyed some success in this realm, with gas stations, stores, a car dealership, and other examples of entrepreneurship. Still, as elsewhere, the flow of dollars from the Navajo Nation to the businesses of Flagstaff, Winslow, Holbrook, Farmington, and Gallup remains considerable.

At the same time, the non-Indian dollar can play a part in Arizona's Indian economy. Forms of artistic expression, including silversmithing, weaving, pottery, basketry, painting, sculpture, and woodcarving, continue to attract not only widespread appreciation but purchase. Arizona Indians have gained justifiable acclaim for their achievements within these areas, and the financial return to individual artists can be considerable, even if most receive a less than substantial hourly wage from their labors. Tribal arts and crafts enterprises also represent an important attempt to obtain a maximum percentage of return to the artists.

Indian country includes some of the most magnificent scenic resources to be found in a state noted for its extraordinary beauty. Westerners traditionally have had highly ambivalent feelings about the behavior and even the mere presence of tourists, ideally preferring somehow to glean their money without having them there at all. Yet tourism, including such related offshoots as film making and advertising, promises to be a valuable addition to the Indian economy. From skiing at Sunrise on the White Mountain Apache reservation to riding a horse down into the canyonland home of the Havasupais, the tourist has the chance to sample some of the best that Arizona has to offer. Tourists from abroad have already discovered the beauty of Arizona's Indian country, and more efforts may be made in the future to garner a larger share of the international tourist market. One controversial aspect of non-Indian entertainment of late has been the rapid growth of bingo and other forms of gambling through tribally sponsored halls. Questions about both the wisdom and the legality of such diversions have been aired in the courts, with a February 1987 U.S. Supreme Court decision ruling against California's effort to intervene in Indian bingo operations. As the various state lotteries and other such games remind us, a lot of money apparently gets diverted into these channels.

In the face of major problems in Indian economic development, the federal government has continued to play a role in providing both direct and indirect assistance. Federal programs offering employment and aid tend to provoke criticism from non-Indians, though it is worth noting in passing, as Walter Prescott Webb, Joe Frantz, and other western historians have remarked, that the American West has gained enormously from federal investment and assistance and from the continuing federal presence through military bases and other institutions. Nonetheless, the degree to which the federal and tribal governments must prop up tribal economies is a fact of consequence and concern.

To what extent can economic development be directed and controlled by Indians themselves? It is easy to support development on Indian terms, but it is more complicated to explain what that means. Leasing is a case in point. We cannot always say with certainty that leasing is a bad economic strategy. Among other things, it depends on the amount of capital needed, the need for equipment, and the size of the resource to be used. In any event, like other rural communities, Indian communities frequently find it challenging to inspire appropriate and rewarding development. Rip-off artists abound; by definition, corporate concerns want to get the most they can while paying the least for it.

It can be useful to look at commonality as well as differences between Indians and non-Indians.[12] Surely Indian and non-Indian values and priorities are not always identical, but many of the problems besetting them in regard to economic development are not dissimilar. In an increasingly urbanized Arizona, we need to reexamine the extent to which cities prosper at the expense of rural well-being. One does not have to embrace a metropolis-satellite theory of economic development (in this instance the rural areas revolving around the needs and demands of the metropolitan areas) to appreciate that urban needs or wants can influence the quality of life in rural Arizona—be it for electrical power or recreation. Does it matter to people from Maricopa or Pima County what life is like in Apache County? Can urban residents understand a world they either left behind or never knew at all? Are we left with only the prospects of fewer farmers and ranchers, fewer people who know the land and work on it?

Such dreary dispatches from the dismal science of economics may not be correct, but we do need to analyze Indian economies with an eye to the year 2012. Sources at hand can tell us a lot. Instead of endlessly playing out tragedies and triumphs of frontier days, more historians ought to be examining tragedies and triumphs of the recent past.

Oral history, when employed for more than antiquarian purposes, surely can be extremely valuable, but we must ask the right questions. In some instances language will pose difficulties, but we should be getting at experiences, insights, and understandings of the recent past. As with other topics in Arizona Indian (and non-Indian) history, economic development is a sensitive subject that must be probed carefully and sensitively. Still, we need to do a more thorough job of examining company records, tribal newspapers, and other sources. Such sources are likely to be even more prevalent as tribal archives are encouraged to develop. We need to solicit the views and opinions of Indian politicians, workers, and unemployed, as well as non-Indian merchants and company representatives. We should be gaining a better sense of what has happened since self-determination became a buzzword and rallying cry. What have been the benefits and the costs of mineral development? What have been the effects of greater or lesser degrees of federal assistance? How different are the situations being faced in different parts of Arizona, or on reservations of different dimensions or with different histories? What challenges are or have been unique at Colorado River or Gila River? How has urbanization within Indian reservations affected tribal economies? How has the migration of Indian people to towns and cities affected matters? What about the changes in national and international economies and their impact upon Indian communities? Could solar energy make a critical difference in the

Indian economic future? Such questions are but examples of vital and pressing issues that need to be examined. Inevitably, it seems, historians, anthropologists, and other observers may take too narrow a view, specializing in one community or one concern. As with other topics addressed here, a broader, more interpretive, and at times comparative perspective frequently may be helpful.

Urbanization

Historians of immigration often speak of push and pull. For people to migrate to another place, they remind us, there are usually considerations that push them from where they are and pull them to where they go. When we think about U.S. history or the history of the American West, we remember that conditions in the old country or birth order within a farming family could prompt migration. Equally, the attraction of a new place that offered a fresh start or specific resources to be exploited could encourage a person to move. The wealthy have a natural tendency to stay put; the old proverb has it that dukes don't move. And often the extremely poor cannot garner the finances or the strength to migrate. Between the dukes and the downtrodden come those willing to relocate. If moving may be perceived as an act of desperation when motivated by adversity, it should also be seen as an act of hope, encouraged by a belief in tomorrow. People who live in Arizona should hardly need to be instructed about that; most of us fall into the category of fellow immigrants at some point in our family histories, to borrow the memorable observation of Franklin Delano Roosevelt.

The image of the American West is usually a rural one. We think of open spaces, desert and mountain country uncluttered by human habitation. While vast stretches of Arizona and other western states remain relatively underpopulated, Gerald Nash and other historians have noted correctly that the story of the West in the twentieth century is to an important degree an urban one. Most people in Arizona live in towns and cities, and a substantial portion of them live in the Phoenix and Tucson metropolitan areas. People are drawn to the cities not because they prefer to see the air they breathe, but because the cities are where the jobs are. We may speak of quality of life, educational opportunities for our children, or whatever, but for most people moving is more than anything an economic decision. And we would do well to realize that many people within the Arizona experience have always been oriented to the urban rather than the rural environment. When we speak of urbanization, we are talking about an intensification of a trend apparent long ago.

Our image of Arizona Indians is also a rural one, yet it is subject to some of the same modifications. Why has the Arizona Indian population become increasingly urban? This transition also may be explained by reference to push and pull. During the 1950s officials of the Bureau of Indian Affairs promoted relocation to metropolitan areas from reservations. Reservations held Indians back from plunging into the American mainstream, they contended. If Indians would move to Phoenix, Los Angeles, and other such places, they would have access to employment, improved housing, better education for their children, and so forth. A not too hidden item on this particular agenda was the renewed desire to assimilate Indians more fully into American society, a task always made more formidable by reservation residence.

Indians who began to make the move to the cities were propelled by more than BIA rhetoric. For many people, the experience of World War II had provided exposure to the urban world beyond the reservation, and this first glimpse made such an urban transition more plausible. Economic conditions on the reservation also could inspire consideration of alternatives. High unemployment and discouraging forecasts concerning significant improvement of reservation economies could push individuals toward town and city.

Not all of that migration would funnel into Phoenix and Tucson, nor indeed would all of it flow off reservations. While primary attention is being paid here to movement into largely non-Indian communities, it is worth noting that within reservations there has been a clear trend toward urbanization. As rural small-scale economies have become more problematic, people have been forced from the land. Towns become the place to shop, to go to school, to find work, and, gradually, to live. This movement, in turn, has affected social and political life on the reservation.

The off-reservation migration has focused either on border towns or on the Phoenix and Tucson metropolitan areas (which, of course, also border some Indian communities). The situation confronted may differ, especially between border towns and large cities. Indians often form a larger percentage of the border town population, and that town will also be a place at least partially dependent upon Indian business. On weekends and special occasions, Indians will be an especially noticeable component in the town. Relations between Indians and non-Indians may be strained by stereotypes as well as by recurring disagreements.

Within cities such as Phoenix and Tucson, as well as in border towns, important matters face the Indian immigrant. Not all migrants have to deal with exactly the same issues or with the same issues to the same degree, but several concerns are common. As members of a minority group, Indians can expect to encounter instances of racism and discrimination. As a consequence, their perspectives may change about U.S. society in general or about approaches to take on the reservation. The urban experience can provoke apathy as well as militancy, especially if ties to a reservation community are more tenuous. Indians who in increasing numbers are born or grow up in the city may find themselves setting different priorities for themselves or for their families. Within the city the Indian community is more likely to be fragmented spatially and is more likely to be multitribal. All along the way, Indians encounter questions about who they are and what they want, and the answers may differ perceptually from those encountered in reservations.

Despite the fact that Arizona Indians represent a more urban group than in earlier decades, relatively little scholarly attention has been paid to this transition. Federal policy in the 1950s is starting now to receive book-length analysis, but urbanization during and since that decade merits much more thorough treatment. Surprisingly little work has been done on border town communities and their relations with Indian residents or neighbors. The growth of towns on Indian reservations has not been widely examined. Urban Indian institutions and organizations—the Indian Center of Phoenix, for example, or the Inter-Tribal Council—should be studied. In addition, Indian celebrations or gatherings could be studied with profit. Demographic trends yield social consequences.

What is the effect of urbanization upon family life or kin responsibilities? To what extent has movement away from reservations affected Indian language retention or the practice of particular ceremonies or rituals? How have off-reservation employment opportunities affected choices made by Indian young people, including those with a college education? And how much will urbanization affect the workings of tribal politics? Can we differentiate among migrants who are permanent off-reservation residents, people who go back and forth, and people who may return to the reservation or even go to live there for the first time? This is one of several instances where more quantitative approaches may be especially instructive in a field that heretofore has been dominated by narrative description. And finally, no discussion of urbanization should neglect at least mention of the forced relocation of people caused by the Navajo-Hopi land dispute. Although two books have already been devoted to this complex issue, much remains to be learned about the impact of this program upon towns such as Flagstaff and Winslow, upon the two tribes in general, and upon specific individuals caught up in this tragic conflict.

Government

Because of the unique status of Indians within Arizona, five different levels of government are of interest: tribal, city, county, state, and federal. Indians in the state must deal with matters relating to the responsibilities and the real or claimed jurisdictions of all five entities. Depending on the issue at hand, several or conceivably all of these levels can be involved at the same time and could be opposing each other. Governmental involvement reflects, of course, the different dimensions of each Indian as tribal member, city, county, and state resident, and citizen of the United States. Matters concerning one kind of jurisdiction versus another quickly may cause disagreement or conflict. Again and again in the past generation in Arizona we have witnessed misunderstandings and misgivings on this score. What is at stake, to be sure, is more than philosophical disagreement. Vital economic, social, and political interests are intertwined in the strands of such debates.

While Indians were once limited to participation within tribal governments, their political activity now extends into other realms. It is worth remembering that the very exercise of the franchise has not always been a given for Indian voters. But changes in the law combined with demographic change to increase involvement. Movement off reservations naturally has involved Indians as citizens of counties, towns, and the state, just as increased registration and consequent voting within the reservation has added to their impact in county and state elections. In close contests, the Indian vote may assume even larger proportions, as Navajo support for Raúl Castro demonstrated in the 1974 gubernatorial race. The Navajos also began to be successful in the 1970s in sending representatives to the state legislature. Particularly in Apache and Navajo counties, Indian voters strongly influence the results, but in other counties they may also affect outcomes. There is not, of course, a monolithic Indian vote, but recent years have shown that even in a state with a rapidly growing non-Indian population, Indians can still be an important force in the political process. Nonetheless, it is within Indian communities that the matter of politics arouses the liveliest sentiments.

Opinions vary enormously on the efficacy and legitimacy of tribal governments. Arizona reservations differ considerably in the degree to which an institution such as the tribal council has been incorporated successfully into the life of the community. Because these systems were imposed upon the Indians by the federal government, one may argue that they are by definition unauthorized and illegitimate creations with no binding authority. Conservative elements within the Hopis would subscribe not only to that argument, but to the additional contention that the United States itself does not have authority over the internal concerns of their villages. A larger percentage of Arizona Indians perhaps may concede the necessity of some form of elected government, but remain unhappy with a particular form, or even more likely with particular strategies, tactics, actions, and leaders. If one subscribes to Macaulay's dictum that the best government desires to make the people happy, and knows how to make them happy, then on a long-term basis most tribal governments (like, to be sure, most governments of any kind) will probably be in some trouble.

One should hardly be surprised that tribal councils and their leaders come under continuing criticism both from within Indian communities and from outside those communities. Their assignment, after all, may not quite qualify for mission impossible, but it surely ranks as a tough task. Today tribal governments take on a staggering array of challenges that cover the full sweep of Indian life. The degree to which they are successful in confronting these obligations will to a significant extent determine the viability of Indian communities in a modern age.

Regardless of how they might assess their performance, most observers would agree that Indian governments are more ambitious in the range of assignments they tackle than they were forty years ago. This transition may be traced to several interrelated causes. First, in the 1950s the federal government and many state governments promoted the notion that they should assume greater civil and criminal jurisdiction in Indian country. Based upon their prior experience with state governments, Indian politicians were understandably reluctant to promote an extension of state authority. The termination era thus forced the more rapid assertion of Indian rights and the more rapid development of tribal institutions. Second, the creation in 1946 of the Indian Claims Commission by the U.S. Congress encouraged many tribes to hire legal counsel for the first time. Attorneys such as Normal Littell with the Navajos and John Boyden with the Hopis nurtured the growth of tribal governments and aided in the affirmation of Indian rights through the courts. In 1959, for example, *Williams* v. *Lee* was contested all the way to the U.S. Supreme Court. Justice Hugo Black's opinion reversed the decision of the Arizona Supreme Court, which had ruled in favor of a non-Indian reservation trader who sued a Navajo seeking to collect for goods sold on credit. The trader had brought the case in a state court, but Black's ruling denied the jurisdiction of Arizona over this matter. And third, the growth of some tribal economies in the decade allowed some tribal governments to take on greater responsibilities.[13]

While the more conservative nature of the contemporary U.S. Supreme Court has limited recent advances in Indian sovereignty, other judicial triumphs were recorded in the past two decades. Issues such as the collection of state taxes on Indian wages earned on Indian reservations were resolved against the state of Arizona in 1973 in *McClanahan* v. *Arizona State Tax Commission*. The ability of Indian governments to tax corporations doing business on Indian lands has not been fully settled in the courts, and the next twenty-five years doubtless will bring other comparable struggles.

Recent and current controversies instruct us about how controversial and complicated many of these matters are. The southern section of Apache County periodically attempts to secede from its connection with Indian land to the north. The Salt River Pima-Maricopa Indian community blockades Pima Road in an effort to wrest a more equitable leasing agreement from the city of Scottsdale for the portion of the road on Salt River land. Homeowners on the west side of Pima Road threatened by the construction of a new freeway suggest that it be built entirely on Indian land, which is described as "empty" and therefore implicitly without value. One remembers how old and prevailing cultural assumptions may be and how we continue to return to essentially the same issues in relations between Indians and non-Indians. In seventeenth-century Massachusetts John Winthrop reasoned that the Indian lands were legally waste and so the English could justify expanding their settlements onto that "empty" territory. One could equally well reason that the best use of open land within a heavily "developed" metropolitan area might just be to leave it more or less as is and not somehow be penalized for not adding yet another row of houses to an already cluttered panorama.

These and other incidents demonstrate that Indian governments continually face intriguing emotional issues. They also show that there are questions to be explored here by historians and others that tell us a lot about assumptions and priorities within various groups of people. What about those normally invisible Indians who suddenly make Pima Road a topic of breakfast conversation all over the city? For that matter, what about the working assumptions of Scottsdale or state officials on this subject? What do we know about Indian political leadership in Arizona? Are more young people now being accepted as participants in the political process? How will the population growth on reservations and the growth of off-reservation populations affect the workings of tribal governments? What kind of effect has the large increase in the number of college graduates had on those governments? Will the nature of legal counsel be altered in the years to come? Are there differences in the styles, methods, and priorities of Indian political leaders in comparison to non-Indian leaders? Has the mushrooming population growth of Maricopa and Pima counties affected the kinds of problems faced by tribal governments within these areas? These are just a small sample of the questions we might be asking during the next twenty-five years.

Education

Schools in the Navajo Nation like to feature the words of the Navajo leader Manuelito on classroom bulletin boards: "Education is the ladder. Tell my people to take it." It is an effective image and one destined to be emblazoned wherever possible. But only since World War II has the ladder grown more steady, with more people willing to try to ascend it. And while important gains have been achieved in Indian education in Arizona, critical and pressing difficulties remain.

Until World War II, Indian education in Arizona was provided by the BIA and by mission schools. Indian students who lived on reservations and who wished to attend high school had to leave home to do so. Even though the Bureau in the New Deal period had featured some innovative approaches to language instruction and had been more sympathetic to cultural concerns, school still was imposed from the outside, with Indian parents little involved in the process. Experiences garnered during the war inspired many to reassess the value of formal education in a changing world.

For education to be more responsive to the perspectives of the Indian community—and simply be more accessible to students—a public school network had to be established. In Arizona and elsewhere such a development proved difficult on reservations, given the absence of property taxes usually employed to support school systems. Two federal laws passed in the early 1950s, Public Laws 815 and 874, originally were designed to aid public school districts affected by military bases; when amended, the laws were broadened to assist Indian reservations with funds both for school construction and for school operation. The growth of public education for Indian students may be traced to this legislation. By the 1970s, most students could attend public schools, from kindergarten through high school, without leaving home. Gradually the Bureau began to withdraw from its function of providing boarding school education, though it continued to operate schools in isolated stretches of the Navajo Nation and the old high schools in Phoenix and elsewhere. Over time, some of the old schools also began to close—Chilocco in northern Oklahoma, Chemawa in Oregon, Albuquerque—and now the Phoenix Indian School is entering its final days, a casualty of changing times.

The movement for public education naturally was accompanied by a determination to gain greater control over the substance of instruction. At the local level, people registered to vote in order to participate in school board elections. Once controlled by non-Indians, reservation school boards began to feature Indian majorities. Several innovative contract schools opened, using Bureau funds contracted through a community board. Such alterations affected hiring, curriculum, and the general environment of Indian schools.

In border towns and cities, the picture remained more clouded. Though Johnson-O'Malley funds had been available since the 1930s and other supplementary funds had become available in more recent years, serious questions continued to surface about how those dollars had been spent. Critics charged that in public schools where Indian students were a minority, federal support had not been used to benefit them. In addition, these students encountered a more standard curriculum and approach. With a multitribal clientele, public schools not on reservations often had a different set of issues to confront. In some urban schools, Indian students could be treated "just like everybody else," which is to say without regard to different needs or perspectives.

Forty years ago, few Arizona Indian students could attend college. Now they are enrolled by the hundreds at the three public universities in the state, at community colleges, and in colleges and universities outside the state. Programs launched by various institutions have had some success in keeping students on the road to graduation, but four major problems can raise obstacles along that path. The first is inadequate academic preparation. The second is the often impersonal and seemingly insensitive environment of colleges and universities. The third is lack of funds. Students often cannot meet the costs, and parents frequently cannot help much. Tribal college scholarship funds are inadequate, and the federal government continues to slash the amount available for student aid. The fourth obstacle is family. Students who maintain ties with nuclear and extended families often wrestle with obligations that may interrupt their classes, sometimes unpredictably. Instructors who try to practice what they deem fairness—again under the guise of treating all in the same way—may not be sympathetic to what they in all likelihood view as lack of dedication.

These roadblocks are critical, when we recall the pressing needs for Indian professional people in Indian communities both on and off the reservation. Certainly the supply of such individuals is larger than it used to be, but there is no surplus of engineers or physicians, planners or accountants. A related concern is placing those people who do have professional training in positions that are appropriately challenging, and adequately compensated. Otherwise, as in developing nations elsewhere, there is an ever-present danger of losing talented people to jobs elsewhere that are more fully satisfying.

When we assess the recent past, we can look back to a period of vigorous change. The degree to which Indian control of Indian education has been achieved, the increase in publication of materials affirming Indian languages and cultures, the rise in the number of Indian college graduates—all rank as important achievements. The interesting question now is, What next? Now that hard-earned local control has been gained on reservations, what will happen? Can the financial resources be obtained to provide superior educational systems? Will interest be sustained in the school boards or will many people become more apathetic now that control has been achieved? And what kind of courses of study will be provided? In the next generation will language instruction be emphasized as much? At the college level, will Indian Studies programs be maintained or will college and university commitments continue to slip? Will pathbreaking institutions, such as Navajo Community College, expand or be restrained in their evolution?

Indian education remains a sensitive subject, one not easily probed from outside or from an insider's perspective. Because it is an area to which so much energy and emotion has been devoted, and because Indian schools and educational programs represent both achievement and aspiration for adults and for young people, this is a sphere where criticism and analysis may not always be welcome. Nonetheless, such review needs to take place to a much greater extent than it has. I expect the next twenty-five years will bring us more scholarly examinations of this subject. In the generation after self-determination, it may be more possible to look back and candidly scrutinize the many significant accomplishments, the controversies, the setbacks, and the problems that remain to be solved. We need histories of the schools themselves, biographies of educational leaders, analyses of the effects of language and culture programs. As more Indian students are enrolled in off-reservation schools, we will continue to need to assist teachers with materials to allow them to incorporate Indian histories and cultures more fully into the curriculum. Publications such as the new source book developed by the Indian Education Unit of the Arizona Department of Education (*A Varied People: Arizona's Indians*) should prove most valuable in this regard. This volume, which includes both a culture-based curriculum unit and an annotated reference guide, should also be most useful in Indian schools. *A Varied People* reminds us that all Arizona schools can and must tell more fully the story of Arizona Indian women and men and reveal more completely the record of continuity and change in Arizona Indian life.

Identity

Seventy-five years ago in Arizona and elsewhere, non-Indians anticipated the eventual disappearance of Indian peoples. Photographs such as Edward Curtis's "The Vanishing Race" and statues such as James Fraser's "The End of the Trail" symbolized, in D'Arcy McNickle's words, "the note of inevitable doom . . . the idea that Indian destiny had run the course." "If this occasioned regret," McNickle added, "it was no more deeply felt than that expressed for the extermination of the passenger pigeon and the buffalo.

Such losses were accepted as part of the cost of taming a wilderness world. Only the Indians seemed unwilling to accept oblivion as an appropriate final act for their role in the New World drama."[14]

Seventy-five years later one may still encounter non-Indians who anticipate that Indians will disappear. And I suppose if there is any prediction one could make about the year 2012, it would be that yes, the same anticipation would be expressed. Some lessons are just difficult to learn. Of course, more than a few Indian stories contain the notion that some day non-Indians will disappear. But we should know by now that in 2012 Indians will still be an important component of Arizona's population. The words with which I concluded my book *The Navajo Nation* seem equally applicable to the Indians of Arizona: "Time and again, they have been pictured as a vanishing race or a people who could not continue to live on their own land, and time and again they have defied the uninformed judgments of others who predicted their decline or demise. If their past and present teach us anything, it should be not to underestimate their strength, resilience, and persistence."[15]

What elements in Indian identity systems have allowed for that persistence? I do not think we can improve upon some of the insight of that distinguished student of the Southwest, Edward H. Spicer. In a masterful essay included in a volume of the same title, *Plural Society in the Southwest*, Spicer stated that each group in the region "has a terminology which is an important feature of the identity system and symbolizes its conception of the group in relation to all other groups." This terminology, he went on, "may be regarded as an instrument employed by a group for the expression and reinforcement of its sense of distinctness and of common identification."[16] For Indian identity systems, then, we should study cultural content, historical experience, and group image.

In regard to cultural content, Spicer mentions such considerations as language, awareness of and willingness to give high priority to traditional forms of kinship obligation, and a record of participation in wider organizations distinctive of the group.[17] Certainly among Arizona Indians these concerns have generally been important. With urbanization, marriage outside one's own tribe, and more universal exposure to formal education where English is employed as a first language, the percentage of native speakers of a tribal language may fall significantly by 2012. Such a trend would be in keeping with national trends among Indians outside the Southwest. Still, the percentage of Indians in Arizona who speak a tribal language remains substantial. Kinship obligations also have continued to be important. In February 1987, for example, Navajo miners lobbied for the right to take days off for funerals of clan relatives. Again, depending on marriage and migration patterns, this priority may lose importance in years to come. A variety of organizations, including those of a religious nature, also command the attention and loyalties of individuals. Religious participation will continue to be expressed within tribal ceremonies as well as in such multitribal associations as the Native American Church.

Spicer remarks that Indian evaluation of their history has tended to grow more positive in recent years.[18] The outpouring of books written by Arizona Indians about their histories and cultures is an important indication of cultural revitalization. There is a continuing need for studies that are both culturally sensitive and academically sound. And the post–World War II era obviously needs more thorough analysis. What about those unsung heroes of the 1950s and 1960s who quietly but firmly pushed for civil rights, for equitable return on tribal economic development ventures, for better schools, for a better tomorrow for their children? Those who investigate this history can gain a recognition of the power and poignancy of historical experience—an understanding that the past has a very real influence on thoughts and actions of the present.

Group image, in Spicer's view, "involves placing value on the cultural differences and historical experience of the group."[19] Indian communities in Arizona have had a clear sense of themselves as distinct entities, with language, history, religion, and other critical elements shaping their perspective. That line between "us" and "them" tends to be drawn firmly and with good reason. The functioning of what anthropologists have termed a working ethnic boundary is unlikely to change. But what of the potentially difficult issue of tribal enrollment? Certainly each community has a right to determine its membership; that right has been affirmed by the U.S. Supreme Court. But will changing times, with attendant fiscal limitations, force certain groups to change the rules of who is and who is not a member?

Spicer and others have perceived the consequence of the reservation system for the maintenance of Indian identities. During the late 1940s and the 1950s, the federal government made a concerted effort to eliminate reservations. Under the authority of *Lone Wolf* v. *Hitchcock* (1903) and other Supreme Court decisions, Congress does not need the permission of an Indian reservation populace to terminate federal protection. If such matters are cyclical, then we are due for another attempt within the next twenty-five years to eliminate the trust status now in place. Such an assault could be prompted either by economics or by the national mood or both, but it should not be entirely surprising. Among the lessons of history for Indians of Arizona and elsewhere: be wary, be watchful; there are always those who would rob you of your heritage and deny you your future.

Though a certain portion of the Arizona Indian population will continue to live and work away from reservations, we should not be mistaken about the significance of that land base. Spicer concluded that Indians differ from other groups in how they see and feel about the land. Rather than perceiving the land in terms of utility and power—a secular, human perspective—Indians are more likely to have as part of their true identity "the symbol of roots in the land—supernaturally sanctioned, ancient roots, regarded as unchangeable."[20] Although non-Indian persons can share this vision, urbanization has cut most of us off from it more than we would care to admit. The Kiowa writer N. Scott Momaday once wrote of people today being more sure of where they were in relation to the nearest coffee break or supermarket than they were to the stars and the solstices.[21] He was right.

That alienation from the land, that assumption that land is a commodity, poses dangers for Indians and for all of us who hope to be around to celebrate the Arizona centennial. For along with its people Arizona's greatest treasure is its land—and a fourth of that land is Indian land. We may not be able to predict the future, but we can accept a common responsibility to remember and protect that extraordinary earth and sky of our state. In that spirit, let me conclude with the words of the Tewa, addressed to that earth and that sky:

> . . . weave for us a garment of brightness;
> May the warp be the white light of morning,
> May the weft be the red light of evening,
> May the fringes be the falling rain,
> May the border be the standing rainbow.
> Thus weave for us a garment of brightness
> That we may walk fittingly where birds sing.[22]

Notes

1. Donald G. Pike, *Anasazi: Ancient People of the Rock* (Palo Alto, Calif.: American West Publishing Co., 1974), 138. In his introduction, Pike notes Anasazi achievements as builders, farmers, craftspeople, and religious people.

2. See the two volumes on the Indians of the Southwest in the Smithsonian's *Handbook* series, cited in "For Further Reading."

3. See Edward H. Spicer, *Cycles of Conquest: The Impact of Spain, Mexico, and the United States on the Indians of the Southwest, 1533–1960* (Tucson: University of Arizona Press, 1962).

4. Bernard L. Fontana, "History of the Papago," in *Southwest, Handbook of North American Indians*, vol. 9, ed. Alfonso Ortiz (Washington, D.C.: Smithsonian Institution, 1983), 137–39.

5. See, for example, Ruth Roessel, ed., *Navajo Stories of the Long Walk Period* (Tsaile, Ariz.: Navajo Community College Press, 1974).

6. Francis Paul Prucha, ed., *Americanizing the American Indian: Writings by the "Friends of the Indian," 1880–1900* (Cambridge: Harvard University Press, 1973), 3.

7. See Peter Iverson, *Carlos Montezuma and the Changing World of American Indians* (Albuquerque: University of New Mexico Press, 1982).

8. Paul H. Ezell, "History of the Pima," in Ortiz, *Southwest*, 158–60.

9. Among other accounts see Harry C. James, "Civil War at Oraibi," in *Pages from Hopi History* (Tucson: University of Arizona Press, 1974), 130–45.

10. See Broderick Johnson and Ruth Roessel, eds. *Navajo Livestock Reduction: A National Disgrace* (Tsaile, Ariz.: Navajo Community College Press, 1975).

11. See Iverson, "Building Toward Self-Determination: Plains and Southwestern Indians in the 1940s and 1950s," *Western Historical Quarterly* 16, no. 2 (April 1985): 163–73.

12. Iverson, "Cowboys, Indians, and the Modern West," *Arizona and the West* 28, no. 2 (Summer 1986): 107–24.

13. Iverson, "Building Toward Self-Determination."

14. D'Arcy McNickle, *Native American Tribalism: Indian Survivals and Renewals* (Oxford: Oxford University Press, 1973), 3–4.

15. Iverson, *The Navajo Nation,* paperback ed. (Albuquerque: University of New Mexico Press, 1983), 226.

16. Spicer, "Plural Society in the Southwest," in *Plural Society in the Southwest,* ed. Edward H. Spicer and Raymond H. Thompson (Albuquerque: University of New Mexico Press, 1975), 24.

17. Ibid., 25.

18. Ibid., 27.

19. Ibid., 27–28.

20. Ibid, 35–36.

21. N. Scott Momaday, "The Man Made of Words," in *The Remembered Earth: An Anthology of Contemporary Native American Literature,* ed. Geary Hobson (Albuquerque: University of New Mexico Press, 1980), 166.

22. Quoted in Margaret Connell Szasz, *Education and the American Indian: The Road to Self-Determination Since 1928,* 2d ed. (Albuquerque: University of New Mexico Press, 1977), 78.

For Further Reading

In addition to the citations in the notes, the following books represent a small sampling of the writing on this subject:

Basso, Keith. *The Cibecue Apache.* New York: Holt, Rinehart, and Winston, 1970.

Bingham, Sam, and Janet Bingham, editors. *Between Sacred Mountains: Navajo Stories and Lessons From the Land.* Tucson: Sun Tracks and University of Arizona Press, 1984.

Dozier, Edward P. *Hano: A Tewa Indian Community in Arizona.* New York: Holt, Rinehart, and Winston, 1966.

Evers, Larry, editor. *The South Corner of Time: Hopi-Navajo-Papago-Yaqui Literature.* Tucson: Sun Tracks and University of Arizona Press, 1980.

Fontana, Bernard L. *Of Earth and Little Rain.* Flagstaff: Northland Press, 1981.

Hinton, Leanne, and Lucille J. Watahomigie, editors. *Spirit Mountain: An Anthology of Yuman Story and Song.* Tucson: Sun Tracks and University of Arizona Press, 1984.

Hirst, Stephen. *Havsuiw 'Baaja: People of the Blue Green Water.* Supai: Havasupai Tribe, 1985.

Ortiz, Alfonso, editor. *Southwest,* vol. 10 of *Handbook of North American Indians.* Washington, D.C.: Smithsonian Institution, 1979. (This volume contains articles on the Pueblo Indians, including the Hopis; volume 9 is devoted to the other Indian groups of the Southwest.)

Painter, Muriel Thayer. *With Good Heart: Yaqui Beliefs and Ceremonies in Pascua, Arizona.* Tucson: University of Arizona Press, 1986.

Spicer, Edward H. *The Yaquis: A Cultural History.* Tucson: University of Arizona Press, 1980.

Weaver, Thomas, editor. *Indians of Arizona: A Contemporary Perspective.* Tucson: University of Arizona Press, 1974.

Zepeda, Ofelia, editor. *Mat Hekid O Ju: 'O'odham Ha-Cegitodag. When It Rains: Papago and Pima Poetry.* Tucson: Sun Tracks and University of Arizona Press, 1982.

HISPANICS
IN ARIZONA

Oscar J. Martínez

The history of Hispanics in Arizona is largely the history of the interaction of that ethnic group with Anglos. Until fairly recently, the ability of Hispanics to exert political and economic power depended on their numbers: when they were the majority—as they were in Tucson as late as the turn of the century— they were able to play an active role in government and society, and racial conflict was minimal. When Anglo immigration increased, and Mexican Americans became a true minority, racial conflict and discrimination began.

Since the 1960s, however, increased political activism and involvement in issues such as civil rights, labor organization, and education have offered Hispanics the ability to participate in, and influence, state and local government as well as economic and social institutions. Martínez suggests that one area in which Hispanics are insufficiently involved is history, which is perceived as a luxury, middle-class activity. If we are to understand the Hispanic past, he explains, this attitude must change.

The history of Mexican Americans reveals complex and heterogeneous experiences that can more fully be appreciated by examining the record of the past at the local and regional levels. Hispanic Arizonans present a somewhat unusual case because of their relative isolation from other Hispanic communities in Texas, New Mexico, and California. This introduction to the history of Mexican Americans in Arizona highlights major events and processes that have shaped their destiny since the days of Spanish colonization. I have focused on selected social, economic, and political trends; I have been able to treat important themes such as cultural and religious experiences only minimally. I encourage readers to consult the available literature for further information on these subjects.[1]

One of the challenges in writing about persons of Mexican descent in the United States is to select the correct identifying term. Lacking the wisdom to choose a single satisfactory term and wishing to achieve variety in style, I have used terms such as *Mexican Americans, Hispanics*, and *Spanish-speaking people* to mean persons who trace their ancestry to Mexico but whose permanent home is the United States. *Spaniards* refers primarily to the early settlers of the Sonora frontier, and *Mexicans* to people with a predominantly Mexican way of life, whether Mexican nationals or Mexican Americans.

The Experience of Hispanic
Arizonans in Perspective

The history of Mexican Americans in Arizona closely resembles the experience of Hispanics elsewhere in the southwestern United States in terms of the general patterns discernible in the standing of the group over time within U.S. society. After a short period of friendly, cooperative, and mutually beneficial relations at the initial stage of contact, Anglos and Hispanics in Arizona, Texas, New Mexico, and California unfortunately diverged greatly in their subsequent evolution. Everyplace where Anglos became the majority or where they assumed economic dominance, political and social control followed. Because of their different ethnic and cultural background, Mexican Americans found it difficult to receive acceptance or fair treatment in a society that had little tolerance for people of Latin American extraction, and particularly those whose racial make-up included Indian or African blood. Thus Hispanic Arizonans, like their counterparts in neighboring states, struggled for many decades to achieve recognition as first-class citizens under the Constitution of the United States. Significant advances in the social status of Mexican Americans as a U.S. minority group did not occur until the 1960s, and Arizona follows that larger pattern.

On the other hand, Mexican Americans in Arizona exhibit unique characteristics that distinguish their reality from that of Mexican Americans elsewhere. Certainly the desert environment of Arizona has shaped the experience of local Hispanics in ways that are different from what is found in the lush areas of south Texas, the coastal zones of California, or the mountain regions of New Mexico. Desert living requires the development of unique survival skills and special living and occupational arrangements. The limited initial European settlement of Arizona, the isolation from the outside world, the difficult relations with surrounding Indian groups, the delayed Anglo immigration into the area, and the group's participation in the mining industry are other significant factors that need to be taken into account in differentiating the historical experience of Hispanic Arizonans.

One might also approach the subject by considering regional distinctions *within* Arizona itself. It is well known that the experience of Hispanic Tucsonenses is very different from the experience of Hispanic Phoenicians. It is also clear that Hispanics who have made rural Arizona their home differ in many ways from urban Hispanics, and especially those who live in the state's two big cities. The people from the mining areas are also unique, as is the population that lives along the international boundary with Mexico. When all these regional variables are taken into consideration, the complexity of the Hispanic experience becomes clearer. Thus, generalizations about Mexican Amerians in Arizona and other areas as well must be made with care. Just as there are "many Mexicos" south of the border, there are many Mexican and Mexican American "worlds" in the United States.

The Early Years

Hispanic Arizonans trace their beginnings in the state to the sixteenth-century Spanish expeditions that originated in New Spain. Famous explorers such as Marcos de Niza, Francisco Vásquez de Coronado, Antonio de Espejo, and Juan de Oñate ventured into Arizona, but the remoteness and aridity of the region prompted them to move on to more promising lands. European missionaries settled among the Hopi Indians in the early seventeenth century, but the Pueblo Rebellion of 1680 ended that venture. Decades passed before the Spaniards could gain a permanent foothold in Pimería Alta, as the northernmost part of Sonora came to be called.

Pimería Alta remained relatively unknown territory until Father Eusebio Francisco Kino familiarized the outside world with the area's unique peoples and natural resources. In the latter seventeenth century Kino explored the region widely, established missions, worked with the Indians, and promoted colonization. In the 1730s, a mining boom in the northern Sonoran frontier stimulated new settlements. In 1752 the Spaniards founded an important *presidio* (garrisoned town) at Tubac to protect colonists. The transfer of the Tubac garrison to a new location led to the founding of Tucson in 1775. The Spaniards also attempted to colonize an area at the junction of the Gila and Colorado rivers, but abandoned the effort after an uprising by the Yuma (Quechan) Indians in 1781.

The pioneers of Pimería Alta carried on a relatively simple lifestyle, sustaining themselves through farming and ranching. Their ancestors had lived in Sonora for many years, and they inherited the ability to survive in a desert setting under the threat of Indian attacks. Given the isolation, the harshness of much of the land, and the Indian problem, it is not surprising that only fifteen hundred Spanish-speaking people lived in Arizona in 1821, at the time of Mexican independence from Spain.

The end of Spanish rule throughout Mexico cau
able disruption in Arizona because resources to sustair
and *presidios* could no longer be obtained. As a newly
country, Mexico had many political and economic problems to co-
front, and it could not meet the needs of the northern frontier
population. Consequently Indian depredations increased, and Arizona suffered significant depopulation. By the end of the U.S.-
Mexico War (1848), only about a thousand Hispanics resided in
Arizona.

Hispanic Arizonans had the good fortune to miss the 1848
conflict, since most of the fighting took place in other parts of
northern Mexico. Nevertheless, U.S. soldiers on their way elsewhere
made two appearances at Tucson. As a depopulated and remote
territory, Arizona did not invite U.S. military interest as did other
provinces such as Texas and California. Indeed, the boundary established by the Treaty of Guadalupe Hidalgo left the Spanish-speaking
communities of Arizona in Mexico. A few years later, however,
Hispanic Arizonans became part of the United States through the
Gadsden Purchase (1854). In exchange for $10 million, Mexico
agreed to transfer 29,640 square miles of its territory to the United
States, most of it south of the Gila River in present-day Arizona.
During the interval between the Treaty of Guadalupe Hidalgo and
the Gadsden Purchase, hundreds of Anglos trekked through Arizona on their way to the California gold mines, and some decided
to stay.

Initial Contact with Anglo Americans

Following the Gadsden Purchase, the flow of Anglo American
migration to Arizona was very modest. This contrasted with heavy
Anglo immigration to Texas and California shortly after those provinces became part of the United States. Limited economic opportunities and danger from Indians discouraged many migrating
Anglos from making Arizona their new home. Nevertheless, some
of them liked the area and decided to settle permanently. Their

numbers remained small for many years: in 1860, only 1,080 Anglos lived in Arizona, compared to 1,715 Mexicans; ten years later Arizona had 4,424 Anglo residents and 5,235 Mexicans.

As a numerical minority, Anglos adapted to local ways and learned to get along with their Mexican neighbors. The latter in turn welcomed the new settlers because more people meant greater physical security and increased economic activity. Thus, interdependence and mutual respect developed in those early years, sparing Arizona the severe racial and cultural clashes then occurring in other parts of the Southwest.

In Tucson, where Anglos made up 20 percent of the town's 925 residents in 1860, ethnic harmony prevailed. Family-oriented Anglos often married Mexican women and found a place in the economy of the area. Some, following the example of Hispanic entrepreneurs, became prosperous by engaging in regional trade and commerce. Because Tucson offered limited opportunity to wanderers and adventurers who sought quick fortunes and were prone to make trouble, the city avoided a large concentration of undesirable elements among its population, and that made a significant difference in the ethnic climate of the community.

It is significant that as economic activity expanded, Anglos came to control a disproportionate share of Tucson's wealth. Census data from 1860 indicate that Anglos had assets amounting to over $500,000, compared to less than $73,000 for the Mexican community. In his excellent book on the history of Mexicans in Tucson, Thomas E. Sheridan explains that Anglos were able to accumulate greater wealth because most of them were males in their prime years, unburdened with family responsibilities.[2] In addition, Anglos had greater knowledge about profitable trade possibilities with the rest of the United States, and probably many of them brought some capital with them to start local businesses or to buy property.

Despite the economic differences, ethnic relations remained amicable in Tucson for many years. Perhaps the crucial factor in the relationship was that both communities genuinely needed each other. Further, the Mexican numerical majority and the presence of a strong Mexican elite lessened the potential for friction; the absence of large-scale economic enterprises also spared Tucson the severe labor tensions that troubled other areas within and outside Arizona.

To the south of Tucson, considerable conflict took place in the mining areas as a result of Anglo mistreatment of Mexican workers and the application of "frontier justice" in settling disputes. Lured by old Spanish stories of lost mines, Anglo entrepreneurs and adventurers moved into the border area in the 1850s, often coming from the California gold fields. The first Anglo-owned mine opened in 1854 at Ajo. Because of high extraction and transportation costs, owners considered it essential to hire laborers as cheaply as possible. They therefore recruited workers from across the border in Sonora who were willing to work long hours for little pay. In 1859, about eight hundred Mexicans worked in the Heintzelman mine just west of Tubac. In many cases the low wages paid the workers did not cover their living expenses, and they became indebted to the company stores where they bought their supplies. Their indebtedness forced them to remain on their jobs. Deep resentments developed, and ethnic distrust, based on class distinctions, emerged.

Anglo mine owners and ranchers in southern Arizona sought to keep Mexican workers under control with the use of "outlaw" hired help, provoking angry employees to take the law into their own hands. For example, mining superintendent Frederick Brunchow and rancher John Ware were killed by Mexican employees in the late 1850s. By May 1859 Arizona had experienced at least one recorded ethnic altercation near the mines around Tubac, which left four Mexicans and one Yaqui Indian dead. News of the killings caused many workers to abandon the mining camps temporarily, bringing production to a halt. The workers returned to their jobs once the threat of violence subsided.

Apart from the friction caused by exploitative employment patterns, negative ethnic attitudes contributed to mutual hostilities. Mexicans viewed Anglos as materialistic and crude, while Anglos saw Mexicans as their inferiors. Influenced by the racist ideology of the period, Anglo writers had little positive to say about the people they encountered in the Southwest. In their view, Mexicans were backward, lazy, unproductive, immoral, dishonest, and incapable of self-government. It was up to Anglos, whose culture and institutions were assumed to be superior to those of the people of the Southwest, to "regenerate" the Mexicans. The following observation by J. Ross Browne, a writer of western travel books in the mid-nineteenth century, illustrates the degree to which racist feelings affected the attitudes of Anglos: "[Arizona] became infested with the refuse population of Sonora—the most faithless and abandoned race, perhaps, on the face of the earth. . . . I think Sonora can beat the world in the production of villainous races. Miscegenation has prevailed in this country for three centuries. Every generation the population grows worse; and the Sonoranians may now be ranked with their natural compadres—Indians, burros, and coyotes."[3]

Ethnic rivalry and economic abuse are central to understanding the conflict between Anglos and Mexicans in southern Arizona. In addition, the frontier conditions of rural areas contributed significantly to the problem. Throughout the late nineteenth century Arizona suffered from extreme lawlessness. Territorial newspapers carried many stories about shootings, beatings, thefts, and other forms of violence. Both Mexican and Anglo bandits roamed the countryside, victimizing people on both sides of the international border. Moreover, the Apache Indians constituted a continuing threat to stability throughout Arizona. The withdrawal of Union troops at the commencement of the Civil War in 1861 to posts along the Río Grande encouraged the Apaches to increase their attacks on Mexican and Anglo settlements.

During the years of extreme lawlessness, Tucson itself remained relatively calm, serving as an island of tranquility in a sea of banditry and Indian depredations. Throughout the 1860s and 1870s, Mexicans and Anglos continued to coexist peacefully. By 1880, 80 percent of the town's population was still Mexican, thus assuring that Mexican culture and customs would prevail. Fourteen percent of all marriages at that time involved Mexican-Anglo couples, surpassing intermarriage levels recorded in Los Angeles, Santa Fe, and San Antonio.

The Tucson economy remained diversified, allowing farmers, ranchers, merchants, and craftsmen from both groups to make a living. In contrast to other parts of Arizona, Mexicans remained a central part of the elite economic sector in the town. Several Mexican entrepreneurs became active in the freighting business, accumulating wealth and status that transferred over into other areas. After the Civil War, freighting was Arizona's most important business, and Mexicans became owners and teamsters. Estevan Ochoa became one of the most prominent businessmen in the region, heading a freighting firm that handled approximately $300,000 in transactions a year. Ochoa also owned mines, ranches, mercantile stores, and a smelting plant.

Other notable Mexican entrepreneurs of the territorial period were Mariano Samaniego (ranching, freighting, transportation), Leopoldo Carrillo (real estate, ranching), Sabino Otero (ranching), and the Aguirre family (ranching, freighting). With few exceptions the wealthy Hispanics of those years were immigrants, primarily from Sonora and Chihuahua, although a few arrived from elsewhere in Mexico and even other Latin American countries. The native-born Arizonans, while often well respected in their communities, tended to work small family farms.

The prominence of the local Mexican elites assured that Tucson would maintain its strong bicultural way of life long after Arizona's annexation to the United States. This is in contrast to other southwestern communities, where wealthy Mexicans quickly lost their privileged position as a result of being overwhelmed by Anglo immigrants. In time, however, Tucson too would change dramatically as advances in transportation precipitated accelerated Anglo immigration.

The Decline of Mexicans in Arizona Society

The arrival of the railroads in Arizona in the 1880s radically changed the territorial economy, precipitating alterations in the structure of local wealth and patterns of business activity. The railroads introduced cheaper means of transportation, thereby making conventional methods of moving people and goods obsolete. With the railroads came giant U.S. corporations eager to extract raw materials from the resource-rich Southwest for shipment to the

industrial eastern states. Agribusiness assumed importance as cotton
began to be grown for export, especially in the Phoenix area. Thereafter the Mexican entrepreneurs who had managed to amass wealth
in Arizona found it increasingly difficult to hold on to it. They
could compete with individual Anglo entrepreneurs like themselves,
but they could not compete with corporations like the Southern
Pacific Railroad and Phelps Dodge. The pattern of decline of Mexican businessmen is most noticeable in Tucson.

When the railroads reached Tucson, local trade with Mexico
dropped precipitously, harming the interests of many merchants.
An indication of the change in economic orientation in Tucson is
the end of the practice of using Mexican pesos as a medium of
exchange. As Mexican businessmen saw their freighting businesses
and other concerns decline because of the new competition, they
shifted their investments to other activities such as ranching or
retreated to servicing the Mexican community. The depression suffered by the city in the 1880s also forced many working-class people
to migrate to the mining towns or the cotton-growing areas. Some
moved to California and others returned to Mexico, where job
opportunities became available during the boom years of the Por-
firio Díaz period.[4]

The railroads brought a fresh wave of Anglos into Arizona,
and most of them had little understanding of or sympathy for the
Mexican way of life. Unlike the first arrivals, whose limited numbers
had encouraged integration with Mexicans in places like Tucson,
the new immigrants saw no need to interact with the Mexican population. To the contrary, they wished to keep the Mexicans segregated
in their own communities and locked into low-paying, low-status
occupations. With the new Anglo immigration, the total population
of Arizona swelled from 30,192 in 1876 to 40,440 in 1880 and
75,000 in 1886.

The force of numbers eventually took its toll on the Mexicans
of Arizona. The pattern of decline is most clearly illustrated in the
reduction of political representation as the nineteenth century progressed. The loss of influence began with the 1863 separation of
Arizona as a separate territory from New Mexico. Earlier Confeder-
ate-leaning Anglos had sought to break away from New Mexico

in part to eliminate the control exercised by Hispanic New Mexicans over both areas. That attitude carried over to the Union sympathizers as well, who succeeded in convincing Congress to establish Arizona as a distinct territory. Throughout the territorial years, not a single Mexican served in a top elective or appointive territorial position, although some did manage to serve in the legislative assembly.

By the early twentieth century, statehood had become an important issue in Arizona. One prime concern for many Anglos was that Arizona would be accepted as a state only if it joined with New Mexico, given that both territories had relatively small populations. That prospect prompted one congressman sympathetic to Anglos in Arizona to ask in 1906: "Can Arizona as a single state control it better by itself, or shall we join the Mexican greasers [of New Mexico] to Arizona and let them control it?"[5] After much debate, Congress finally passed and the president signed the Arizona Enabling Act in 1910, clearing the way for statehood. Of the fifty-two delegates at the Arizona state constitutional convention, only one was a Mexican. This contrasts sharply with California's constitutional convention (in 1849), where eight of the forty-eight delegates were of Mexican heritage, and New Mexico's constitutional convention (in 1910), where about one-third of the one hundred delegates were of Mexican descent. Considerable debate at the Arizona convention centered on the possible curtailment of employment opportunities for Mexicans, but the delegates—a large number of whom represented mining interests that were unwilling to give up access to cheap labor—approved only a provision to exclude Mexicans from public works projects. In contrast to the California and New Mexico constitutions, which recognized the bilingual nature of their states, the Arizona constitution remained silent on the matter.

The only place in Arizona where Mexicans had any significant political influence during the years of decline was Tucson. As a town where a pioneer Mexican elite maintained continuity well into the Anglo period, Tucson managed to provide native leadership for local and state positions. For example, Estevan Ochoa, the merchant and freighter, served in the territorial legislature on three different occasions in the 1860s and 1870s and became mayor of

Tucson in 1875. Another Tucson entrepreneur, Mariano Sama-niego, was elected to several offices at the local, county, and state levels during a political career that spanned a generation. According to Sheridan, by the 1890s Samaniego wielded more power and influence than any other person of Mexican descent in Tucson, and at one point there was even a movement to make him governor of the territory. Other Spanish-surnamed persons from Tucson and elsewhere who served in the legislature include Francisco León, Jesús Elías, Juan Elías, Ramón Romano, José María Redondo, N. González, and Alfred Ruiz. Apart from holding offices at the state level, Mexicans also managed to get elected to local positions. Several Tucsonenses, for example, became city councilmen, county supervisors, and law enforcement officials. Hispanics continued to achieve leadership positions in Tucson, but beyond this town political representation was practically nonexistent for Spanish-speaking Arizonans.

The years of Hispanic political decline witnessed a deterioration in ethnic relations as well. By the 1870s incidents of violence against Mexicans had become common. In 1873, for example, one Mexican was lynched at Phoenix and three at Tucson. In 1882, another was lynched at Bisbee. Four years later a Mexican citizen named Manuel Mejía was arrested in Wickenburg and held for seventeen days because he was suspected of having participated in the murder of an Anglo man. Upon release, he was strung up and beaten severely by a mob; he lost an eye and an arm in the fracas. Such cruelty, of course, was not unique to Arizona. Texas and California have the distinction of surpassing Arizona in the number of lynchings and other forms of violence against Mexicans and other minorities. Nevertheless, the brutality in Arizona precipitated great resentment and bitterness among the Spanish-speaking.

Institutionalized discrimination in the criminal justice system further estranged the Mexican community from the mainstream society. An examination of court records from Pima County from 1882 through 1889 reveals that Mexican prisoners routinely received harsher sentences than Anglo prisoners. For instance, Mexicans convicted of murder served sentences almost four times as long as those given to Anglo killers, and Mexican larcenists drew sentences twice as long as their Anglo counterparts. Part of the explanation lies in the fact that few Mexicans were allowed to serve on juries.

The story of the "forty blonde babies" is perhaps the most revealing and poignant incident in the history of ethnic relations in Arizona. One day in 1904 Father Mandin, a new priest in Clifton, announced to his predominantly Mexican congregation that many children from New York were available for adoption. The parishioners enthusiastically expressed desire to adopt "blonde" babies, and the priest wrote back to the foundling home expressing that sentiment. Shortly thereafter forty small children, accompanied by an Anglo nun, arrived in Clifton-Morenci. The nun was shocked to learn that most of the adoptive parents were Mexicans, whereupon she unsuccessfully attempted to stop the delivery of the children. After much argumentation, the nun agreed to go along with the original arrangement and, with some exceptions, the Mexicans took their new babies home and celebrated the occasion. When the Anglo community in Clifton learned that Mexicans had "bought" Anglo babies, a rude mob forcibly took the children from their new parents and placed them in "proper" homes pending a permanent solution. At Morenci, pressure exerted by Anglo residents prompted Father Mandin to retrieve the children from the Mexican homes. Apparently twenty-one of the children were then taken from Arizona, but nineteen remained in the hands of the Anglo community. The foundling home in New York then attempted to recover the remaining children, but the Anglo "foster parents" had already initiated legal adoption proceedings. The case went before the Arizona Supreme Court and the U.S. Supreme Court, and both institutions upheld the adoption of the children by the Anglo parents. For the Mexicans of Clifton-Morenci, this was a tragic event not only because they lost the children, but because they were viciously maligned and degraded as "unfit" parents by their Anglo neighbors, the press, and the courts.[6]

As early as the 1870s it had become clear to Tucson's Mexican leadership that the community needed better and more formalized organization in order to preserve its culture, protect its interests, and care for the needs of the less fortunate. Thus in 1875 several prominent Tucsonenses founded the "Mexican Society for Mutual Benefit," which provided help for its own members and to those unable to help themselves. Other communities followed suit, and soon there were *mutualista* groups in Florence, Phoenix, Solomon-ville, Clifton, and St. Johns. These societies inspired the founding in Tucson in 1894 of the Alianza Hispano-Americana, one of the most important grassroots organizations in the history of the His-panic Southwest. Like its predecessors, the Alianza was primarily a fraternal and mutual aid society, but its activities spilled over into the political arena as well. Many of its members were deeply involved in civic affairs, and having a network of fellow *aliancistas* available to render assistance made a significant difference to those seeking to become public figures. The Alianza's program of promoting unity and providing moral, financial, and other help appealed to many *mexicanos;* this is evident in the steady rise of the membership, which reached eleven thousand throughout the Southwest by 1932.

Struggle for Economic Survival After 1880

The railroads, mines, and agribusiness all required cheap labor in large quantities, and the immigrant Mexicans fleeing their home-land in the late 1880s became the major labor source for the develop-ing industries of Arizona. For example, the Southern Pacific, which came to dominate Tucson's economy, hired large numbers of Mex-icans. By 1920, one-fourth of all the Mexican men in Tucson worked for the Southern Pacific.

The Southern Pacific was eager to employ Mexicans as laborers but did not allow them into upper-level blue-collar jobs or white-collar jobs until the mid-twentieth century. Major responsibility for the discrimination against Mexicans rested with the Anglo-controlled railroad unions, which consciously kept Mexicans locked in the lowest-paying jobs. To a significant degree job discrimination in the railroads was rooted in racism, but lack of education and linguistic ability on the part of the Mexicans also contributed to their disadvantaged situation.

The presence of so many immigrant Mexican laborers, desper-ate to work for whatever the bosses would pay, led to much inequity in the workplace. Differential wage scales for Anglos and Mexicans were common. For example, in the late 1870s, Mexican miners made from $.50 to $1.50 per day, while Anglos doing the same work made $2.00 to $3.00. By 1895, the average wage for unskilled Mexican workers stood at about $2.00 per day, remaining at that level for the next fifteen years. By contrast, the wages paid Anglo workers rose steadily to about $4.00 during the same period. Copper companies routinely placed Mexican workers in a lower-wage payroll category labeled "Mexican labor," creating a dual wage structure that remained in effect through the 1940s. Unequal treatment on the job also extended to community life, where Mexicans lived segregated from Anglos in the mining camps and towns. Anglos often referred to the Mexican sections of mining camps as "frog-towns" and "jim-towns."

The mining companies' strategy of keeping Anglo and Mexican workers at odds worked so well that certain mining communities became known as "Mexican" camps, while others were identified as "white" camps, and there was little desire on either side to mix in the workplace or the community. The Globe-Miami mining district, for instance, was manned primarily by Mexican laborers, most of whom remained Mexican citizens.

In their misguided desire to elevate themselves above the Mexican workers, Anglo miners seriously hampered unionization efforts. The first strike in the copper mines of Arizona actually centered around the issue of hiring Mexican workers. The Western Federation of Miners struck the Old Dominion mine in 1896 in an effort to drive out Mexicans, reinforcing an unfortunate ethnic division among the workers that would weaken the struggle against the powerful mining companies for many years. Employers derived significant advantage from the proximity of the border, since they could import low-paid Mexican labor, thereby frustrating unionization efforts and strengthening antagonistic feelings among Anglo miners toward Mexican workers.

Without the help of Anglo unions, Mexicans found it difficult to force employers to improve working conditions and grant them higher wages. Nevertheless, they fought for their rights as best as they could. A major confrontation involving thousands of Mexican miners took place at Clifton-Morenci in 1903 over a decrease in worktime in the mines, which in effect reduced the earnings of the workers. Since unions like the Western Federation of Miners had largely written off Clifton-Morenci because of its predominantly Mexican work force, the strike caught nearly everyone, including labor leaders, by surprise. In the absence of union assistance, Mexican miners were able to coordinate their protest by other means, particularly through *mutualista* organizations. Strikers halted production for several days, but a flood and the intervention of Arizona Rangers and federal troops ended the strike.

Unfavorable publicity given the Clifton-Morenci strike by pro-employer newspapers hurt the image of Mexican workers among the public at large, but their determination caused Anglo unions to take them more seriously. In fact, the Western Federation of Miners temporarily suspended its anti-Mexican strategy during the strike. Once the strike was over, however, the Anglo unions reverted to their entrenched opposition to Mexican labor. The growing presence of "alien" workers in the Arizona mines, including many Europeans and Asians, became an increasingly bitter issue for the Anglo miners in the early part of the twentieth century.

In 1910, the Anglo unions joined forces with the Democratic party in a legislative campaign to restrict the hiring of Mexican workers. One successful bill in the Arizona territorial legislature excluded noncitizens from working on public works projects. Another bill which did not pass sought to prevent employers from importing aliens as contract workers. The most controversial initiative during the legislative session required that 80 percent of all workers hired by any individual or firm be U.S. citizens; the same bill also ordered employers not to hire non–English-speaking workers for hazardous jobs. Such legislation was mainly aimed at the Mexican workers, and there was considerable support for it among the voters; the 80 percent rule passed overwhelmingly through an initiative in 1914. The following year, however, the U.S. Supreme Court ruled the initiative unconstitutional. Thereafter, attempts continued to drive out Mexican workers from Arizona jobs, but the labor-Democratic coalition soon faltered and the movement lost steam.

Despite the unfavorable climate, Mexican workers kept migrating into Arizona and steadfastly demanded justice in the workplace.

In 1915, about five thousand Mexicans struck the mines at Clifton, Morenci, and Metcalf over discriminatory wages and the custom of foremen's selling jobs and forcing workers to buy raffle tickets to keep their employment. The strike lasted almost five months, but the arrest of hundreds of miners by the National Guard finally ended it. Two years later, a strike at Bisbee and at Jerome became infamous because of the inhumane treatment of the strikers. Close to 1,200 workers, both Anglo and Mexican, were rounded up and shipped in railroad boxcars to the desert in New Mexico, where they were turned over to federal troops.

By the late 1910s, organized labor found itself in a demoralized state, although workers could point to some accomplishments. Mexican miners had made significant progress in bringing workers together to press their demands for fair wages and decent treatment; after many years of struggle, they had also managed to enlist at least some participation of Anglo union members in their cause. Yet the public perception that radical and disloyal elements permeated the labor movement in Arizona played well into the hands of the mining companies, making it easier for them to utilize repressive measures to break the strikes. Even the Spanish-language press at times condoned the actions of the mining companies, arguing that Arizona should not tolerate the activities of "enemies" of the United States when the country was at war. *El Tucsonense*, for example, denounced the actions of the Industrial Workers of the World (Wobblies), encouraged Mexican Americans to vote for antilabor candidates, and expressed agreement with the kidnapping and expulsion of workers at Bisbee. One effective tactic used by law enforcement agencies against Mexican workers was deportation, especially of strikers identified as leaders. For many years after the confrontations of 1915 and 1917, Mexican workers concentrated on surviving the unfavorable climate, hoping that in the future better conditions for labor organizing would prevail in Arizona.

Revolution, Migration, and Hard Times

In the 1910s Arizona became an important destination for thousands of Mexicans fleeing the turmoil of the Revolution in

Mexico, one of the most significant events in the history of that country. Sonora played a prominent role in the fighting, providing troops for both revolutionary and federal forces and acting as a decisive battleground on several occasions. For example, in 1911 revolutionary forces captured the town of Agua Prieta, opposite Douglas, in a battle in which some Americans were wounded or killed. In 1913 the Constitutionalists took Naco, Sonora, after several weeks of fighting, and the following year the Villistas attacked the town repeatedly, seeking to drive out the Carrancistas. In 1915 the Villistas lost a crucial battle in Agua Prieta when Carrancista reinforcements were allowed to travel to the area through U.S. territory. Nogales, Sonora, was the scene of two important battles, one in 1915 and the other in 1918. In both cases U.S. troops, who were stationed at the border to prevent violence from spreading into U.S. territory, participated in the fighting. All these battles produced hundreds of casualties and drove many Mexicans into the United States.

Arizona towns such as Nogales, Naco, Douglas, and Bisbee provided asylum for many refugees from Sonora, just as border communities in Texas like Brownsville, Laredo, and El Paso served as a haven for refugees from Tamaulipas, Nuevo León, Coahuila, and Chihuahua. Many of the refugees returned to Mexico once things settled down, but a large number of them lost so much or became so disillusioned with perpetual instability in their homeland that they settled permanently in Arizona. The adjustment to life in the United States was not always easy, as the recollection of one man who made Tucson his new home reveals: "Having lost everything in our hometown of Fronteras we crossed the border at Naco in 1914 and went to Bisbee. They tried to take care of all us new kids in the schools there, but the building was so crowded that they had to throw up other ones in a big hurry. What they built looked more like chicken houses than anything else, and the Mexican kids who went to classes in them were known to the others as 'gallineros' which means 'people who live in chicken houses.' We thought when we came to Arizona that we would go back when the fighting was over, but there wasn't anything to go back to."[7]

As a result of the migration spurred by the Revolution, the Mexican-born population of Arizona more than doubled between

1910 and 1920, increasing from 29,987 to 61,580. In Tucson, the Mexican-born population increased from 2,441 in 1910 to 4,261 by 1920. Most of the new arrivals belonged to the working class, but a significant portion came from the middle and upper classes. Journalists, attorneys, physicians, and businessmen from Sonora settled in Tucson's Mexican American community, providing a needed infusion of new talent and leadership for a group in decline. In the years that followed, the well-educated and affluent refugees made significant contributions to Tucson through their professional work and their involvement in civic activities. Their presence also assured that Tucsonenses would have an an expanded middle-class pool from which to draw the next generation of leaders. On the other hand, the emigration of these refugees represented a serious loss for Mexico because it would take many years before that country recovered sufficiently from the upheaval of the 1910s to be able to produce more educated and skilled people to replace them.

An indication of the revitalization of Tucson society during the 1910s was the publication of several Spanish-language newspapers, including *El Tucsonense,* which appeared continuously from 1915 to the 1950s. *El Tucsonense* was the most successful of a long line of newspapers going back to the nineteenth century that kept the Spanish-speaking community of Tucson informed and at the same time provided literary entertainment. The cultural milieu of the Hispanic community was also strengthened by the founding of theater groups, orchestras, bands, and other forms of recreation for the educated elite. *Teatro Carmen,* the most important local Mexican theater of the early twentieth century, was founded in 1915. It presented a variety of serious and light dramas as well as musical concerts. Mexican Americans were also favored by many talented performers. One of the best folk singers produced by Tucson was Luisa Espinel, who received training in Europe and delighted audiences throughout the United States between the 1910s and 1930s. While Hispanics with a liking for high culture attended concerts and theater productions, working-class people with down-to-earth tastes frequented such amusements as horse races, bullfights, and cockfights. Of course other forms of entertainment appealing to all sectors of society, such as movies and sports, were also available.

The poor migrants who left Mexico during the period had the

good fortune to find employment in a variety of occupations. Arizona's mines were in the midst of an economic upswing, and many of the newcomers gravitated to the state's mining centers. Others went to the cotton-growing areas around Florence, Casa Grande, Yuma, and Phoenix. When the United States entered World War I in 1914, great labor shortages developed in Arizona, and American employers went into Sonora to recruit workers. In 1917, a controversy developed between U.S. labor recruiters seeking workers for the cotton fields and the Sonora governor, who attempted to put a stop to the practice by requiring a $1,000 bond for every person who left the state. Despite the opposition of the Mexican government, employers succeeded in luring the workers to jobs north of the border. By 1919, almost six thousand had been recruited to work in Arizona. In the Phoenix area, the cotton growers association spent more than $320,000 to import Mexican workers to the Valley; the investment paid handsomely, as the employers realized savings in the millions of dollars by fixing wages at very low levels.

The working-class migrants who settled in the cities for the most part toiled in low-paid, low-status jobs and lived in segregated barrios. They lived a life apart from the Anglos as well as the middle-class Hispanics, who looked down on them and made every effort to demonstrate their superior status. The arrival of the downtrodden elements from Mexico rekindled racist, nativist, and anti-foreign sentiments throughout Arizona, but especially in those areas where Anglo workers felt threatened by the competition from laborers willing to work for low wages. Union members deeply resented Mexican and other "alien" workers because they had arrived at the height of the struggle against the powerful mining and railroad companies.

Anti-Mexicanism again flared up among the state's politicians. In 1918, the legislature debated but did not pass a proposal to restrict employment in the mines to people who could speak English. In 1923, the legislature passed a resolution endorsing proposed legislation restricting immigration then being debated in the U.S. Congress. The Arizona resolution stated in part: "Arizona, the youngest of the States and the last frontier of the continental United

States, is the home of a citizenry animated by the virile Americanism of the great southwest, devoted to the upbuilding of the character of its people and maintaining a very high rank in the standing of educational institutions, yet handicapped by an appalling percentage of illiteracy due, in a large measure, to the steadily increasing number of its foreign population."[8]

Anti-immigrant sentiments held by elected officals reflected attitudes that prevailed in society and in the mass media. The *Arizona Republican* considered the growing numbers of immigrants "the biggest problem and greatest menace that faces the American people." This newspaper was so caught up in the anti-alien and anti-Mexican hysteria of the period that it wrote an editorial in 1919 supporting the lynching of a Spanish-speaking person in Pueblo, Colorado.[9]

In Phoenix, where the Hispanic population had grown from 2,323 in 1920 to 7,293 by 1930, institutional racism was a fact of life. Anglo officials kept Mexicans, Blacks, and Asians at the bottom of the social order through policies and legislation that permitted pervasive job and housing discrimination. The Mexican barrio grew larger as older residents and new migrants clustered together for mutual support and protection.

The extreme poverty that characterized life in the Phoenix barrio bred many social problems that in turn engendered ethnic tensions. Alcoholism, drug abuse, and prostitution flourished in some parts of the Mexican community. Anglos who desired pleasures not permitted in their own neighborhoods frequently visited the barrio to satisfy their needs. On occasion, the presence of outsiders caused problems with the Mexican youth, who resented them. For example, in 1923 a fracas broke out when "white boys showered too much attention on Mexican girls" at a dance hall. The fight had the potential of turning into a "race war," but police intervened and limited the damage to a few stabbings inflicted on the visitors.[10]

In 1929, the Mexican community in Phoenix learned the extent of its powerlessness when it was unable to apply sufficient pressure to convict a group of Anglo police officers involved in the execution of two Hispanic burglars who were victims of an entrapment. While four policemen waited inside a drug store, another officer, acting as a thief himself, drove the would-be burglars to the site, where they were seemingly shot without warning. One of the burglars was apparently killed instantly and his two companions were wounded. Later testimony revealed that an officer shot one of the two wounded men in the face in an attempt to finish him off. Despite the details of the case, it took a jury only thirty minutes to acquit the policemen who set up the ambush. The only officer convicted was the driver of the car, who turned out to be a member of a major Anglo burglary ring that operated in the area. He and other fellow gang members received lengthy prison terms.

Life in poor Mexican neighborhoods in Arizona was not easy in normal times, and it became very difficult during periods of economic distress. In 1920–21, for example, at a time of nationwide depression, barrio resources in Phoenix became severely strained when hundreds of unemployed workers from the cotton fields and the mining areas streamed into the city seeking relief. Officials attempted to keep these unfortunate people out by ordering police to arrest and fine them for vagrancy. Yet the numbers were too large, and city fathers could do little but grimace at the sight of tent communities in the barrio and makeshift settlements along the main arteries leading into Phoenix. The situation of the stranded people became so pathetic that Mexico's President Álvaro Obregón ordered an investigation through the Mexican consul general in Los Angeles, who visited Phoenix and sought an appropriation of $17,000 from his government to provide emergency aid. Local newspapers, charity groups, labor unions, and ordinary Phoenicians rendered assistance in a variety of ways, including making cash contributions and donating food. Eventually thousands of Mexicans throughout Arizona returned to their homeland in a repatriation drive sponsored by the Mexican government, but many, fearing that conditions would be worse south of the border, decided to take their chances in Phoenix and in other Arizona communities.

A decade later Mexicans in the Phoenix area faced similar hardships again, although this time the economic crisis lasted much longer. As elsewhere in the United States, the Great Depression had a devastating effect on Arizona, and of course the greatest suffering fell on those at the bottom of society. By 1933, nearly two-thirds of Arizona's Mexican population lacked the means to generate steady income. Non-U.S. citizens were particularly vulnerable, for they could not participate in the public works projects sponsored by the federal government. To make matters worse, poor Anglos and Blacks arrived constantly to compete with Mexicans for field jobs. This created a very favorable situation for the growers, who cut wages so drastically that many workers refused to take jobs, which prompted the state to order removal from the relief rolls of all field hands who refused to work. Tragically, while economic devastation took its toll, a typhoid epidemic broke out in the migrant camps, forcing officials to evacuate people en masse from their shacks.

The poor in Tucson also endured severe privations, as the story of Teresa García Coronado illustrates. At one point Mrs. García Coronado's family had so little to eat that she and her husband found it necessary to take drastic measures in order to survive. Her husband stole eggs from the neighbors' chicken coops and she searched wherever she could for food. "I was going around to gather up whatever there was. One time the men of the C.C.C. [Civilian Conservation Corps] threw out two dead cows, and I grabbed a quarter which a man cut into three portions for me. They [the C.C.C.] had thrown them out for the people who were scavenging in the garbage dump of Hollywood [a local westside Tucson barrio]. There were apples and rotten oranges. There were long lines to receive the food that they gave away. That which I did for my children gave me no shame."[11]

The drastic unemployment problem prompted the federal government to threaten a massive deportation of foreigners, creating a climate of fear and apprehension among Mexicans. Arizonans apparently did not organize formal "repatriation" programs as occurred in other states, but certain sectors of Anglo society worked to have foreigners deported. In Phoenix, a small group of Anglos accused Mexicans of receiving welfare assistance and demanded that the U.S. Immigration Service look into the matter. The accusation turned out to be false. In Douglas, the Chamber of Commerce sought to initiate a repatriation program much like the one in place in Los Angeles, but local officials turned down the plan. Even without officially generated pressures, however, it is estimated that eighteen thousand Mexicans left Arizona between 1929 and 1937 as a result of the unfavorable economic and social climate. It is likely that a significant percentage of the repatriates were U.S. citizens, because many Mexican families included members who had been born in the United States. Nationwide, the number of Mexicans who returned to Mexico during the Depression years numbered about half a million.

Sadly, most of the repatriates encountered even worse economic conditions in Mexico, and within a short time many made their way back to the United States. The experience of many families with American-born children was painful, as the following excerpt from a 1943 report of the Children's Bureau of the U.S. Department of Labor makes clear: "Children of repatriated parents, including many American-born children with alien parents, are causing great concern to the welfare authorities in these areas [Arizona-Mexico border]. It was reported that some 15,000 such children with their parents went through Nogales, Arizona, just across the border from Nogales, Mexico, on their way back to Mexico. Many of these children have drifted back to the United States, particularly older children, and are living from hand to mouth in Arizona."[12]

World War II and Its Aftermath

A reversal of the losses in population experienced in the 1930s as a result of the repatriation movement to Mexico began to be felt during the World War II years, when Mexicans entered the Southwest again in large numbers. In 1950 the Census Bureau reported that 128,318 persons of Spanish surname lived in Arizona, and that number had increased to 194,356 ten years later. While most Mexican Americans remained in the working-class sector during the 1940s and 1950s, the group recorded important gains in the middle-class ranks, and that in turn had significant implications in the effort to improve conditions in the barrios and colonias throughout the state.

World War II and the Korean conflict transformed the lives of many young men who served in the armed forces. The military acted as a powerful agent of socialization for large numbers of Mexican Americans who previously had had limited opportunities to interact with members of the dominant society. In addition to learning more about the nature of Anglo American society, Mexican Americans had an opportunity to see different parts of the country and also traveled abroad as participants in the European and Asian war zones. Military service entitled Hispanics to benefits under the G.I. Bill of Rights, and many took advantage of the opportunity to attend colleges and universities. With the availability of higher education, members of the working class were able to enter professional and business occupations. That new status allowed them to become more aware of the problems that beset their communities, and many became involved in organizations that sought to eliminate discriminatory practices that continued to harm the interests of the group.

One of the least-known chapters of Mexican American history is the contribution of women to the war effort in the 1940s. While the men served abroad, the women engaged in many activities at home to help the country. In Tucson, for example, La Asociación Hispano-Americana de Madres y Esposas (The Hispanic-American Association of Mothers and Wives) sold war bonds and stamps, collected clothing for shipment to war-torn countries, collected scrap metal and other materials useful for industrial purposes, provided child care for women who worked in defense industries, and organized many functions to lift the morale of servicemen. In Phoenix, women were also centrally involved in assisting with war-related activities in the Mexican American community. Aside from participating in bond drives and the like, Hispanics organized the "Victory Labor Volunteers," whose members sought to meet the labor shortages in the cotton fields around Phoenix. An estimated five thousand Mexican Americans participated as "labor volunteers" through this effort. Community organizations and religious groups also encouraged unassimilated Mexicans to learn English and become American citizens, thereby paving the way for involvement in civic affairs.[13]

Despite the significant contribution of Mexican Americans to the war effort both in the military and in civilian life, the dominant society still felt reluctant to accept them as first-class citizens. Returning servicemen often encountered discrimination in employment,

housing, and in public facilities such as restaurants. Just before the
state was to honor Pfc. Silvestre S. Herrera, Phoenix's only Congressional Medal of Honor winner during World War II, the governor
had to order the removal of signs in the city that read "No Mexican
Trade Wanted." Such experiences convinced many former servicemen to become involved in the civil rights struggles of the period.[14]

In the 1950s, when the issue of segregation had assumed great
importance nationwide, the Alianza Hispano-Americana became
very involved in legal battles in Arizona. School segregation assumed
the highest priority for the Alianza because the continued separation
of Mexican American children from the mainstream implied prolonged marginalization in society far into the future. Communities
such as Miami, Glendale, Tolleson, Douglas, Safford, Duncan,
Tempe, Ajo, and Flagstaff maintained de facto separate schools for
Mexican American students. In 1950 Alianza attorneys, in conjunc-
tion with the Committee for Better Americanism, filed a federal
suit against the Tolleson School District in the Phoenix area, charging school officials with unlawful segregation of Mexican American
children. The court agreed with the plaintiffs, noting that the schools
that served Mexican American students were clearly inferior to
those that served Anglo children. Following this victory, the Alianza
made an attempt to end school segregation in the whole state by
filing suit against the Glendale School District as well as the Arizona
Board of Education. The strategy yielded only partial results because the Glendale school officials decided not to fight the case in
court, choosing instead to close down the Mexican school and to
build a new one for all the children of the district. The decision of
the Glendale School District undercut the ambitious objective of
eliminating segregation statewide through a single court case, and
the problem continued for years.

Segregation in other spheres of life in Arizona prompted Mexican Americans to take appropriate action. In Winslow, Mexican
Americans suffered the humiliation of being allowed in the town's
public swimming pool only on Wednesdays, the day before the pool
was emptied and cleaned. In 1954 the Alianza took the matter to
court, using as precedent a federal court ruling ten years earlier in
California that desegregated a swimming pool in San Bernardino.

Recognizing the illegality of the Winslow policy, city officials chose to settle the matter out of court. Henceforth Mexican Americans would have access to the pool along with everyone else anytime it was open.

Arizonans were so race conscious and so influenced by stereotypes that the harmful effects of segregation could be found even in religious life. In Miami's Catholic church, Mexican American parishioners sat on the right side of the altar while everyone else sat on the left side. This practice reportedly began in the 1920s when a few Anglo parishioners accused Mexican Americans of stealing purses inside the church. To solve the problem, the priest ordered the separation of the two groups, and the tradition lasted at least into the 1940s. Another pathetic scene in Miami involved three churches along the town's main street. An Anglo church, the "Miami Community Presbyterian Church," faced another church of the same denomination, the "Mexican Presbyterian Church." The Mexican church was noticeably run-down and unattractive, while the Anglo church was an imposing concrete structure. Nearby, a dilapidated shack known as the "Colored Baptist Church" served the religious needs of a segment of the town's black community.[15]

The Chicano Generation and Beyond

By the 1960s, racial minorities in the United States had become increasingly aware of their disadvantaged status. Blacks in particular stirred the American conscience with massive civil rights demonstrations, forcing the government and the private sector to respond with more enlightened policies toward the poor. Internal dissent over the Vietnam War and the rebellious mood of the youth added to the turbulence and confusion of the period. As the nation examined itself, Mexican Americans likewise began a process of introspection, seeking to clarify their position in U.S. society and to determine the path to follow in their long struggle to achieve equality. New organizations such as the United Farm Workers, La Raza Unida party, the Crusade for Justice, the Alianza Federal de Pueblos Libres (Federal Alliance of Free Communities), and the

Movimiento Estudiantil Chicano de Aztlán (Chicano Student Movement) introduced a more activist and militant approach to the solution of community problems. "Chicanismo" had arrived, and the Mexican American people would never again be the same.

As elsewhere in the Southwest, activists in the Chicano movement in Arizona chose education as one of the prime targets for reform. Specific problems identified in the public schools included segregation, substandard facilities, high dropout rates, inadequate curricula, poor counseling, and lack of Mexican American teachers and administrators. Some of the same problems existed at the university level, with the added concern that relatively few Mexican American students actually pursued higher education.

In 1968, students at Arizona State University formed the Mexican American Student Organization (MASO), a group patterned after similar organizations that had been established on California campuses beginning in 1966. MASO first displayed its ability to pursue Chicano-oriented goals in the fall of 1968 when it persuaded the university food service to halt the purchase of California grapes, which at the time were being boycotted by the United Farm Workers. Shortly thereafter MASO organized a widely supported protest to pressure the university to reassess a contract it had with a laundry that was accused of practicing discrimination against its workers. The university responded favorably to the demands of the Chicano students, boosting their confidence that through effective organization and calculated militancy much could be accomplished to better conditions on campus.

In 1969, tensions that had been building for years at Phoenix Union High School exploded into protest marches and a boycott of classes that lasted several weeks. At the time, Phoenix Union had an enrollment of 43 percent Mexican American students, 35 percent Anglo, 20 percent Black, and the rest "other." The controversy began over conflicts between Chicano and Black students and the question of campus security, but it quickly escalated to embrace other important issues such as curricula and school personnel. Undoubtedly the decision to call a boycott by the Ad Hoc Chicano School Board that was formed at the height of the turmoil was influenced by well-publicized walkouts that had taken place earlier in predominantly Mexican American schools in California and Texas. After the boycott ended at Phoenix Union, apparently some of the concerns raised by the protestors were addressed satisfactorily, but the fundamental change that many sought to bring about did not take place.

In Tucson, Chicanos and Blacks in 1974 expressed their dissatisfaction with the educational establishment by suing Tucson School District #1, charging that the district had historically segregated Mexican American and Black students. The plaintiffs accused school officials of promoting "discriminatory construction policies, segregatory zone lines, racially imbalanced feeder patterns, free transfer policies, tracking, and discriminatory staff assignments." In their view the district fostered a "system in which most minority children attend minority schools and most Anglo students attend Anglo schools." The defendants denied intentional segregation, arguing that the separation of the different groups was a product of residential segregation. Four years later the judge who ruled on the case found school officials innocent of the segregation charge, although he noted that instances of discrimination had taken place in the district.[16]

The civil rights movement nationwide greatly encouraged Mexican Americans to challenge institutions in Arizona and elsewhere. Yet little would have happened during those years if the Hispanic community had not been ready to sustain the level of activism necessary to achieve change. In earlier times the Hispanic community had lacked the resources and expertise to file lawsuits or to conduct demonstrations. Before the 1960s relatively few Mexican Americans were businesspeople or professionals, precisely the people with the time and resources necessary to pursue societal change in the courts and elsewhere. Chicano student activism was an outgrowth of the expansion of the middle class and the resultant presence of greater numbers of Hispanics in the universities. Prior to the 1960s relatively few Mexican Americans went beyond high school, especially students from working-class backgrounds. Thus the pressures for change on a national scale brought on by the turmoil of the 1960s and early 1970s coincided with the maturing of the Mexican American community to the point where it too had the means to express its discontent in ways that produced positive results.

The intense attention focused on Hispanic issues stimulated many young Mexican Americans to continue their involvement in community affairs beyond their university experience. In Tucson and Phoenix former student leaders from working-class backgrounds, replicating what occurred in other urban centers throughout the Southwest, took their talents and organizing abilities to the barrios and middle-class neighborhoods where their people lived. By the late 1970s many of them ran businesses, headed community organizations, practiced law, occupied professional positions, and held elective office.

Politically Mexican Americans became more visible in Arizona than ever before, as the increase in the number of elected state officials makes clear. The advances in politics during the period are reflected in the number of state legislators: by 1973 the state had a total of twelve Hispanic state legislators, compared to only four in 1960 and none in 1950. That represented very impressive gains, given that in previous years extremely few Spanish-surnamed persons had been elected to such offices. For instance, from 1912 to 1940, the state legislature included only four persons of Hispanic descent (three of them were Tucsonenses). Between 1913 and 1934, not a single Hispanic served in that body. Mexican Americans also managed to win elections to many offices in city and county governments starting in the mid-1960s. By 1980, Spanish-surnamed mayors served in communities such as Nogales, Miami, Clifton, and Tolleson, and Hispanic supervisors could be found in five of the fourteen counties in the state. Reflecting trends in society in general, relatively few of these public servants have been Hispanic women. Yet a few women have been elected to such offices as mayor, state representative, and other lesser local positions. Hispanic women have served as mayors of Miami, Hayden, and South Tucson; Pima County has sent a Hispanic woman to the state legislature; and Santa Cruz, Graham, Apache, and Pima counties have elected Hispanic women to a variety of secondary offices. Finally, significant progress has been achieved in appointive positions. For example, of 845 appointments made by Governor Bruce Babbitt in the early

1980s, 105 went to Hispanics. By contrast, in 1965 only 8 Hispanics occupied such positions, out of a total of 449 appointees.[17]

The most impressive political triumph among Hispanics in Arizona historically has been the election of Raúl Castro as governor. Elected in 1974, Castro symbolized the success of many Mexican Americans who started at the bottom and through hard work and determination made it to the top. Castro was born in poverty in Cananea, Sonora, in 1916. The death of his father in 1929 forced him to struggle in a variety of occupations to obtain an education; he eventually became an attorney in Tucson. Having practiced law and served in various local political offices, he became a diplomat in the 1960s, acting as U.S. ambassador to El Salvador and Bolivia. In 1970, he returned to Arizona and ran unsuccessfully for governor, and four years later he won the state's top job. In 1977, he accepted an offer to become ambassador to Argentina, and he left the governorship. The prominence achieved by Raúl Castro was a great source of pride and inspiration for the Hispanic population of Arizona.

Substantial as the political advances of recent years have been, they have perhaps tended to focus too much attention on Hispanics who have "made it" and blurred the reality of widespread poverty and destitution among the masses. Census data from 1980 revealed that over one-fifth of all Hispanics in Arizona lived below the poverty line, compared to less than a tenth of the Anglo population. Less than 2 percent of Arizona's Hispanic families had incomes above $50,000, compared to more than 5 percent of Anglo families. Only 5.6 percent of Hispanics twenty-five years and older had completed college, compared to 18.9 percent for Anglos (Table 1). In Phoenix, the median home value among Hispanic homeowners in 1984 was $54,500, compared to $72,100 for the city's population as a whole; comparable figures for Tucson revealed only a slightly better situation, $57,600 for Hispanics and $72,500 for the total population.

In Phoenix, Hispanics have been integrated into the mainstream of community life very slowly. The 1980 census actually indicated a significant growth in the level of segregation of Mexican American neighborhoods. A report issued by the Department of Housing and Urban Development characterized low-income Hispanic areas of Phoenix as a deteriorating inner city zone surrounded

Table 1. Education, Income, and Poverty Levels of Anglo (White)
and Spanish Origin Population, Arizona, 1980

	Number		Percentage	
	Anglo (White)	Spanish Origin	Anglo (White)	Spanish Origin
Education				
Persons 25 Years or Older	1,363,150	192,709	100.0	100.0
Completed High School	485,815	50,298	35.6	26.1
Completed College	257,493	10,874	18.9	5.6
Income				
Number of Families	614,400	96,286	100.0	100.0
Income below $15,000	97,380	18,062	15.8	18.8
Income above $50,000	32,986	1,684	5.4	1.7
Poverty				
Persons Sampled	2,219,510	437,512	100.0	100.0
Income below Poverty Level (1979)	214,878	91,783	9.7	21.0

Source: U.S. Bureau of the Census. *Census of Population and Housing. Advance Estimates of Social, Economic, and Housing Characteristics. Arizona.* Washington, D.C.: 1982.

by a modern and booming metropolis. The spread of commercial and industrial establishments into the barrios has posed a serious threat to many low-income people who face permanent displacement. In 1982, five hundred Mexican Americans demonstrated against the threatened destruction of their neighborhoods by the sale of land for purposes other than the construction of housing. The demonstration included persons from Tempe, Glendale, Tolleson, and Phoenix. Besides the problem of housing, protestors also complained about the closing of minority schools, unemployment, and police brutality. When asked why they felt the need to take to the streets, the leaders replied: "Because officialdom has turned a deaf ear to the problems of the Mexicano communities."[18]

Another major problem besetting Phoenix is the destructive activity of barrio gangs. Many young people who apparently have given up on society have engaged in deviant activities such as drug abuse, theft, and violence. Numerous neighborhoods have felt terrorized by roaming bands who threaten to disrupt the peace that law-abiding citizens desire. In the 1970s stories appeared frequently in the press detailing problems caused by gangs, including the frequent victimizing of innocent persons caught in the crossfire.[19]

One of the most compelling issues in recent decades for Hispanics in Arizona and elsewhere in the Southwest has been immigration from Mexico. Controversy over undocumented migration escalated in the 1970s as a result of the increased flow of immigrants and the prolonged national debate over restrictionist legislation, culminating in the passage of the Simpson-Rodino law in 1986. In the national context, Arizona has attracted relatively small numbers of undocumented workers. Considerable attention, however, has been focused on Arizona because of union activity involving Mexican nationals and because of exploitation and mistreatment of workers.

In the late 1970s the Arizona Farm Workers, an arm of the Maricopa County Organizing Project, became involved in organizing farmworkers, including persons without documents. The AFW took this step because the United Farm Workers, the union headed by César Chávez, had accomplished very little since it first began organizing in the state in the 1960s. Apparently the limited success of the UFW stemmed from the conservative political climate in Arizona as well as from Chávez's need to concentrate staff and resources in California. The Agricultural Employment Relations Act of Arizona in particular has severely restricted the rights of workers to organize, thus making it difficult for either union to succeed.

Nevertheless, some important advances have been made as a result of the efforts to organize the workers. Both the UFW and AFW have assisted workers with a variety of social service programs, and both can point to some legislative and court victories. The AFW in particular can claim unprecedented success in its drive to organize undocumented workers and in its efforts to negotiate contracts that include contributions by employers into a fund for economic development projects in Mexico, in the areas from which the workers come. Combining those resources with funds obtained from foundations, in 1982 the AFW invested some $350,000 to help workers in various rural areas of Mexico build their future in their own country. The activities of the AFW have been led by Guadalupe Sánchez and Jesús Romo.

Most farmworkers remain unorganized and therefore lack the protection offered by unions and other agencies. Reports of workers living in the fields under primitive conditions and of callous employer disregard for their welfare have appeared frequently in the media. Abuses of undocumented people have also been publicized. The most notorious incident involved the kidnapping and torturing of three Mexican nationals by the Harrigan brothers in the late 1970s in southern Arizona. Acquitted by a state jury, the Harrigans were eventually tried in federal court. In early 1981 one of the brothers was convicted and the other was acquitted. Other recent cases have involved killings by U.S. Border Patrol agents and deaths or injuries of workers through the negligence of employers and others.

Future Historical Research on Hispanic Arizonans

The current state of historical scholarship allows us but a partial picture of the experience of Mexican Americans in Arizona. Much more is known about Hispanics in Texas, New Mexico, and California because historians have focused greater attention on those states. In order to reconstruct a more complete record of the Hispanic past in their state, Arizonans will need to build a historical consciousness and support more historical research on this group in both academic and nonacademic circles.

Plenty of topics await those interested in writing about the history of Hispanic Arizonans. One type of study deserving more attention is local history. In *Los Tucsonenses,* Thomas Sheridan demonstrated the great potential of using this approach to understand the Hispanic past at the community level. His methodology might be applied in other towns and cities where Mexican Americans have lived in significant numbers. A longitudinal study of Phoenix would be particularly valuable. Every effort should be made to bring community studies as far into the present as possible in order to illuminate our understanding of long-term evolutionary processes.

Another fruitful approach is to focus on important themes that illuminate fundamental aspects of the group's overall experience. Histories might be written about such topics as Hispanic immigration into Arizona, the farm labor movement, Hispanic political involvement, entrepreneurship in the Hispanic community, the Chicano movement in Arizona, and Hispanics in the mining industry.

A third important approach involves the study of individuals whose lives represent important facets of the evolution of the Hispanic community. Prominent figures such as Raúl Castro are obvious candidates for such biographies, but the experiences of "ordinary" people are equally significant. Fascinating persons can be found in all parts of the state. In gathering biographical data, the tape recorder can be used with considerable effectiveness. Oral history, however, requires some expertise, and new practitioners of this methodology should seek training through historical societies or university programs.

Perhaps the greatest challenge is to convince the public at large that historical research is important and worthwhile. Even in the Hispanic community itself there is little appreciation for the value of knowing the past. That reality is largely explained by the low level of education in the Hispanic community and the ever-present preoccupation among many working-class members of the group simply with making a living. Under such circumstances history is seen as a nonessential, "luxury" activity pursued only by well-established middle-class and affluent sectors of the population.

For this enterprise to succeed, more bridges will need to be built among different levels of society and among professional historians, university programs, historical societies, community groups, and the "average people" in the Hispanic community. By engaging in such an effort, Arizona might point the way for Hispanics in other states to recapture and popularize their heritage for the benefit of this ethnic group and of society as a whole.

Notes

Strict space limitations prevent me from footnoting this essay comprehensively. I am deeply indebted to many authors who have written about Hispanic Arizonans, and I regret that I cannot list all the works I have consulted. I would like to express my sincere appreciation to numerous colleagues whose excellent writings made my task easier. I owe special gratitude to Christine Marín, Assistant Archivist at the Arizona Collection, Arizona State University Library, for giving me valuable and kind assistance during the research phase of the project. My thanks also to James E. Officer and Phylis Cancilla Martinelli, who provided helpful comments for revision of the manuscript.

1. Two outstanding works provide an excellent starting point for delving into the history of Hispanic Arizonans: James E. Officer, *Arizona's Hispanic Perspective* (Tucson: Arizona Academy, 38th Arizona Town Hall, and University of Arizona Press, 1981), and Thomas E. Sheridan, *Los Tucsonenses: The Mexican Community in Tucson, 1854–1941* (Tucson: University of Arizona Press, 1986). Both books were extremely helpful in the preparation of this chapter.

2. Sheridan, *Los Tucsonenses,* 37–38.

3. J. Ross Browne, *A Tour Through Arizona, 1864, or Adventures in the Apache Country* (Tucson: Arizona Silhouettes, 1950), 171–72. Cited in Cecil Robinson, *Mexico and the Hispanic Southwest in American Literature* (Tucson: University of Arizona Press, 1977), 72.

4. Officer, *Arizona's Hispanic Perspective,* 79–80.

5. Cited in David J. Weber, ed., *Foreigners in Their Native Land: Historical Roots of the Mexican Americans* (Albuquerque: University of New Mexico Press, 1973), 145.

6. A. Blake Brophy, *Foundlings on the Frontier: Racial and Religious Conflict in Arizona Territory, 1904–1905* (Tucson: University of Arizona Press, 1972).

7. Officer, *Arizona's Hispanic Perspective,* 102.

8. Mary R. Titcomb, "Americanization and Mexicans in the Southwest: A History of Phoenix's Friendly House, 1920–1983" (M.A. thesis, University of California—Santa Barbara, 1984).

9. Ibid., 21.

10. Michael J. Kotlanger, "Phoenix, Arizona: 1920–1940" (Ph.D. dissertation, Arizona State University, 1983).

11. Sheridan, *Los Tucsonenses,* 211–12.

12. Raymond J. Flores, *The Socio-Economic Status Trends of the Mexican People Residing in Arizona* (M.A. thesis, Arizona State College, 1951; R and E Research Associates reprint, 1973), 6.

13. Christine Marín, *La Asociación Hispano-Americana de Madres y Esposas: Tucson's Mexican American Women in World War II* (Tucson: University of Arizona, Renato Rosaldo Lecture Series Monograph, vol. 1, Summer 1985).

14. Christine Marín, "Patriotism Abroad and Repression at Home: Mexican Americans in World War II" (unpublished manuscript, May 1977, Arizona Collection, Arizona State University Library), 26.

15. Flores, *Socio-Economic Status Trends,* 48.

16. Sheridan, *Los Tucsonenses,* 219–21.

17. Officer, *Arizona's Hispanic Perspective,* 143–49.

18. *New Times* (Phoenix), June 23–29, 1982.

19. See, for example, the following newspaper accounts: "West Phoenix Neighborhood Terrorized," *Phoenix Gazette,* June 22, 1977; "City Focuses on Gang Violence," *Phoenix Gazette,* September 19, 1978; "Gangs Proliferate," *Tucson Citizen,* November 11, 1979.

RESHAPING ARIZONA'S ECONOMY: A CENTURY OF CHANGE

Gerald D. Nash

There is probably no field of study in which the desire to predict the future is more intense than economics. In this essay, Gerald Nash discusses past trends in national, western, and Arizona history that help us understand the possibilities of our economic future. He suggests that using such broad, historic trends is a more reliable basis for projection than the more present-minded techniques of futurists, and he offers some predictions of his own.

The main problem with this approach, as Nash himself points out, is that we lack detailed studies of Arizona's industries, work force, entrepreneurs, and economic development that would provide data for such projections. With very few exceptions, Arizona's economic history remains unwritten.

During the 1980s a growing number of Americans became aware of far-reaching changes in the nation's economic life. Factories were closing, thousands of workers were losing their jobs, and whole industries—such as steel and textiles—were in a period of serious decline. Moreover, international competition was threatening the vitality of scores of other industries in which Americans had once been preeminent. What was happening? Many Americans were befuddled, confused, and bewildered. Others looked anxiously for answers. Why had the United States lost its competitive edge? Was it the slowdown of productive efficiency, or perhaps the lag of American technology? Those who searched for easy answers to such questions found none, for the circumstances leading to major changes in America's economic structure were complex.

Yet the 1980s were not the first time that Americans were forced to undergo the travail of reorganizing their economy. In fact, technological changes—among many factors—had stimulated Americans to restructure their economic life about once every generation (approximately every thirty or forty years) since the early nineteenth century. The process was never easy; it forced millions of individuals to change not only their means of livelihood, but as often as not their geographical location, their social status, and, indeed, their entire lifestyle. Much of the American success story in the twentieth century was to some extent related to the adaptability of previous generations, to their willingness to innovate and to experiment with new technological processes and ideas. Like a snake that sheds its old skin, so Americans were positively disposed toward change, which they often equated with progress.

The National Economy

The processes of change in the 1980s, therefore, must be viewed within the context of similar transformations in previous years. That the decade after the American Revolution required substantial adjustments in trade and commerce is well known. So, too, did the War of 1812 force Americans to become more self-sufficient, particularly in manufacturing. By the 1840s Americans bore the full brunt of the Industrial Revolution as New Englanders and entrepreneurs in the Middle Atlantic states founded new factories to replace cottage industries. That disruptive phase of industrialism lasted for about one generation. By the 1880s another economic cycle was in full swing with the rise of Big Business. Family-owned entrepreneurial enterprises of an earlier period were now replaced by large corporations staffed by expert managers. Whether organized in holding companies or trusts, these new business firms often encompassed entire industries and embodied vertical as well as horizontal integration of auxiliary industries. The new corporate giants made the United States the world's leading industrial nation and changed the face of American society. But the pace of change did not abate. By the 1920s another breed of corporations was reshaping the national economy. The dynamic business enterprises of the 1880s had been based largely on the exploitation of raw materials, but those of the 1920s were rooted in technological innovations such as radio, moving pictures, consumer appliances, or cars. So rapid was their rise, however, that they also brought economic dislocations in their wake and contributed to the Great Depression of the 1930s.

Somewhat unexpectedly, World War II ushered in another phase in American economic growth. After a decade of stagnation, war mobilization stimulated the slumbering economy. While promoting a rapid restructuring of the industrial base that sustained the nation's military effort it also transformed a Depression-wracked people into the consumers of the postwar affluent society. A country that had been gripped by notions of scarcity and limitations emerged from the war as one inspired by visions of abundance and unbounded economic expansion. Profound feelings of pessimism fueled by the unemployment of the 1930s now gave way to unbounded optimism and new expectations of material affluence and consumer indulgence.

This changed perception of America's future was possibly the most important consequence of World War II. But of course that mood was only a reflection of substantial changes in American life wrought by the conflict. The American economy had been a sleeping giant, drugged by the Depression, but awakened by the war. Mobilization not only spawned great increases in the productive capacity of American industry; it also stimulated new industries in such fields as electronics and created a vast pent-up demand for consumer goods. In addition, it brought considerable expansion to the service industries—banking, tourism, health care, and education.

Above all, World War II demonstrated that full employment was not a utopian ideal but, as the years between 1941 and 1945 demonstrated, a fully realizable goal. To strive for a rising standard of living was one goal on which most Americans could agree.

The far-reaching economic changes of the 1940s had a recognizable social impact. The new economic prosperity greatly expanded the American middle class and made their aspirations part of the rising expectations of most Americans. That was particularly true of minorities who, after the war, became more determined than ever to join the American mainstream. Economic affluence clearly stimulated the civil rights revolution of the 1950s. The improved material well-being of a majority of Americans led them to move from inner cities to newly built suburbs where the split-level ranch house became the visible symbol of the American Dream. The prosperity ushered in by World War II also led to a higher birth rate in the postwar decade as Americans chose to raise larger families. Suburban living, contemporaries claimed, tended to promote conformity and standardization, as well as an increasingly relentless pursuit of materialism to the exclusion of most other values.

Social and economic currents stimulated by World War II also affected the political climate. The years between 1945 and 1960 witnessed "consensus politics," well represented by Ike in the White House and by governors like Earl Warren in California who attracted voters from both major political parties. Given the fears of a nuclear holocaust and the tensions of the Cold War with the Soviet Union, Americans desired a measure of placidity at home. Nonconformist groups such as purported Communists or radicals were obviously disturbing elements in the context of such a view of the world, and the Red Scare of the McCarthy era was a major reflection of such paranoia. But, above all, Americans believed that the prime goal of their political leaders—apart from providing for national security—should be to maintain and improve the economic stability of the nation.

The patterns created by World War II served the American people for at least one generation. By the early 1970s, however, it became clear that changing conditions in the United States and the world required another cycle in the reshaping of the American economy. The changing structure of the economy, bringing with it vastly altered social and political conditions, now necessitated fundamental readjustments. A decline of older manufacturing industries such as steel and textiles, the growth of new technological industries involving electronics and computers, and the vast expansion of service and information-processing industries profoundly altered American economic life. Moreover, the postwar boom had run its course, and the rate of economic growth slowed. The restriction of growth created increasing social tensions among the unemployed, farmers, and minorities and recent immigrants who feared that they might become members of a permanent underclass. And just as their demand for social services increased, the rate of economic growth declined. Meanwhile, the extraordinary expansion of government bureaucracy aroused fears and concerns in a wide spectrum of social groups in the United States, leading to a growing distrust of politicians and the political system.

In the 1980s, then, Americans were engaged once more in an attempt to reshape their economic life. The direction of this effort was not as yet clear in 1987. It appeared that Americans were resigned to losing their basic manufacturing industries to foreign competitors, and to concentrating their efforts on developing newer technology and information-processing industries. Although aware of their more limited economic resources, they were not as yet able to restrict either their expenditures or the demand for a wide range of social services. And they had not decided whether to have more government or less. These issues were to be resolved not by rigid ideological dictates but by a pragmatic process of trial and error within a loose framework of basic American values.

The Western Economy

The economic development of the trans-Mississippi West in the nineteenth and twentieth centuries in many ways paralleled major changes in national life, but in some respects it was unique. Since the days of the California Gold Rush in 1849, westerners had also undertaken the task of reshaping the economy of their region about

once every generation. In the years from 1849 to 1880 they con-
quered the virgin wilderness that was the trans-Mississippi West to
develop agricultural, livestock, and mining industries. By the 1880s
the beginnings of manufacturing and commercial agriculture expanded the western economy, a trend that was to dominate until
1940. A great leap forward did not occur until World War II, which
generated enormous economic booms throughout the region, bringing great diversification. In addition to stimulating expansion of
the raw materials industries, it added new manufacturing and service industries to the economy and bequeathed a scientific research
complex where almost none had existed before. Thus, by the 1980s
the West had developed a far more diversified and complex economy
than it had a century before.

In addition to an agricultural and mining base the West now
had a small but significant complex of manufacturing industries,
in part engaged in the fabrication of raw materials such as oil,
chemicals, and aluminum. Increasingly more important than manufacturing, however, was the growth of the service sector in the
years after 1945, particularly tourism, education, health care, and
financial institutions. Beyond these mainstays of the western economy the region now also boasted new technological industries,
perhaps the most dynamic sphere during this period. Computers,
electronics, and information-processing systems became a vital element of the regional economy. California's Silicon Valley came to
symbolize the most advanced forms of American technology, but
similar research and manufacturing complexes dotted many communities throughout the West. In addition, in the four decades
after 1945 the West retained a significant share of the military-indus-
trial complex fathered by World War II. These national defense
industries embraced rocketry and missiles, and scores of components for the nation's large new military establishment. Perhaps not
quite so dramatic, the large network of federal military installations—including air bases, supply depots, and training sites—came
to constitute an important factor in the western economy, contributing jobs and income. The fact that the two major wars of this
period—in Korea and in Vietnam—were fought exclusively in the
Pacific was clearly felt in the western states, whose proximity to the

Pacific theater of war emphasized their strategic importance as staging and supply areas. In addition, the West was a beneficiary of vast federal expenditures for the environment, for ambitious federal dams and water projects including the Central Valley Project in California, the Big Thompson in Colorado, and the Central Arizona Project.

By the 1980s, however, the economic structure that had developed over the course of the twentieth century began to show fissures. The raw materials industries, beset by declining domestic demand and increasing foreign competition, experienced increasing difficulties. Manufacturing and fabricating industries such as steel—laboriously created in World War II—now faced hardships serious enough to challenge their very existence. Processing industries such as petroleum and copper were directly affected by the downturn. And these trends placed pressures on the region's service establishments, whether banks, educational institutions, or tourist-oriented enterprises. As western natural resource industries slackened, as jobs were lost in these as well as in fabricating industries, the service sector could not help but be affected by the downturn. And declining revenues led most state governments in the West to embark on financial retrenchment, and to be more cautious in allocating their resources and services. Even the West's proudest hope for the achievement of economic affluence—the technological and electronics industries—began to face serious setbacks by 1980, when increasing international competition, particularly from the Japanese, brought serious depression to Silicon Valley and similar areas. At the same time, a slowing of the federal government's space exploration program and more cautious dispersal of funds for national security dampened, even if it did not end, public expenditures for military purposes in the West. Moreover, by 1980 the Bureau of Reclamation and the United States Corps of Engineers had dammed over many of the more obvious sites for production of electric energy and irrigation development so that the prospects for major new federal reclamation projects in the West seemed less bright in the 1980s and 1990s than they had half a century before. By the mid-1980s it was becoming apparent that the pattern of economic growth generated by World War II, which had characterized the region's economic development for almost four decades, required reshaping. Such a perception was conditioned by changing economic conditions in the region, the nation, and, indeed, the world. What the next stage in western economic development would be was not as yet altogether clear in 1987.

But the challenge of reshaping the region's economy was hardly a new phenomenon. Like other Americans, westerners had been restructuring their economic life about once every generation since the first settlement of the region. A major change in developing the trans-Mississippi region had come in the middle of the nineteenth century when it was still largely a virgin land. But then the gold, silver, and land rushes between 1849 and 1880 transformed the area. That hectic period came to an end in most, if not all, parts of the West in the 1880s with the founding of new towns, the finality of Indian removal, nascent manufacturing and processing industries, and the growth of service establishments embracing retailing, distribution, and banking. Although the basic pattern did not change appreciably until 1940, the western economy grew gradually in this period. During the 1920s increasing population resulted in some expansion of the natural resource and manufacturing sectors, and some diversification. Tourism, in particular, came to be a more important source of income as highway and railway networks ended the isolation of hundreds of communities in the West and tied them more closely to the regional and national economies. The Great Depression created a real impediment to rapid western economic growth until World War II provided the impetus for rapid reshaping of the economy. In fact, the war triggered the most significant boom the West had ever experienced. Wartime demands boosted mineral production, stimulated new manufacturing, introduced new technology, greatly expanded the service sector, and brought large federal investments to the West in the form of military expenditures. Until the 1980s the imprint of World War II set the parameters of western economic life.

The middle of the nineteenth century was one of the greatest watersheds in the economic growth of the trans-Mississippi region. That era saw an enormous influx of new population—more than 1.5 million between 1850 and 1880. Although the California Gold Rush accelerated the development of mining in that state, and the

production of more than $1 billion in precious metals, the develop-
ment of agriculture there and in the Rocky Mountain region was
hardly less significant. This included the vast wheat-growing areas
in the Pacific Coast states, and in the Red River Valley of the Dakotas.
It also saw the beginnings of fruit and vegetable production in the
Pacific, Rocky Mountain, and Plains states. Together with the cattle
and sheep industries in the West, the exploitation of such raw materials provided the backbone of the region's economy. And the lure
of wealth provided by these natural resources was sufficient to draw
successive waves of settlers to the region in the three decades after
1850. Their lobbying for even more rapid growth resulted in the
building of railroads to link the still isolated region to the national
economy. That demand was heard consistently during this period
and found fruition by 1882 with the completion of no less than
four transcontinental railroads.

The linking of the trans-Mississippi West to the Northeast and
the Middle West tied the region more closely to the national economy
and ushered in a new stage of economic growth. In the generation
after 1880 westerners began to build nascent manufacturing industries and developed a more highly commercialized form of agriculture. Specializing in grains and fruits and vegetables tied the West
more closely to national as well as international markets. An enthusiastic movement for more irrigation and reclamation of arid and
semiarid lands in the West opened up vast new areas for production
of specialized crops. Completion of the railroads led to a decline
of the cattle industry but brought a new source of income in the
form of tourism. That was a welcome addition in view of the West's
extreme dependence on the exploitation of raw materials. Such
dependence had led to the development of a colonial mentality on
the part of many westerners who feared the consequences of
economic dependence on the East. In fact, the relationship of the
newer and the older regions was not unlike the colonial connection
between a mother country and its colonies. From the Populists in
the 1890s to the Progressive reformers between 1900 and 1914 in
the West came cries of protest and a call for greater economic
independence for the region, and a new effort to reshape its economy, particularly through diversification.

But westerners had to be patient, for these cries were not

answered in the decades between the two world wars. The West continued to depend mainly on mining, agricultural, and livestock industries, despite continuing growth. Establishment of the national park system in 1916 and the expansion of automobile travel during the 1920s did add a major new industry to the regional economy. Manufacturing grew more slowly, although, on the Pacific Coast, Los Angeles in 1940 ranked eighth among U.S. cities in manufacturing, measured by value of production. And service industries grew notably between 1920 and 1940 despite the obvious dampening effect of the Great Depression after 1929.

World War II transformed the economy of the trans-Mississippi West. Domestic mobilization diversified the western economy as had no other influence before. In four short years it accomplished a reshaping of western economic life that would have taken at least forty years in peacetime. Federal expenditures induced by the conflict greatly expanded the volume of western manufactures. Although most funds were funneled into the shipbuilding and aircraft industries, thousands of other products were affected. The federal government also created new industries such as aluminum, magnesium, and synthetic rubber. At the same time it built a vast new scientific research complex for the West, with major laboratories at Los Alamos, New Mexico, and Hanford, Washington, and lucrative contracts for what was to become the Jet Propulsion Laboratory in Pasadena. The Office of Scientific Research and Development awarded scores of contracts to western universities for special projects. Such facilities stimulated establishment of new technologically oriented industries in the West. A vast influx of population to the Pacific Coast and the Southwest also stimulated the growth of service industries and financial institutions. Meanwhile, the armed services undertook an unprecedented expansion of military installations in the West, building scores of new storage facilities and arsenals, and hundreds of new airfields and training centers. Western proximity to the Pacific theater of war added a new dimension to the importance of the West in the context of national security. The net result of all of these wartime changes was the diversification of the western economy, partially fulfilling a long-awaited dream of many people in the region.

Western economic growth between 1945 and 1980 proceeded within the pattern created by World War II. In many ways the West now set the pace for the rest of the nation because it constituted a veritable laboratory for economic change. The diversified economy with which the West emerged from the conflict continued to expand in the ensuing decades, although not at the frenetic wartime pace. Especially noteworthy were the new technologically oriented industries in the West such as electronics and computers, in addition to large-scale commercial agriculture, mining, lumbering, and extensive energy development, particularly with a newcomer like natural gas. Manufactures and the tourist industry also saw unprecedented expansion. But by 1980 each of these sectors began to feel the slackening of national economic growth; the post–World War II boom was exhausted. Economists postulated that the expansive economic cycle that had begun in 1945 had run its course, to be followed after 1980 by several decades of more limited and restrained economic growth. Western farmers now faced increasing costs, and tough international competition. Much the same could be said for copper producers, lumber interests, and the petroleum industry. Western manufacturers in steel and aluminum faltered under intense foreign competition. Even the glamorous computer and electronics manufacturers buckled under the pressure of foreigners, losing some of the luster that had given them a special place in western economic growth. Growing national budget deficits led to more cautious and restrained disbursement of federal funds for national security, and even the closing of some facilities. By the 1980s, therefore, westerners were groping for a sense of direction to cope with economic problems that clearly required some reshaping of their regional economy.

The Arizona Economy

Although the economic development of Arizona has in many ways been unique, nevertheless it took place within the broader context of national and regional trends. Until World War II, Arizona's economy grew very slowly. From 1880 to 1920 irrigated agriculture and stock raising were emphasized, as in other western states, and the northern part of the state provided the basis for a lumber industry. Arizona's main pursuit, of course, was mining, since copper and gold provided a major portion of total income. By the 1920s increased emphasis on irrigation allowed for somewhat greater diversification in specialized farming, especially cotton and fruit. After World War I tourism emerged as a significant source of income. Not only the Grand Canyon, but dude ranches and resorts near Tucson and Phoenix began to draw a national clientele. But the Great Depression stymied the hopes for diversification that Arizonans had nourished in the prosperous twenties.

The more rapid economic expansion of the Arizona economy did not occur until World War II. That conflict spurred the growth of urban centers such as Phoenix and Tucson, which developed nascent manufactures, including electronics and technologically oriented industries. During the war, mirroring the experience of other western states, Arizona's economy became more dependent on federal largesse. New jobs were created in part due to the proliferation of a complex of military bases. The war may also have hastened some new technologies that changed the course of Arizona's history. Among these the development of air conditioning was preeminent. The vast expansion of commercial air travel also ended Arizona's erstwhile isolation. These developments were to influence Arizona's economic expansion in the next four decades.

After 1945 the patterns brought on by the war, as elsewhere in the West, determined the course of expansion in Arizona. With a burgeoning urban population, manufacturing grew more rapidly than at any previous time in the state's history. Irrigated agriculture grew significantly as Arizona became one of the nation's leading producers of cotton and specialized crops. If the mining industry did not enjoy a boom as in wartime, it prospered until foreign competition by 1975 inaugurated a decline. And a new, dynamic component in the state's economy was the "post-industrial" industries emphasizing technology which clustered in Phoenix and Tucson. To a considerable extent they served the federal military establishment, for military bases and military scientific research activities proliferated in Arizona during these years. And in underwriting the Central Arizona Project the federal government brought a major infusion of government funds into the state. By 1964 fully one-half of public expenditures in Arizona came from congressional appropriations. With the astounding increases in population during each of the three decades after 1945 (from 749,000 in 1950 to 2.7 million in 1980), Arizona became the nation's fastest growing state. That growth created new local markets and led to an enormous boom in the service sector. Financial institutions, health care facilities, schools and universities, and tourism grew more rapidly in Arizona in this period than anywhere else in the United States. In short, as in the nation and the region, Arizona built an affluent society in these years.

By 1975, however, this hectic expansion showed some signs of a slowdown. Increased international competition in agriculture left its mark. The decline of copper mining was a hard blow for Arizona, the nation's largest producer of the metal. Japanese competition in the computer and software industry seriously affected the companies Arizona harbored. And the scale of federal water projects will be much reduced once the Central Arizona Project is completed. As they face the twenty-first century, Arizonans, like other Americans and westerners, have begun to ponder the reshaping of their economy. This is not the first time they have had to consider such a problem, because it has occurred at various stages of the state's history.

To a considerable extent Arizona's economic growth can be traced to 1863, when it became a territory, with no more than 4,573 non-Indians. In this first stage of economic development the mining industry played a major role. Although gold and copper were also mined extensively, between 1865 and 1890 silver dominated the state's economy. Successive mining rushes dramatized important finds at Tombstone, Superior, and in the Bradshaw Mountains near Prescott. A contemporary traveler, Richard Hinton, estimated in 1878 that there were perhaps as many as 13,000 miners in the territory and at least 6,500 mining operations. Until a significant decline in 1893, silver was dominant. Prospecting for gold and silver continued until World War I, but copper became the state's most important mineral. New inventions created enormous demands for telephone wires and electric circuits, opening new markets for Arizona miners. Arizona was blessed with some of the richest copper mines in the United States, at Clifton-Morenci, Globe-Miami, Ray,

Bisbee, Jerome, and Ajo. Since the Southern Pacific Railroad had reached Tucson in 1880, Arizona copper producers had transportation available to reach nationwide markets. By 1888 the value of Arizona copper production exceeded that of the precious metals.

The mining industry triggered a population boom and the growth of auxiliary economic pursuits. Visions of wealth had lured 88,243 people to the territory, according to the Census of 1890, and 204,354 by 1910. This phenomenal growth stimulated farming and a bevy of service establishments as well as banks. Some of the entrepreneurs who became the founding fathers of Arizona's economy included Charles Trumbull Hayden and Michael Goldwater, whose names became household words.

Once farming became more profitable, the demand for water and irrigation systems grew more insistent. During these years the Salt River Valley, the Yuma Valley, and artesian wells in San Simon and Sulphur valleys made the desert bloom. Increasing demand for food supplies also promoted cattle raising. Between 1865 and 1885 Arizona cattle ran on the open ranges, as in other western states. But the coming of the railroads ended that era in the 1880s as barbed wire restricted the ranges and led to the establishment of large ranches. The largest in the state during the late nineteenth century was the Aztec Land and Cattle Company near Holbrook, which ran 60,000 head on a spread measuring 40 by 90 miles. But by 1900, as irrigation became more common, growing numbers of cattlemen opted for smaller operations on which they could control breeding practices to produce higher-quality stock. The years from 1880 to 1914 also witnessed the emergence of a significant sheep industry. The Daggs Brothers near Flagstaff had more than 50,000 head and helped to lay the foundation for one of Arizona's most stable industries in the years to come.

Between 1863 and 1914 new settlers in Arizona laid the foundations for its economic development. Development here in many ways was similar to that in other western states. It was characterized by a raw materials economy in which mining, farming, and ranching were preeminent, accompanied by a modest growth of banking, merchandising, and related service industries.

As it did elsewhere in the West, World War I accelerated

Arizona's economic growth. Moreover, Arizona's admission to statehood in 1912 attracted new settlers, while the completion of the Panama Canal in 1914 expanded commercial and trading opportunities, not only for the Pacific Coast but for adjoining states. To a lesser extent, the completion of a Southern Pacific line from Tucson to Nogales in 1910 provided a direct railroad link to Mexico. And construction of short railroad links such as a branch of the Atchison, Topeka and Santa Fe Railroad from Wickenburg to Cadiz, California, reduced Arizona's erstwhile isolation. The World War I era also saw enthusiastic support of Arizonans for the Good Roads movement and the increase of automobile travel. The desire to lessen the remoteness of the state by developing transportation also found expression in early enthusiasm for aviation. It was not an accident that Tucson opened the first municipal airport in the United States, in 1917. Economic expansion, it was clearly recognized, was directly dependent on establishing links with other parts of the West and the nation. Arizonans profited from this perception when the wartime demand for copper doubled prices and stimulated a boom that made the state the leading copper producer in the United States. Similarly, the war boosted cotton culture in Arizona. In 1912 only 400 acres of Pima (long-staple) cotton had been planted. But by 1917 rising prices prompted the planting of 41,000 acres, making it the leading Arizona crop.

The stimulus of war extended to Arizona's economy in the 1920s. So profitable was cotton that large growers planted 230,000 acres in 1920 as new markets for cotton developed, particularly for automobile tires and airplane fabrics. The boom collapsed within a year, but expansion continued later in the decade. In fact, the Goodyear Tire Company planted 75,000 acres in the Salt River Valley and smaller acreages in the Yuma region. In this decade tourism also emerged as a major source of income for the state. The extensive improvements in transportation of the preceding decade now made it possible for Americans to use Arizona as a winter resort. Fred Harvey had built El Tovar Lodge at the Grand Canyon as early as 1901, and Isabella Greenway opened the famed Arizona Inn in 1910. But in the 1920s scores of entrepreneurs built new hostelries to create the industry. Meanwhile, some ranches began to accept guests and advertised themselves as dude ranches for easterners who wanted a taste of "roughing it." Some observers in this period noted that Arizona's economy was based on 4 C's: copper, cotton, cattle, and climate.

This observation was accurate except that it neglected to include a new but major source of income, increased federal expenditures. The Newlands Act of 1902 already had made some federal monies available for reclamation, but in the 1920s dam-building projects of the U.S. Corps of Engineers and the Bureau of Reclamation on the Salt and Verde rivers brought many new jobs to the state, as did the building of Hoover and Parker dams. Although income from the state's major industries stagnated or declined during the Great Depression, federal investment in Arizona did not. With the advent of the New Deal, the federal presence in Arizona increased mightily. New Deal programs such as the CCC and the WPA and PWA became significant factors in the state's economy, as did manifold farm and livestock aid activities of the Department of Agriculture. Whether or not Arizonans wanted to acknowledge it, by 1939 national government programs were making an important contribution to the state's total income and were becoming a vital aspect of its economic structure.

But even more than the New Deal, World War II led Arizonans to reshape their economy in order to contribute to the mobilization program. One immediate effect was to revitalize the ailing copper industry since now the demand for the metal was virtually unlimited. Arizonans opened mines that had been closed and geared up for maximum production. The Metals Reserve Corporation, a federal agency, bought up whatever Arizona's miners could produce at guaranteed high prices. The state's cattle growers profited from rising meat demand. And cotton growers found the demand for textile and rubber products insatiable.

But the war did more than stimulate the raw materials industries. It did much to encourage Arizonans to diversify their economy. The state's year-round good flying weather and its proximity to the aircraft manufacturing complex of southern California attracted auxiliary enterprises to Arizona. Consolidated Vultee built a plant in Tucson, and the Aluminum Corporation of America established a large aluminum extrusion factory in Phoenix. There the Garrett

Corporation also located its new AiResearch facility for building airplane components. Goodyear Aircraft constructed a new manufacturing operation at Litchfield Park in Phoenix to fabricate airplane parts and balloons. During the war years Phoenix also attracted the Allison Steel Company, which built portable bridges for the armed forces, particularly in the Pacific theater. Meanwhile, several dozen smaller subcontractors in Arizona built special parts for airplanes as well as tanks. In fact, Arizona's industrial expansion proceeded so rapidly that it encountered a labor shortage. That led Arizona's new entrepreneurs to undertake extensive recruiting throughout the United States and resulted in a large influx of newcomers, especially from the South and the Middle West. They, in turn, did much to stimulate the state's service industries. A number of the migrants went to work in the expanding network of military installations in Arizona which were now adding a significant component to the state's total income. Notable were air training fields such as Luke and Thunderbird near Glendale, Falcon Field at Mesa, Williams Field near Chandler, Davis-Monthan Field near Tucson, and Marana and Ryan fields in southern Arizona. Huge federal storage depots, such as the Navajo Ordnance Depot at Bellemont, west of Flagstaff, further added to the federal presence. Several prisoner of war camps as well as Japanese relocation centers also dotted the Arizona landscape.

The frenzied pace of wartime expansion resulted in an extraordinary population boom in Arizona. By 1950 its population had jumped to 749,000, a gain of over 250,000 since 1940, constituting an increase of more than 50 percent. Much of this increase was in the cities. Phoenix nearly doubled its inhabitants in the World War II decade, from 56,000 in 1940 to 105,000 ten years later. Tucson, which had 35,000 residents in 1940, was home to 45,000 in 1950. This enormous urban growth stimulated construction and service industries—whether food services, finance, education, or health care—as had no other single event since the mining rushes of early territorial days. In historical perspective, World War II was one of the great watersheds in Arizona's economic growth.

Indeed, during World War II Arizonans succeeded in reshaping their economy. In place of a raw materials economy dependent primarily on the East for capital and markets, Arizonans emerged

from World War II with a far more diversified economic structure
than they had ever had before. In 1945 Arizona's economy included
not only raw materials industries, but manufactures, service establishments, and a wide range of government installations. This was
the economic heritage of World War II, and it was to provide the
framework for the enormous economic expansion the state experienced in the ensuing three decades. Between 1945 and 1975 a
steady stream of people moved west, not only to the Pacific Coast,
but also to the Southwest, and particularly to Arizona. In the affluent
society that arose in the United States and much of the West, Arizona's mild climate and scenic amenities now provided an irresistible
magnet for newcomers. True, natural resources were still significant
in the state's economy, but they no longer had the primacy of the
prewar years. In 1963 the state continued as the nation's leading
producer of nonferrous metals—first in copper, second in silver,
and third in gold—but minerals were no longer the major source
of income. And although Arizona was still a leading cotton producer—the nation's leader in production per acre—increasing
worldwide competition and higher costs of water were slowing the
expansion of that industry by 1975.

More significant during the period from 1945 to 1975 was
manufacturing, which became the main source of the state's income.
Much of that increase came with the establishment of thousands
of new technologically oriented businesses in the computer and
electronics fields, rather than in old-type smoke industries. Some
of the capital required for these new enterprises was provided,
directly or indirectly, by the federal government, which embarked
on vast expenditures for national security during this period. Familiar corporate names established themselves in Arizona, such as
Hughes Aircraft, which built a large plant in Tucson; Motorola,
which established the first of several facilities in Phoenix during
1947; and Sperry Electronics and General Electric, who specialized
in fabrication of computers. Special incentives offered by local and
state governments lured clothing manufacturers and construction
enterprises to the state, already becoming known for its trained
labor force and attractive climate. Right-to-work laws and a non-
union environment made the state even more attractive.

A continuing influx of large numbers of people also provided increasing momentum for the service industries. Arizona nearly doubled its population in the 1950s (to 1.3 million by 1960) and again to 2 million a decade later. The 1980 census recorded 2.7 million in the state. Such a rapid increase boosted retail and a wide range of service establishments, including an impressive banking system. The tourist industry became a major source of income, to a large extent because of the development of air conditioning after 1945, which allowed climatic control as in no previous period. By 1975, therefore, Arizona's economy had become diversified, and increasingly complex. In part, this reflected national as well as regional trends, but the state had also become a role model and trend setter for older regions like the Northeast and Middle West which were seeking to reshape their older industrial economies.

After 1980 Arizona's economic growth did not abate, but it was clearly tempered by international, national, and regional trends also affecting other areas in the United States. Worldwide competition in the copper industry hit Arizona's mining establishments hard and resulted in a decline of that proud industry. Agricultural producers, especially the cotton growers, also found themselves beset with more intense competition and falling prices. The sometimes ruinous competition from Japan and other nations in the computer and electronics industries clearly damaged the manufacturing complex for high-tech components that had grown in Arizona since World War II. At the same time, concern over federal defense expenditures curbed the expansiveness that had characterized the previous three decades. Such a slowdown in the pace of economic growth was bound to have some impact on the service sector. In addition, an increasing concern over the availability of water supplies for an expanding population in the twenty-first century raised questions about the state's economic future. By the 1980s, thus, Arizonans, like Americans elsewhere, were pondering the reshaping of their economy in the light of changing conditions in the world as well as at home.

The Future

What will the future bring? As they pondered that question, Arizonans turned to diverse sources for guidance. One such source was professional futurists, individuals who throughout the twentieth century made a profession of forecasting the immediate decade or two ahead. Basing their studies on statistical as well as social science analysis, futurists have at times come up with imaginative and stimulating forecasts. Another, more traditional, alternative is to utilize historical research to identify significant trends of the past which might be used for projections into the future. Clearly, stargazing is not a science, but past experience may be helpful in determining the parameters of future change.

One of the ablest blueprints of Arizona's future, sponsored by a conglomeration of business and public interest groups, was made in 1979 by Herman Kahn and his collaborators at the Hudson Institute, a major think tank. They infused their projections with a strong sense of optimism, reflecting the expansive years of the affluent society. In their projections they envisaged an economy largely shaped by the lifestyle choices of Arizonans, which they identified in terms of preferences expressed in the 1970s. They included an emphasis on outdoor life, on informality, and on water sports. To sustain such preferences they predicted that business leaders would diversify the state's economy further—with an emphasis on computer and service industries. Mining and agriculture, they felt, would not grow as rapidly as in the past. Assuming that economic prosperity would continue, and was not really a major concern, their optimism focused on elaboration of affluent lifestyles. The entire report reflected a preoccupation with the distribution of wealth, with very little consideration given to problems of production, or the generation of wealth.

Like many futurists and social scientists, the bright minds at the Hudson Institute were exceedingly present-minded and lacked the historical dimension. Almost unaware that they were reading the concerns of the immediate past into the future, they shared most of the suppositions of Americans in the years from 1945 to 1975. Those assumptions presumed that technological changes had solved many of the problems associated with the production of wealth and affluence, and that the major problem for Americans was the equitable distribution of wealth and the abolition or reduction of poverty. Professional economists and social scientists strengthened this claim in the 1950s and 1960s by assuring Americans that they had developed tools to engage in social engineering and to fine-tune the economy. Economic growth and stability, they declared, were the products of their professional expertise. The decline in the rate of economic growth that began to be visible after 1975, however, belied many of their more grandiose claims. It indicated also that problems of production and productivity had by no means disappeared, and that an undue emphasis on the distribution of wealth to the exclusion of such problems could lead to economic turmoil.

An alternative approach to divining Arizona's economic future is to project economic trends of the past into the present and the future, although such an attempt should also be accompanied by caution. The poor record of many economic and business forecasters in the past decade bears eloquent witness to the difficulties encountered in such stargazing—even with the benefit of economic models and sophisticated computers. Some economic variables may simply defy quantification; others may not receive adequate attention.

Projection of historical patterns cannot claim precise accuracy either, but it can at least delimit parameters of economic change in a broad macroeconomic context. In light of Arizona's past experience, it is likely that in the next quarter-century increasing diversification will characterize the state's economy. Within that framework, at least seven charatestics of Arizona's economic development in the past are likely to be operative in some form during the next twenty-five years, for historians are aware that despite their apparent rapidity, such changes in fact take place only very slowly.

First, Arizona's economic growth will be fueled by a combination of private and government enterprise. Much of the expansion will be guided by the ingenuity of private entrepreneurs. But economic development will continue to include a prominent role for government at all levels. Despite much rhetoric, governmental responsibilities will neither shrink nor wither away. The influx of federal funds into Arizona's economy—whether through farm benefit payments, water projects, social service programs, scientific research, or military installations—may not expand as rapidly as it did between 1945 and 1975, but it will continue to provide a significant percentage of the state's total income. Government expenditures are likely to continue to be a significant component of economic stability in Arizona.

Second, economic expansion will continue, but at an uneven pace. Older industries such as agriculture and mining will not disappear, but neither will they undergo significant expansion, except in case of a national or international emergency (such as war). But these industries will no longer have the same primary importance they had before 1940. Major growth will occur in technologically oriented enterprises, particularly information processing. Although some sectors—for example, banking and finance—may witness increasing corporate concentration because of growing requirements for large amounts of capital, in the newer technologically oriented fields, smaller enterprises may play a vital role in the innovation and application of new products and processes. Some of these products and processes will affect Arizona's arid lands, either to make them economically more productive, or to provide room for an increasing population.

Third, industries based on science and directly oriented toward research—such as genetics—are likely to expand more prominently. This will lead to a much closer relationship among business, educational institutions, and scientific laboratories. Businesses and universities will be closely involved in cooperative ventures in the development of new products and processes, some of which cannot as yet be identified, as well as in the training of specialized personnel.

Fourth, service-oriented industries will continue to expand more rapidly than other sectors and to assume a more significant share in contributing to Arizona's income. This will include retailing, which is likely to adapt electronic communications to a greater extent than in the past. Health care, education, and financial services will grow in importance, in addition to tourism. Americans will not only live longer in the next twenty-five years, but segments of the population will also enjoy more leisure time.

Fifth, increasing automation and mechanization will diminish the demand for human labor and will weaken the organizational efforts of labor unions. The work force will become even more white collar than in 1987. Moreover, increasingly it will consist of part-time employees and people over the age of sixty; brains rather than brawn will constitute a major element of job performance.

Sixth, the economy of Arizona will increasingly be affected by international influences. Some of Arizona's corporate enterprises will very likely be engaged in worldwide operations. Price levels for some of Arizona's major products, whether of mining or agriculture, will be determined on world markets. At the same time, foreign investors will enter Arizona's economy to a larger extent than in previous years and will acquire significant stakes in real estate and business. And the condition of the Mexican economy will affect Arizona profoundly. In short, Arizona's economy will become more internationalized.

Seventh, Arizonans will become more conscious of their attitudes and values as these relate to the state's economic growth. With the decline of the work ethic in a society emphasizing leisure, how can Arizonans continue to emphasize the importance of creativity and high levels of performance in business, education, and science? What alternative values can be substituted for the Protestant ethic to achieve excellence? How can Americans retain—or regain— the competitive edge that some in 1987 fear has been lost? How can business best motivate employees after a decade of lagging work performance and productive efficiency?

Clearly, then, projection of historical trends makes no pretense to accurate forecasting of the future. But such projections do limit the parameters of likely change and indicate spheres of continuity and likely change.

Any attempt to appraise Arizona's economic past brings into sharp relief the enormous gaps in our present knowledge of that past. Our projection of future trends would be far more accurate if we had more detailed studies of Arizona's economic history. But, in truth, the state's economic history has not yet been written. We do not have a multivolume work, or even a single book, that surveys the exciting record of economic accomplishments. Perhaps more has been written about mining in the nineteenth century than about other industries, but most of this literature seeks to appeal to antiquarian interests. A solid history of mining in Arizona after 1890 would be greatly welcomed, as would histories of particular industries such as agriculture, including cotton, fruit, and vegetables, and of water and irrigation development. Some research has touched on lumbering, but the subject has by no means been exhausted. Corporate histories would be welcomed, whether of Hughes Aircraft, Goodyear, or General Electric—as their operations relate to Arizona. It is difficult to understand why the important history of service industries in Arizona is largely untouched, with the exception of banking. Studies of the history of retailing, health care, and above all tourism would be as interesting as they would be significant. And what has been the economic impact on communities of government installations such as air bases or supply depots? Military histories of these installations are available in manuscript form, but these generally do not address issues of economic impact. Nor has the history of government economic policies in Arizona been written—at the local, urban, state, or federal level. What is the record of state policies toward business, agriculture, or labor? We do not have histories of state agencies affecting economic development—whether corporate regulation, insurance and banking regulation, licensing of the professions, or even water policies. A more thorough understanding of Arizona's economic heritage would contribute to a fuller understanding of the present, and would allow more precise planning for the future.

The reshaping of Arizona's economy to meet the challenges of the twenty-first century will not be easy. Yet it is reassuring that past generations of Arizonans have faced a similar problem of reshaping their economies and have met the challenge. The task confronting Americans in 1987 is perhaps more complex. It will require much of that same pioneering spirit, much of that same imagination, much of the same creativity, much of that same drive and determination that characterized Arizona's Anglo pioneers more than one hundred years ago when they dreamed of the blooming of what was then a desert. The reshaping of Arizona's economic life in 1987 provides its citizens with a major challenge, and only the next twenty-five years will demonstrate how successfully they confronted it.

Suggested Readings

National Economy
Berle, Adolph A. *The Twentieth Century Capitalist Revolution.* New York, 1954.
Galbraith, John K. *The New Industrial State.* Boston, 1967.
Rostow, W. W. *The Stages of Economic Growth.* Cambridge, Mass., 1960.

Western Economy
Arrington, Leonard. *Great Basin Kingdom.* Cambridge, Mass., 1958.
Morgan, Neal. *Westward Tilt.* New York, 1961.
Nash, Gerald D. *The American West in the Twentieth Century.* Albuquerque, 1977.
———. *The American West Transformed: The Impact of the Second World War.* Bloomington, 1985.

Arizona's Economy
McKnight, Thomas L. *Manufacturing in Arizona.* Berkeley, 1962.
Pare, Madeline F. *Arizona Pageant.* Phoenix, 1965.
Peplow, Edward H. *History of Arizona,* 3 vols. New York, 1958.
Powell, Lawrence C. *Arizona: A Bicentennial History.* New York, 1976.

The Future
Naisbet, John C. *Megatrends: The New Directions Transforming Our Lives,* 6th ed. New York, 1987.
Reich, Robert. *The Next American Frontier.* New York, 1983.
Reich, Robert, and Ira C. Magaziner. *Minding America's Business: The Decline and Rise of the American Economy.* New York, 1982.

"WATER, WATER EVERYWHERE, NOR . . ."

Karen L. Smith

Karen Smith divides Arizona's water history into three periods: the establishment of water rights, development of the water supply, and the insurance of water quality as well as the allocation of water in ways that match current and future needs. As in the past, economic, political, and legal issues will intertwine to determine how successful we will be in managing a scarce resource. Population growth, urbanization, the loss of agricultural land, and varied attitudes toward natural resources on the part of the state's political and ethnic groups continue to complicate the issues. Although the history of water cannot be studied in isolation, neither can it be ignored by economic, political, and social historians.

Nor is water the only environmental issue ripe for examination by both historians and policy makers. Air quality and climatic alteration are also of concern, and the relationships among economic development, land use, and environmental quality need to be better understood.

Throughout its seventy-five years of statehood, Arizona has witnessed dramatic change: what was a sparsely populated agricultural and mining state in 1912 has become a fast-growing urban state with dense pockets of population working primarily in electronics and service industries. Arizona has changed but has scarcely missed a beat during that change. The same things that made it grow in 1912 make it grow in 1987: a great climate, natural and scenic wonders, innovation and imagination in its people, and a dependable water and energy supply. It is important to take stock after seventy-five years, to assess our successes and failures as well as we can, and resolve to improve our shortcomings. Arizona has problems after seventy-five years of growth, some of which are large, expensive, and nearly impossible to solve. One issue that will surely continue to be at the top of our list is maintaining a dependable supply of water.

Over the past seventy-five years, we have thought maintaining a dependable supply of water meant simply building more water supply projects: more dams, canals, pumps, and treatment plants would create more usable water. Our past has reaffirmed this view. We have built dams on nearly every major river in the state, and our latest water supply project is the most expensive and complicated of all: bringing water about two hundred miles from the Colorado River to Phoenix and then on another hundred miles to Tucson. But recent history has shown us that maintaining a dependable supply of water means more than creating additional water. Over the past ten years, a host of hazardous alphabetical compounds have surfaced in our wells, ranging from PCB to TCE. We are learning that maintaining a dependable supply of water also means ensuring its quality.

There have been three periods in Arizona's water history. The first, beginning roughly in 1864 and lasting to about 1919, focused on establishing the rights to use the water of Arizona's rivers and streams. The second period, from about 1890 through the late

1970s, concentrated on developing the supply. We are now in the transition to Arizona's third period, one that will focus upon two concerns: water quality and appropriate allocation.

Determining Rights in the Rivers

There is a saying in the arid West that "water is more precious than gold and more explosive than dynamite."[1] This philosophy emerged in a West that was more dependent on water for its survival than on any other resource. Mining and agriculture were the first major economic activities in Arizona; water is a critical ingredient for both. Miners worked claims along the major river valleys of the state, near the Santa Cruz, San Pedro, Gila, Verde, San Francisco, and Hassayampa. Farmers settled in areas with rich alluvial soil along the Salt, Gila, Agua Fria, and Verde rivers.

Early settlers in the region took the water they needed, following local customs based on Mexican law which allowed for water to be taken from a river and used on lands far from the stream. This broke with custom in the eastern United States, where riparian practices based upon English common law are followed. These provide for water to be used only on lands adjacent to the stream. These pioneer Arizonans and others in the West established a body of law to handle the special role water has in sustaining life in the desert. Termed the *doctrine of prior appropriation*, it embraced a set of beliefs which determined that water in streams, rivers, lakes, and creeks was a public resource. One could acquire a right to use the water, however, and the first person in time to use the water had the first right to it. The amount of the water right was limited only by the added principle of beneficial use.

The doctrine of prior appropriation promotes the goals of settlement and development of the West because it allows for a water right to be treated as a property right. The water right then becomes security for the heavy capital investment necessary to develop mineral resources or build irrigation projects. The priority feature of first in time, first in right, acts to limit growth to the

capability of the existing water supply. Judge Joseph Kibbey, a
territorial governor and water law attorney, wrote in 1903 that "no
greater calamity can happen to a community dependent upon the
artificial application of water to the soil than the attempt to distribute
the available water supply over too great an extent of land."[2] This
method of allocating the water ensured that these economic investments would remain on a stable footing. The doctrine of prior
appropriation, outlined in Arizona initially in the Howell Code of
1864, and later reaffirmed in the State Water Code of 1919 as
amended, provides certainty regarding rights to the water supply.
It allows for growth, but it limits and allocates water without creating
a government bureaucracy to do so. The doctrine "cuts off" the last
person in time using the water rather than providing for sharing
a water shortage. The courts are the arena for settling disputes,
creating a stand-by water allocation mechanism rather than a continual process. This was of critical importance in an Arizona with
few institutional resources to devote to allocation, but which depended exclusively on its water resources to attract its main industries: mining and agriculture.

Even with this relatively simple means of allocation, there is
nothing easy in the doctrine of prior appropriation. There is another saying in the West that "you can kick a man's dog, or you can
steal his wife, but you'd better leave his water alone." Arizona's
history would not be quite so colorful without stories of men with
shotguns guarding their irrigation headgates. But the mechanism
to resolve disputes worked; the courts were full of water cases during
these years. Farmers turned to the courts to establish further the
principles outlined in the doctrine of prior appropriation. In a
critical case in 1892, Judge Kibbey ruled that a water right could
not be sold separately from the land for which it was appropriated,
but was appurtenant or attached to that specific parcel of land.[3]
The Kibbey Decree, as it was known, was disregarded, however, as
water rights continued to be sold and leased apart from the land.

In 1900, settlers in the Salt River Valley in Maricopa County,
by then the most populous county with more than 20,000 people,
looked for steady growth, not the quick "boom and bust" kind they
saw in Los Angeles. As more speculators tried to sell land without

water rights to unsuspecting would-be farmers, Valley leaders attempted to stabilize the land and water situation. The Valley, which was also the center of agriculture in the territory, lacked a dependable water supply. Desert rivers like the Salt are flashy and unpredictable, one year sending torrents of water downstream, and the next, barely enough to keep the streambed wet. A severe drought that began in 1897 reminded them of the need for a water storage dam to hold back the floods of one year for use in the dry year that would surely follow.

The national irrigation movement swept the nation during this time much like a religious crusade. Irrigated farming on the lands west of the one hundredth meridian was thought to provide a panacea for most of the nation's ills, and public policy makers, led by Theodore Roosevelt, made it a national commitment. The federal government would lend the money to farmers to build large water storage works and water distribution systems so that the desert might be reclaimed and made into small family farms.

The national reclamation program required that all water disputes be settled before the government would lend any money for water storage. Leaders in the Salt River Valley seized the opportunity to have the federal government help them with their water storage plans and in 1904 began a process to settle the water disputes in the Valley. They filed a friendly suit in what is now the Superior Court to adjudicate the rights in the Salt River, known as *Hurley* v. *Abbott*.[4] In his decision, Judge Edward Kent tabulated all the lands in the Valley according to the date when they were first cultivated and the amount of water they had historically used. Judge Kent returned to the Kibbey Decree and reaffirmed that water was appurtenant to the land. He also reaffirmed Kibbey's decision that canals were simply carriers of water and could not hold water rights themselves. The water belonged to the land, not to canal companies or individuals. He did not apportion shares of any water to be stored on the rivers to landowners. The Kent Decree of 1910 remains today the case of record adjudicating the rights of the land in the Salt River Valley to the Salt River. Other water cases decided since *Hurley* v. *Abbott* on different watersheds all maintain the doctrine of prior appropriation as the state's public policy.

As the population in the state increased to a point where more water was claimed than flowed normally in the major streams, reliance on the courts to settle the growing number of water disputes proved ill founded. Because a water right is treated as a property right in Arizona, there is general reluctance to allow any governmental body other than a judicial one authority over water matters. The increased need for technical information in the way of hydrographic reports and soil surveys before water rights could be determined led the major water interests in the state to the conclusion that some governmental agency to provide administrative form to the water rights process was in order. The Legislature passed in 1919 the State Water Code, which codified existing law and precedent and established a centralized machinery for the administration of water law. Where before individuals simply posted their claims to water at the point where they intended to divert it, after 1919, they had to apply to the state for a permit to divert and use the water. The code made no radical departure from the practices that had obtained since the earliest days in Arizona. The doctrine of prior appropriation, the principles of beneficial use, appurtenancy of water to the land, due diligence in construction of diversion facilities, and the application of water to the beneficial use were integral parts of the state's new water law. Although the courts continued to refine Arizona water law, the State Water Code provided for appointment of technical and staff support for the administrative determination of water rights.[5]

Developing the Water Supply

Throughout the last part of the nineteenth century, farmers in Arizona raised crops in two ways: they "dry farmed" in Yavapai and Greenlee counties, among others, or they found some method of artificially applying water to the soil, known as irrigation. Most of the irrigated farming in the territory was done in the Salt River Valley, although there was extensive farming in Pima County using wells and water from the Santa Cruz River, and in Pinal County using water from the Gila River.

Irrigated farming required technology, capital, and energy to succeed. Since most of the land under production was located away from the stream, farmers needed some sort of diversion works at the stream to turn the water into an irrigation canal. In the nineteenth century, these were typically built of timber and rock. Farmers had to dig a canal at a slope sufficient to allow the water to flow to the land by gravity. For Salt River Valley farmers, the canal digging was often the easiest part, as they simply dredged the remains of prehistoric canals. After the main canal was dug, farmers needed a distribution system that would take water out of the main canal and bring it directly to the lands. A headgate, usually built of timber, would divert water from the canal into lateral ditches, which were narrow and often crooked but nonetheless got the water to the land. Settlers typically organized cooperative irrigation associations so that many people could share the work and the cost of constructing the main irrigation canals. These associations were not communal, though, in the sense that decisions about the amount of water necessary to grow crops were made individually, and water shortages were not shared.

By 1900, nearly 123,000 people lived in Arizona; about 20 percent lived in Maricopa County in the Salt River Valley. The increasing numbers strained the water supply system, as more water was claimed than would normally flow through the Salt River. In times of drought, new settlers received no water to irrigate their crops. In times of flood, the diversion works and headgates were washed away, leaving farmers to begin again. This relentless cycle of drought and flood frustrated Valley settlers and prevented the Salt River Valley from reaching its economic potential. Men like Benjamin Fowler, a newly transplanted Yankee; Dwight Heard, well connected in both midwestern financial and eastern political circles; John Orme, an engineer turned farmer; and Joseph Kibbey led Valley citizens in a campaign to secure a water storage dam. The major obstacle for private citizens building large storage projects was financing. Capital was difficult to obtain in Arizona, and eastern financiers wanted a relatively high per-acre charge to ensure a return on their investment. In 1901, Fowler, Kibbey, and others sought to persuade the federal government to allow Maricopa County to bond itself to cover the approximately $3 million cost of the proposed storage dam on the Salt River.

It soon was obvious to Fowler, who had gone to Washington, D.C., to lobby the Congress on the bonding bill, that the national reclamation program had greater advantages for the Valley. The federal loans were to be repaid over ten years at no interest. Fowler, who had met leaders of the national irrigation movement like George Maxwell, Frederick Newell, and Gifford Pinchot, was convinced that the Valley had a very good chance to be selected as a national project. He was correct: the National Reclamation Act was passed in June 1902, and the Salt River was selected in March 1903.

Reclamation Projects

Most water users in the Valley united behind Fowler and Kibbey's plan to organize into one association to deal with Washington. They formed the Salt River Valley Water Users' Association to oversee the development of the project, which would store more than 1 million acre-feet of water behind a high masonry dam built at the confluence of Tonto Creek and the Salt River.[6] The Salt River Project plans called for the storage dam, for a diversion dam at Granite Reef to send the water into both the northside and southside canal systems, and for power generation at the dam. The Roosevelt Dam was built to irrigate approximately 190,000 acres of the 250,000 that were part of the Salt River Reservoir District; it cost about $10 million. Because the water supply stored behind the dam was inadequate to irrigate all the lands within the reservoir district boundaries, the federal government left the door open to enlarge the water supply project at some future time.

Completed in 1911, the Roosevelt Dam began immediately to store water, although it did not fill until 1916. Crop values rose dramatically, and cotton, alfalfa, citrus, and vegetables had banner production years due in large part to the great demand created by America's entrance into World War I. The boom of the war years quickly faded, however, when the armistice was declared in 1918; cotton fell from $1.25 to $.35 per pound.

The Great Depression came early to agriculture, and the 1920s were lean years all over Arizona. The Association had been unable to pay the United States, even though the terms of the loan were extended to twenty years in 1914. In order to pay for Project operation and maintenance and repay the United States, C. C. Cragin, the general manager of the Salt River Project, proposed to the United States that the reclamation project be enlarged by constructing three hydroelectric dams on the Salt River. Mormon Flat, Horse Mesa, and Stewart Mountain dams would produce electricity to sell to the mines east of the Valley in the Globe-Superior area, and the revenues would help the Association repay its debt. The United States agreed on the condition that the Association finance the projects itself; the landowners issued general obligation bonds with their land as collateral.

In 1935, the United States agreed to build Bartlett Dam on the Verde River to augment the water supply of the Salt River Project and to provide an additional water supply for the Salt River Pima-Maricopa Indian Community. In 1944, the United States Defense Plant Corporation and Phelps Dodge joined together to build Horseshoe Dam on the Verde River for the Project in a water exchange project: Phelps Dodge would divert water upstream on the Black River, a tributary of the Salt, and the Association would take that amount off the Verde. By 1945, the Salt River Project had completed its dam construction with four dams on the Salt and two on the Verde, having a total capacity of approximately 2 million acre-feet of water for the lands in the Salt River Valley.

In 1977, approximately 127,000 acres were irrigated on the Salt River Project on about 3,500 farms. More than 1 million people were served municipal water from Project supplies.[7] The remaining people living in the Salt River Valley received their water from other water agencies and corporations, and relied primarily on groundwater for their domestic and agricultural needs.

The Salt River Project was the largest and most ambitious of the early water supply projects undertaken in Arizona, but it was not the only one. A second federal reclamation project was also approved in 1903 at Yuma, whereby a small dam, the Laguna Dam, was built to divert the Colorado River into a distribution system to irrigate approximately 85,000 acres in that area; an additional 25,000 acres would be irrigated by pumps. The Laguna Dam presently serves as a regulating dam, and the Imperial Dam, completed in 1948, now diverts water into the All-American Canal for the Yuma Project. As of 1977, about 60,000 acres were still being irrigated under the Yuma Project on 372 farms; approximately 34,000 people received municipal water service.[8]

A third federal project was begun in 1924 on the Gila River near Florence, when the United States Indian Service built Coolidge Dam to irrigate lands on the Gila River Pima-Maricopa Indian Community and on non-Indian lands adjacent to the reservation. The Indian project was managed separately from the non-Indian; the San Carlos Indian Irrigation Project and the San Carlos Irrigation and Drainage District operate independently of each other. Coolidge Dam has hydroelectric capabilities, but they are at present inoperative. The Indian Service today operates and maintains both the dam and the power facility. Coolidge Dam irrigates approximately 50,000 acres in Pinal County.[9]

About the same time that citizens in the Valley explored the possibilities of building a water storage project, entrepreneurs along the Agua Fria River began planning their own water storage project on a more modest scale. William Beardsley, a developer from Ohio, financed and constructed a diversion dam to irrigate about 20,000 acres northwest of Phoenix. The project fell apart in the 1890s due to financing problems, and it was not until 1924 that Beardsley hired Carl Pleasant to complete it, building what is now called Waddell Dam, which provides water service to an area of approximately fifty-five square miles. The Waddell project was privately constructed, without financial assistance from the federal government. In March 1987, the Maricopa County Municipal Water Conservation District #1, which operates Waddell Dam, celebrated its sixtieth birthday.[10]

In addition to these large water supply projects, farmers, ranchers, miners, and municipalities sank wells to pump groundwater to augment the often meager surface supplies. Before electricity was widely available in rural areas, they used wood and gas to fuel their steam pumps. The city of Tucson, for example, relies entirely on groundwater for its domestic supply. In the Salt River Valley, the Roosevelt Irrigation District and the Roosevelt Water Conservation District use groundwater for irrigation. Groundwater is expensive to pump, and its continued pumping has left the water table in the most populous areas of the state at great depths from the surface. This makes it even more expensive as a source of supply. Even with all of its water storage projects, groundwater accounts for almost 60 percent of Arizona's total water resources.[11]

The Central Arizona Project

It is no wonder, then, that Arizona residents banded together as early as the 1920s to persuade Congress to build the state's most controversial surface water supply project to date: the Central Arizona Project, a nearly 300-mile aqueduct, with water storage and flood control dams, to carry Colorado River water from Lee's Ferry to the Salt River Valley, Tucson, and farms along the way. Senators Carl Hayden and Ernest McFarland first introduced legislation to authorize the CAP in 1947. The Central Arizona Project Association, a private, nonprofit organization of Arizona civic leaders, was formed in 1946 to educate the public about the importance of the CAP. Because there was no state agency at that time dedicated to working on Arizona's water situation, the Central Arizona Project Association took upon itself the role of coordinating the state's effort.[12]

Ever since 1922, when the Colorado River Compact "allocated" the water in the Colorado between the four states of the upper basin and the three states of the lower basin, an unofficial order to the big reclamation projects on the river had been in place. California would have the first, with the Boulder Canyon Project, today's Hoover Dam. Arizona would be next with the Central Arizona Project, and the upper basin would follow with the Colorado River Storage Project (CRSP). The state of California never agreed with the unofficial order of projects, however, and mastered the art of political delay of both the CAP and the CRSP.

After several years of frustrated attempts at congressional hearings, Arizona filed suit in the United States Supreme Court in August

1952 to adjudicate the rights to use the water of the Colorado River between the two states, Arizona and California. Eleven years later, the Supreme Court ruled in Arizona's favor, supporting the state's claim to 2.8 million acre-feet of Colorado River water as allocated by the Colorado River Compact. Senator Hayden immediately introduced new legislation to authorize the CAP.

The problem about the Colorado, however, was just beginning to clarify itself: while the Colorado River Compact based its allocation among the states on an average annual virgin river flow of approximately 15 million acre-feet, the true average flow of the river was perhaps closer to 13 million acre-feet. Still, the Bureau of Reclamation continued to plan its projects using the larger number. Moreover, when one added all the planned uses of the Colorado River, the total was nearly 17.5 million acre-feet of water. The Colorado River Storage Project, which Congress authorized in 1956, is an elaborate project of mainstem hydroelectric dams and smaller participating irrigation projects. If the upper basin project is developed as planned, there will not be enough water in the river to satisfy California, the treaty with Mexico, which guarantees 1.5 million acre-feet of water to that nation, and then Arizona's CAP. The CAP plan, then, is partially based upon the assumption that the upper basin will not develop all those participating irrigation projects until some unforeseeable time in the future.

It was not until 1965 that CAP legislation surfaced again in Congress. This time the opponents included not only the state of California but some of the upper basin states as well. Senator Hayden was an expert at congressional "horse-trading," and CAP provided a vehicle. The original project was modified extensively. The hydroelectric dams at Bridge Canyon and Marble Canyon were "swapped" for a federal government ownership share in the Navajo Generating Station, a coal-fired power plant near Page, Arizona, on lands of the Navajo Nation. The state of New Mexico supported Hayden's CAP in exchange for inclusion of the Hooker Dam in that state. Utah came on board the CAP bandwagon after its Dixie Project was included as part of the CAP authorization. The state of Colorado dropped its opposition when five participating projects of the Colorado River Storage Project were included in an accelerated planning and construction track as part of the CAP legislation. Finally, in September 1968, Congress passed the Colorado River Basin Project Act authorizing construction of the Central Arizona Project.

Senator Hayden was not alone in Arizona's major effort to make the CAP an authorized federal project. Stewart Udall, as secretary of the interior, pushed and prodded the Bureau of Reclamation and other federal officials to gain the Johnson administration's approval. John Rhodes and Morris Udall were key figures in securing the bill's passage in the House of Representatives, and Sam Steiger also assisted. Senator Paul Fannin stood at Carl Hayden's side. Perhaps the most critical element in obtaining passage of the CAP legislation, however, was California's decision to support the bill after that state was guaranteed the first 4.4 million acre-feet of water in the Colorado River below Lee's Ferry.

Despite its authorization and continued funding, controversy continues to plague the Central Arizona Project. Construction on the Navajo Generating Station was complete and work on the first stretch of the Granite Reef aqueduct begun, when citizens concerned about the effects of building Orme Dam, a CAP water storage and flood control dam at the confluence of the Salt and Verde rivers, raised serious questions as to its viability. The Bureau of Reclamation and civic leaders created a new community decision process to identify a scheme that would perform the same functions as Orme Dam, but without the problems of removing the Fort McDowell Indian Community. The Central Arizona Water Control Study, as it was called, identified nine alternatives to Orme Dam. By 1982, community leaders, the Bureau of Reclamation, and the secretary of the interior had identified Plan 6 as the best alternative.[13]

Yet the nearly fifteen years between CAP authorization and the decision to build Plan 6 have taken their toll. The political climate is much different in the 1980s than it was in 1968. Federal funding for water projects has become linked to local cost-sharing. The state and community unity that had been a hallmark of the CAP is stretched thin over the corresponding arguments, agreements, and compromised agreements which have become the new way of life for Arizona's biggest water supply project. Costs have increased dramatically: the original plan for CAP was estimated at about $1 billion, and present costs are anticipated to be closer to $4 billion.

Although local participants have agreed to cost-sharing in order that the CAP may keep to its present construction schedule, the agreement itself is fragile and rests upon a foundation of assumptions that may not continue to hold true.

New issues arise every day to threaten that agreement. A lawsuit was filed in 1986 by the Audubon Society to prevent construction of a portion of Plan 6 because of perceived harm to the environment. Citizens Concerned About the Project are convinced the project has become too big and too expensive for the amount of water it will bring to Arizona. The United States Army Corps of Engineers and the Federal Emergency Management Administration issued in 1986 a revised flood plain map which calls into question some of the calculated flood control benefits of the Plan 6 Cliff Dam on the Verde River. Ironically, one of the most immediate water policy issues facing the state is what to do with the surplus CAP water which is ready to flow into central Arizona, but which few of its users need or are prepared to take. Twenty years have passed since authorization of the CAP legislation, and the aqueduct is completed to a point approximately twenty miles south of Florence, yet customers have signed up for only 500,000 acre-feet of water, well below the 2.2 million acre-feet the CAP aqueduct can carry to central Arizona. In order to prevent California from taking the 1.7 million acre-feet that would bypass Arizona and flow south past the aqueduct, CAP water may be sold at bargain prices.[14]

The benefits of CAP have changed dramatically. When it was first conceived in the 1920s, the Central Arizona Project was a water supply project for agriculture. No one really foresaw the improved technology for groundwater pumping that has augmented Arizona's surface water supply far more than anyone anticipated in 1922 or, indeed, in 1947 when Carl Hayden introduced the legislation for the first time. As Senator McFarland told the Senate in 1947, "If Central Arizona is unable to supplement the present supply of water by 1.2 million acre-feet from the Colorado, our farmers will have to move off the land, and ground once fertile and productive will go back to desert waste."[15] McFarland's lament was echoed several times throughout the legislative process by others; without the Colorado River, central Arizona would become a wasteland.

These dire predictions, which were high drama when they were first made, have become somewhat embarrassing reminders that disaster has not arrived on schedule.

Urban development in the Salt River Valley is changing land use patterns. Agricultural land, once planted with highly water-consumptive plants like cotton, is being converted to places for homes and businesses. Although some very dense business developments do use more water per acre than agriculture, the majority of residential and business uses require less. In 1968, CAP was largely seen as an agricultural water supply project; in 1987, it is primarily a municipal water supply project.

Groundwater Management

This is not to say, however, that Arizona did not have a water supply problem when CAP was first introduced and that it does not have one now. The problem of water resource scarcity will always be with those who choose to live in the desert. The issue has formed in a different way, though, than those who contemplated CAP in 1947 and 1968 thought it would. Central Arizona Project water has become closely linked to achieving a "safe yield" of groundwater use, where the amount of water recharging the aquifer, through natural or artificial means, is nearly equal to the amount of water pumped. Groundwater overdraft, in which far more is being pumped from the ground than is replenished, has been a serious problem in Arizona since the 1930s. Numerous legislative attempts to solve the problem have been made, but until recently all have failed. As part of the CAP authorization, Congress instructed Arizona to enact certain water conservation measures, including effective groundwater management. Over the years, however, the Department of Interior neglected to enforce this demand for groundwater reform.

The Arizona Supreme Court decided a case in 1976 which dramatically changed the groundwater management picture in Arizona. In *Farmers' Investment Company* v. *Bettwy,* the court ruled narrowly on the issue of groundwater pumping and transfer, holding with FICO that groundwater pumped must be used on the land from which it was pumped. The city of Tucson and the mines were stunned by the court's ruling. The mines had purchased every available farm in the lower Santa Cruz River Basin to preserve a water supply for their operations; ironically, FICO was the only major farm not to sell. Both Tucson and the city of Prescott transported large amounts of water from wells outside their service territory, and the court's decision would seriously hamper their efforts to provide water for their growing populations.

The FICO decision turned out to be a hollow victory for farmers, though, because political reality would not allow the courts to issue an injunction to stop pumping against either the mines or the cities. The mines and the cities therefore turned to the legislature to initiate reform. The mines' primary goal was to change the rules regarding the transportation of groundwater, while the cities were after nothing less than comprehensive groundwater management. The 1977 amendment to the 1948 Groundwater Code focused solely on the issue of groundwater transportation, but leaders in the state legislature agreed to pursue further the idea of groundwater management.

This proved to be a delicate political issue. The cities used about 5 percent of the state's water resources in 1977, the mines about 3 percent, and agriculture about 89 percent. In order for groundwater conservation to occur, agriculture, for many years the most potent political power in the state, had to be restricted and forced to conserve. Representatives of agriculture, sensing that time was not on their side in this battle, agreed to join a groundwater study commission that would review the problem and draft legislation.

Formed in November 1977, the Arizona Groundwater Management Study Commission defined eight broad objectives for groundwater management legislation:

1. Resolution of conflicting groundwater rights and uses
2. Management of the groundwater overdraft
3. Groundwater transportation
4. Conveyances of groundwater rights
5. Accommodating growth needs

6. Environmental protection
7. Management efficiency
8. Recognition of federal and Indian water rights

The work of the commission was accelerated by Secretary of the Interior Cecil Andrus, who wrote Congressman Morris Udall in September 1979 that he would not allocate CAP water until Arizona passed a new groundwater code. For the first time, the Department of Interior had established a deadline for groundwater management reform in Arizona. Since the allocations had to be made in 1980 to keep the project on schedule, the legislature needed to act during the 1979–80 session.

Then Governor Bruce Babbitt personally led the final negotiations for the proposed state legislation, which was ambitious in scope and without precedent across the nation. The bill provided for strong state management rather than control vested in independent local groups. Agriculture recognized that local agencies would be controlled by the cities, and Governor Babbitt and the mines recognized that local bodies would be reluctant to enforce demanding conservation requirements of people in their communities. A new water "czar" would have enormous power under the law to direct the state's management program. It was ironic that these interests—the cities, agriculture, and mines—which had long resisted any notion of sharing control over their water operations, agreed to place enormous powers in the state. As one observer noted, "Much of the director's discretion is a result of the parties' inability to agree on a management program."[16] The Groundwater Management Act became law in Arizona on June 12, 1980.[17]

The Groundwater Management Act has two goals. The first is to control the groundwater overdraft which is occurring within the defined active management areas in Arizona by requiring programs in place to achieve safe yield by the year 2025; Phoenix, Tucson, and Prescott are the most significant cities within these areas. The second goal is to provide a means to allocate Arizona's limited groundwater resources to meet changing circumstances more effectively. Two fundamental policies of the Groundwater Management Act are designed to achieve these goals: (1) agriculture may not expand within the defined active management areas, and (2) developers of land outside the boundaries of a city service area have to prove a hundred-year water supply before they can proceed with their development.

The director of the Arizona Department of Water Resources, the designated water "czar" of the state, will require increasingly stringent conservation requirements in five successive state groundwater management plans. The director may also develop programs to augment the water supply through watershed management, artificial recharge, and other feasible means. The director also has the power to levy a pump tax to raise the funds to implement the Groundwater Management Act.[18]

It is a measure of Arizona's ambitious effort to manage this critical resource problem through the Groundwater Management Act that the Ford Foundation recently awarded the Department of Water Resources a $100,000 prize for innovation and imagination.

Water Quality

Beginning in the 1970s, revelations about toxic wastes contaminating Arizona's aquifers were made almost daily. A number of wells in the Phoenix and Tucson areas were closed, and water from several other wells had to be blended with cleaner water in order to reduce concentrations of contaminants. Just as the state had ineffective groundwater management laws on the books prior to enactment of the Groundwater Management Act of 1980, so, too, did Arizona have some water quality and pollution control laws as part of the regulatory framework. Their problem, as with groundwater management, was that they were not the product of consensus and were not well enforced.[19] Existing law contained some regulatory authority, but this was insufficient to cope with the water quality problems. Critically, the law did not identify a responsible agency to deal with the problem. Six years after the Groundwater Management Act became law, state legislators, business, municipal, and agriculture leaders, and representatives of many environmental interests produced another piece of landmark legislation for Arizona, the Environmental Quality Act. They were led in the final negotiations by Governor Babbitt. While the Groundwater Management

Act protects the quantity of Arizona's groundwater, the Environmental Quality Act seeks to protect the quality of those same groundwater resources.

The Environmental Quality Act is primarily a law of prevention. Basically, it declares that all groundwater in Arizona should be pure enough for drinking. All important discharges of groundwater-threatening pollution are prohibited without a permit from a new department in Arizona government, the Department of Environmental Quality. This new department, activated on July 1, 1987, has broad authority to carry out the provisions of the act, including the responsibility to prepare and enforce strict regulations to prevent future contamination. This new legislation makes polluters liable for the cost of cleaning up tainted water and establishes a state fund to do so when the polluter cannot be identified. Finally, the act strengthens regulation of agricultural use of fertilizers, pesticides, and herbicides to protect groundwater and the health of farmworkers. It is, as former Governor Babbitt has written, "the most comprehensive, and toughest, groundwater quality legislation in the country, and one of the most important environmental bills ever enacted on the state level."[20]

Confronting Reality: Managing the Water Supply

The Environmental Quality Act is yet another example of Arizona providing leadership in water management legislation which is already being heralded as "far-reaching" for the nation as a whole,[21] but the real work for the state will lie in its implementation. The road ahead will be paved with hard politics; there is no turning back. The Central Arizona Project and the groundwater management plans will provide adequate water supplies for Arizona over the next twenty-five years. The amount of water will not be important, though, if we are confronted with a situation similar to that in *The Rime of the Ancient Mariner:* "water, water, everywhere, / Nor any drop to drink."

Although the Central Arizona Project is not yet complete, it has already left a legacy here in Arizona and, indeed, throughout the nation. Large, complicated, and prohibitively expensive water supply projects will no longer receive blanket authorization and funding from the federal government. Local residents will have to pay increasing shares of the cost to secure a dependable water supply. As needs for water compete with other municipal needs, the available dollars will not be adequate to provide for all at the present rate of growth and water use. The price for raw water will increase from an average of $22 an acre-foot available to shareholder members of the Salt River Project to a price in the neighborhood of $200 an acre-foot. Like the price of energy, the price of raw water will not become expensive, but it will go from "cheap to inexpensive."[22]

Water resources will have to be conserved, not simply because the Groundwater Management Act requires that all water users conserve certain percentages in each of its ten-year management plans, but because we will have to do so to continue to grow and still enjoy what we love best about our state. We will also need every bit of imagination and character we can muster to allow us to make the increasingly difficult decisions about Arizona's water future. Fortunately, there are many exciting prospects for water management over the next twenty-five years.

Much has been said and written about water marketing, the 1987 version of yesterday's federal reclamation. Just as with the federal irrigation program, water marketing proponents claim that allowing water to function as a fluid commodity—to be bought, sold, and valued in an open market—will provide many of the answers to the West's water problems. Historical events will show, as they usually do, that there is no panacea to problems. Although water marketing may work better in states without river basin compacts ratified by Congress, the institutional barriers against major interbasin transfers are so significant that they are unlikely within the next twenty-five years. Although the Western Governors Association has endorsed water marketing as a viable way of allowing water to find its best use, a spokesman for the Metropolitan Water District in California indicated the difficulty in that approach when he said, "Selling water in California will never be as easy as selling grapes or watermelons."[23] Even in a strict marketplace, water must always carry with it some allocation scheme to ensure its availability at the lowest reasonable cost to those least able to pay; unlike grapes or watermelons, water is a commodity we cannot live without.

Water marketing in Arizona probably will not happen so much as a business deal, a way to make money, as from need. Opportunities to benefit from a water marketing scheme will be greatest for areas without established water rights, for example, from agriculture to recreation or something else. We will see more in the way of "water ranching" in Arizona than strict buying and selling of established water rights. In this way, land is retired from agriculture, and the water that was attached to that land and that use then becomes available for other purposes. The cities of Phoenix and Scottsdale have become municipal water ranchers, investing in a water resource as part of their long-term strategic planning. Their water ranches will not be used in the next ten or even twenty-five years, but fifty or more years from now.

Arizona will experiment with—and we hope master—the science of groundwater recharge over the next twenty-five years. Groundwater recharge is, simply put, water storage underground. It may allow for storage of flood and surplus water in the underground aquifers to be pumped out later in periods of drought. We do not know yet whether the geology of the state will allow for such underground storage, but several projects on the table will answer the question in those areas of Arizona where flood and surplus water exists.[24]

Other possibilities to enhance our water supply over the next twenty-five years include cloud seeding and watershed management. Perhaps the best possibility to make our existing water supplies serve more people better, however, is that of better management and planning. First steps have been taken, with the Groundwater Management Act and the Environmental Quality Act. In 1986, several Salt River Valley cities, the Arizona Department of Water Resources, and the Salt River Project joined to develop a first-ever comprehensive regional water plan that will project needs for the next fifty years. The first phase of the study is expected to be completed in 1988 and will project the demand and supply to the year 2035.[25]

Our tendency to seek technological solutions will not free us, however, from making tough decisions about how we use our surface water supplies, our groundwater, and our "gray" water, or treated effluent. Although the projected water supply for Arizona over the next twenty-five years is adequate to meet our need without compromising too dramatically that famous "Southwest lifestyle," there is an old story in water circles that still reflects the importance of water to Arizona:

Recent years have witnessed a scramble to appropriate every drop of water available in the state. The director of the department of water resources related that a leak occurred at one of the steam power plants in central Arizona, and a small trickle of water flowed out of the power company's property for a brief distance. Before the leak could be repaired, three persons had filed for an appropriation with the Arizona Department of Water Resources.[26]

It is a truism in the arid Southwest that there is only so much water available to use. Arizona cannot use water suitable for drinking in artificial lakes and golf courses, continue to dump toxic wastes in landfills where they can seep into the underground reservoir, and then plead with the federal government to build water supply projects when a drought cycle begins or domestic wells become tainted. We are past the point where the answer to every controversy over water supply is to build more dams. Even if there is something left to fill them with, we cannot afford them, nor can we afford to bring the Great Lakes to Phoenix.

We are confronting, in 1987, the new reality of western water. It is going to be more expensive. It will have to be regulated to maintain its quality. It will be reallocated in the urban areas from agriculture to municipal use, either naturally, through the marketplace, or politically, through the legislature.

An added wrinkle to Arizona's water supply picture over the next twenty-five years is the outcome of Indian water rights claims now under litigation in several basin-wide adjudications. A probable outcome will be that some of the Indian claims will be met, further reducing the water supply available under the old rules.

This does not mean, however, that Senator McFarland's 1947

predictions for an Arizona without the CAP will come true in the next twenty-five years. It does mean that public policy makers, business leaders, and citizens generally need to prepare for a different water environment, where the critical problems are water quality and efficient allocation. Whether or not current Arizonans have the courage and spirit of their predecessors is something for the historians of the future to analyze. We can manage our water supply and make it work for all of us if we will accept the harsh realization and the hard politics that we really have no other choice.

Notes

1. Dean Mann, *The Politics of Water in Arizona* (Tucson: University of Arizona Press, 1963), 67.

2. Joseph Kibbey, "Brief on the Articles of Incorporation of the Salt River Valley Water Users' Association," May 25, 1903, 40.

3. *Wormser* v. *Salt River Valley Canal Company,* Case Number 708 in the District Court of the Second Judicial District of the Territory of Arizona, in and for the County of Maricopa, 1892.

4. *Patrick T. Hurley* v. *Charles F. Abbott and 4,800 Others,* Case Number 4564 in the District Court of the Third Judicial District of the Territory of Arizona, in and for the County of Maricopa, 1910.

5. Mann, *Politics of Water,* 41.

6. An acre-foot of water is roughly equivalent to 326,000 gallons of water. It is enough water to cover one acre of land with one foot of water, or enough to supply a family of five for one year.

7. United States, Department of Interior, Bureau of Reclamation, *Project Data,* 1981, 1089–90.

8. Ibid., 1357–60; United States Geological Survey, *Third Annual Report of the Reclamation Service, 1903–1904,* 63.

9. David M. Introcaso, *Water Development on the Gila River: The Construction of Coolidge Dam,* HAER AZ-7, 1986.

10. David M. Introcaso, "Waddell Dam," brochure prepared for the United States Bureau of Reclamation, April 1987.

11. Desmond D. Connall, Jr., "A History of the Arizona Groundwater Management Act," *Arizona State Law Journal* 2 (1982): 313.

12. Rich Johnson, *The Central Arizona Project, 1918–1968* (Tucson: University of Arizona Press, 1977).

13. Plan 6 consists of New Waddell Dam on the Agua Fria River as a CAP water storage dam, Cliff Dam on the Verde River for flood control and new water conservation storage, and a modified Roosevelt Dam on the Salt River for flood control and new water conservation storage.

14. The Central Arizona Water Conservation District, which is responsible to the federal government for CAP repayment, is considering selling CAP water not

now under contract for $35 an acre-foot, which is the cost to pump the water. The contract price of $50 an acre-foot is well below the cost to operate the system, $115 per acre-foot.

15. Johnson, *Central Arizona Project,* 32.

16. Connall, "History of the Arizona Groundwater Management Act," 334.

17. Ibid., 313–44.

18. Kathleen Ferris, "The Arizona Groundwater Code: A Model of Strength in Compromise," in *Water Management in Transition,* A Special Report by the Freshwater Foundation, Navarre, Minnesota, April 1986, 41.

19. A. J. Pfister and Larry Hawke, "Struggle to Get Act Frustrating, Rewarding," *Arizona Waterline,* Winter 1987.

20. Bruce Babbitt, "Protecting Arizona's Future—The Environmental Quality Act of 1986," *Arizona Waterline,* Winter 1987.

21. *Los Angeles Times,* May 12, 1986.

22. Paul Bracken, "A Vision of the 21st Century, Looking Back and Forward," *The Arizona Republic,* January 11, 1987.

23. "What's a Free Market for Water?" *U. S. Water News,* July 1986.

24. The Central Arizona Water Conservation District plans a joint groundwater recharge project with Signal Oil Company in the Butler Valley using surplus CAP water. The Salt River Project and several Valley cities are talking about a project in the dry Salt River just downstream of Granite Reef Dam.

25. "Regional Water Plan Proposed," *Tempe Daily News,* September 24, 1986.

26. Mann, *Politics of Water,* 41.

Suggested Readings

Byrkit, James W. "A Log of the Verde: The 'Taming' of an Arizona River." *The Journal of Arizona History* 19 (Spring 1978): 31–54.

Dobyns, Henry F. "Who Killed the Gila?" *The Journal of Arizona History* 19 (Spring 1978): 17–30.

Hundley, Norris J. *Water and the West.* Berkeley: University of California Press, 1975.

Reisner, Marc. *Cadillac Desert: The American West and Its Disappearing Water.* New York: Viking Penguin, 1986.

Smith, Karen L. "The Campaign for Water in Central Arizona, 1890–1903." *Arizona and the West* 23 (Summer 1981): 127–48.

————. *The Magnificent Experiment: Building the Salt River Reclamation Project, 1890– 1917.* Tucson: University of Arizona Press, 1986.

Weatherford, Gary D., and F. Lee Brown, eds. *New Courses for the Colorado River: Major Issues for the Next Century.* Albuquerque: University of New Mexico Press, 1986.

Worster, Donald. *Rivers of Empire: Water, Aridity and the Growth of the American West.* New York: Pantheon Books, 1985.

PRESERVING
THE PAST

How much do we really know about our years of statehood? Is our grasp of the events of those seventy-five years strong enough that we can understand our present circumstances and thoughtfully consider plans for the future?

The preceding five essays outlined important research and writing agendas. In some cases their suggestions can easily be followed through. In others the agendas call for complex studies and careful, thoughtful, painstaking research. What has become clear from the observations of these authors is that only the highlights of Arizona's statehood years have been examined. Much remains to be done. If we are to seize present opportunities confidently and plan intelligently for the future, we must know more about our past. We do not need a recital of facts surrounding obscure events and mindless repetitions of the actions of various people and groups; we do need a fundamental examination of what Arizonans have accomplished, and of how they came to make the decisions that brought us to where we are today.

At the moment we have only a rudimentary picture of Arizona at 75. We lack richness in detail and clarity in understanding the changes that have emerged over those years. In the essays of this section the authors examine some strategies to overcome this paucity. They consider whether or not the needs can be met. They wonder whether the time and resources are available.

173

Can we preserve the historical resources necessary to accomplish the essential tasks before us? Are the resources still available, or have they disappeared? What commitments must we make to fulfill current needs for information as well as those to come in the twenty-first century?

In the discussions that follow, the authors suggest the opportunities that lie before us. They point out that action can still be taken, that it is not too late, but that we must act quickly and decisively. The historical landscape of buildings, documents, photographs, and living memories is in jeopardy. Yet Arizona's history can still be read through its remaining buildings, uncovered in documents and photographs, and retold and systematically collected from our memories. Sadly, bulldozers indiscriminately level the built environment, depleting our visual ability to read the history of the state in its structures. Similarly, records are routinely thrown out according to systematic records destruction schedules. And, of course, our citizens die leaving their memories unrecorded.

Our identity as a state, our state of mind over time, is recorded in our taste in buildings, either official or vernacular. That record, for example, of our cultural history, of our business and political history, is fast disappearing. In some instances new structures appear, but in others the land lies vacant. If we are not careful, newcomers and children will lack all ability to read the history of Arizona development through its buildings and will be unable to tap into the network of structures that reveal Arizona's heritage and show how our former citizens coped with their surroundings.

In the first essay, Roger Brevoort, an architectural historian in the State Historic Preservation Office, discusses the importance of identifying and retaining a record of past development in the structures of urban and rural Arizona. We need more than the "historic zoos" of Pioneer Arizona and Heritage Square. We need to preserve structures in their context so that we understand that context and have a yardstick against which to measure and evaluate change, consider our self-worth, and better understand ourselves.

Just as important as the record of the built environment is the record found in documents and photographs. As David Hoober and John Irwin point out, the documentary and photographic heritage of Arizona remains scattered, in disarray, and endangered. Yet with adequate thought and planning we can conserve our written and photographic resources. The first task is to conserve existing records. Organized plans are needed to collect materials and minimize rivalry among collecting agencies. In addition, the state archives celebrates its fiftieth anniversary this year. The agency lacks an adequate home to store materials and has only a skeletal staff to collect materials and inventory, monitor, and manage the collections. Hoober and Irwin examine the possibilities we have to capture and preserve our documentary heritage.

Much knowledge of what constitutes the entity called Arizona is reflected in neither its buildings nor its documents and photographs. It lies in the collective memory of the citizens of the state. Many actions have gone unre-corded. Yet, as Reba Wells points out, the memory of our residents extends back to the turn of the century. It is a memory to be captured on tape by oral historians. While we need to better organize our oral history materials, we must carry on active outreach work. Memories need to be tapped and recorded on tape. Collections need development and better planning. Institutions must cooperate to gather information and make it available to researchers. The promise of oral history lies in its ability to bring past memories into the open so that we have an opportunity to understand specific events or developments.

Finally, if we are to preserve and understand the past, we must broaden our concept of history. Arizona history is more than cowboys and the frontier; it includes city dwellers and economic development since World War II. History is not made exclusively by famous Anglo men, but includes the stories of the unknown, the woman, the Black, Hispanic, Asian, and Indian. Historic buildings are not all Victorian mansions; some are railroad stations, dams, motels, and postwar tract houses. Business records, underground newspapers, and videotape are as much documents as are government records and nineteenth-century diaries. We cannot build a broad understanding of the present on a narrow interpretation of the past.

HISTORIC PRESERVATION: AN AGENDA FOR KEEPING ARIZONA HISTORY TANGIBLE FOR THE FUTURE

Roger A. Brevoort

Historic preservation can be defined as a method for saving visual references to the past. Preservationists view history from the perspective of the buildings, sites, and structures that physically attest to historic events and places and see structures as an interpretable manifestation of historic themes. Preservation historians look at the land as an environment of human "built" resources, all of which have a place in documenting historic events, architectural designs, and technological developments.

The motive behind historic preservation arises from a desire to retain the physical references to past events or earlier architecture that convey an area's history. Knowing when and how things were constructed allows us to read history through the structures built in a particular area or during a specific time period, much as an archaeologist interprets a site from the fragments left behind. It is a basic premise of historic preservation that the structures are integral to an awareness, understanding, and appreciation of history. It is the job of the preservationist—ideally working in consort with more conventional academic historians—to endeavor to preserve the structures that form tangible links to past developments in order to maintain a visual record of the past within our everyday environment.

An agenda for historic preservation in Arizona in the next twenty-five years must revolve around the fact that, as the state reckons with both its current population and the explosive projections of growth and development, historians and preservationists must develop a constituency that is both aware of our history and committed to its preservation. At the same time, we must work to preserve properties and districts that represent our past development. Historic structures are vital to our conception of history, and we need a committed constituency to preserve them. At the same time, we must identify the problems, shortcomings, and challenges facing the historic preservation movement in Arizona today.

The Physical Environment and the Past

Throughout Arizona, cliff dwellings, pueblos, and a host of other archaeological remains attest to the presence of various prehistoric cultures. The subsequent era of Spanish influence is evident from the remains of missions established by the Spaniards in the eighteenth century. The 1880s witnessed the establishment of mining, and in towns like Bisbee, Jerome, Tombstone, and Clifton the ancillary mining structures still stand. The arrival of the railroads in 1879 and the concurrent rise of the railroad towns is reflected in the 1880s buildings in towns such as Flagstaff, Winslow, and Holbrook in the north, and Willcox and Yuma in the south.

In the early twentieth century, agriculture and citrus farming emerged. The railroad helped initiate the tourist industry, and attributes of the state such as the Grand Canyon became nationally known as tourists arriving on the railroad began enjoying the luxury of El Tovar Hotel. By the time of statehood in 1912, the completion of Roosevelt Dam had assured a stable water supply for the central portion of the state and led to the construction of irrigation systems of the Salt River Valley, stimulating the growth of Phoenix. Later, irrigation networks established the central Arizona cotton belt and introduced a major new economy to the state.

The early state highway system initially paved in the 1910s can be seen through remnants of old roads and early bridges throughout the state. The highways advanced as we see from the resorts and tourist courts that appeared early in the 1930s. By the late 1920s Phoenix and Tucson were both major urban centers featuring Moderne style skyscrapers of the day, as well as expanding suburbs composed of hundreds of bungalows in various Craftsman, Western Colonial, and Spanish Colonial Revival designs. Architectural styles tell us the age of these suburbs and testify to their association with prevailing national trends in architecture. By the 1920s Arizona was no longer an isolated western territory. The state was linked architecturally, socially, and culturally with mainstream America.

Thus, one can trace the history of the state and its major historic themes and developmental influences by looking at the components of the built environment visible on the Arizona landscape. These structures provide a visual, three-dimensional picture of the state from which its history can easily be explained to the general public.

A major problem, however, is that the general public, by and large, is not attuned to perceiving the environment as a history book and does not realize that altering this environment fundamentally changes the text. Looking toward the future, we must ask how the absence of key structures would inhibit, or perhaps prohibit, the honest interpretation of state history for historical research or educational purposes. Our response to this question is the compelling reason to broaden public awareness and build a constituency for preservation in order to retain an accurate historical picture for the future.

To illustrate the importance of public perception, consider the city of Phoenix. The city is popularly perceived as being new and without a history, despite its prehistoric heritage. This misconception can be traced to a lack of physical historic references. The original barrio neighborhood of adobe houses, built in the 1870s by Hispanic and Anglo settlers along the Salt River, lies beneath the runways of Sky Harbor Airport. When the periodic flooding of the Salt River forced the residents to move north to the present urban core, wealthy residents built Queen Anne style houses along both sides of Central Avenue immediately north of downtown in the period between the 1890s and the 1910s. The area was quickly named "Millionaire's Row," a title it held until the 1950s, when the northward march of commercial buildings up Central Avenue caused the primary structures to be demolished. Only one of these Central Avenue mansions survives. In the downtown area, the 1892 Rosson House stands as a symbol of Phoenix history, but because it is virtually surrounded by the parking lots of the Phoenix Convention Center, it is difficult to imagine the former status of the house as the showpiece of a residential neighborhood.

Similarly, in the mile between downtown Phoenix and the State Capitol, only one of the original Victorian-era residences still stands. The others have given way to the contemporary state government complex and its associated parking lots. And just to the northwest of downtown, the Roosevelt Neighborhood, the city's affluent streetcar suburb of the 1910s, has been bisected by the alignment of Interstate 10.

The Need for a Constituency

Although all of those later developments had their own rationale and responded to specific needs, it should come as no surprise that it is very difficult to make the history of Phoenix prior to the 1930s believable to anyone but a handful of Phoenix natives and a few perceptive historians. It is no wonder that Phoenicians do not perceive their city as historic. When the visible references to the past are gone, the picture of development is broken and inaccurate. Among Phoenicians, the preservation constituency is small, and the movement is only beginning to achieve the level of awareness essential to its success. Despite the adoption of a City Historic Preservation Ordinance and creation of a Historic Preservation Commission, a recent public hearing to determine the fate of the Patio Royale Hotel attracted only a few interested citizens— and no public comment. The neighborhood outcry of a few months before had fizzled, and the building that was a haven for Hollywood film stars in the thirties and forties was written off—a victim of the economic argument of "not worth saving." Montgomery Stadium, the 1928 Spanish Colonial Revival stadium at Phoenix Union High School, was not given historic designation because the owners argued that they could not find an economically viable reuse and that the historic status would create an economic hardship. These decision are made despite the historic values and associations of the buildings partly because there is no preservation public to voice a sufficiently strong objection. The preservation process simply cannot work without a public constituency to challenge the short-sighted and short-term thinking that puts current economic values above historic importance.

A similar and more tragic example of low public response was the hearing held concerning the dramatic alteration of Roosevelt Dam, a designated National Historic Landmark that is virtually the cornerstone of contemporary Arizona. No public attendance, no media, no comment. Although its alteration is admittedly part of a much larger plan that has been debated on many fronts for several years, the dam is a victim of its own success and is about to be buried without a funeral. Unfortunately, the general public will probably remain unaware of the fate of the dam until demolition is actually underway, and then there will be a massive cry of protest several years too late to do anything.

Problems and Perceptions

Another problem is the narrow public view of what is historic— or what in actuality was significant to the state's past, regardless of prevailing attitudes. Arizona history is commonly identified with the mythology of the cowboy and the folklore of the ghost town. People generally consider Prescott, Jerome, and Tombstone to be the historic towns. The reason is simple. The Victorian image of Prescott is promoted in numerous magazines and tourist publications. The legend of the OK Corral gunfight is taught in elementary schools coast-to-coast. Yet the reality that Tombstone was a mining camp with little relation to the cowboy, and that copper mining—not cattle—is the primary reason for the state's existence is essentially unknown. As we develop an agenda for the next twenty-five years, we must immediately begin communicating knowledge of history to the diverse population of the state, establishing a constituency among the current residents, and instituting educational programs at all levels.

We must continue to foster public and governmental support for existing preservation projects. Ideally this should include public funding for restoration of significant properties which suffer from inadequate maintenance. Major buildings are too often owned by municipalities or individuals without sufficient capital to repair or maintain them. Equally problematic is the number of buildings that stand idle and unmaintained owing to budgetary constraints. Numerous structures fall into this category, with railroad stations perhaps the best example. Usually large and centrally located, without passenger service they have lost their intended use and are generally viewed as surplus property. Warehouses and older commercial buildings, schools, and even courthouses find themselves on the under-utilized list. However, if we consider these historic resources as a public good, their care deserves and requires support from the public trust.

Older neighborhoods also face problems of neglect, especially neighborhoods that have shifted to low-income status, with the concomitant absentee ownership, poor maintenance, transiency, and eventual demolition of a "blighted" neighborhood. Oddly enough, politicians and planners still like to boast about clearance efforts as progressive accomplishments, and the public never challenges these statements.

The problem is again one of perception. If vacant buildings and older neighborhoods are to survive, we must educate the public to see their original architectural characteristics or their rehabilitation potential, not the deficiencies of current use or current appearance. As we can see increasingly in Tucson, and are beginning to see in Phoenix, inner city neighborhoods do have the potential to recover. Old houses are attracting investors and a growing core of residents, yet they still disappear in the fringe areas of the cities. The commercial development potential of central city property is still winning in the real estate office and on zoning maps. Tackling the problem of neighborhood attrition, either through zoning ordinances or creative real estate financing—an untraditional task for historians—is nonetheless an important item on the historical agenda.

Priorities and Possibilities

At some point we need to set priorities for what is worthy of being preserved and make some choices, because growth and development are inevitable. The preservation movement must be accountable and historically credible. Identification and evaluation bring us to the balance point.

One of our priorities needs to be ensuring the long-term survival of Arizona's preservation program. At present the program is supported by an equal share of federal and state funding. Cuts at either end will shrink the program, something we cannot permit. Nationally the program has strong advocates and has survived several rounds of zero budget allocations thanks to grassroots support. But this support needs to be continually nurtured to keep abreast of political changes—both state and national—in years to come.

Preservation efforts are based on a continual inventory and identification process that locates, researches, and formally recognizes sites. Already in Arizona we have made major progress in the inventory of historic properties, with over two thousand historic sites and twenty thousand archaeological sites catalogued in the State Historic Property Inventory. Arizona has five hundred entries on the National Register of Historic Places. This program, operated through the State Historic Preservation Office, functions as the official inventory of significant properties. National Register status becomes the benchmark for establishing priorities or initiating negotiations. In many cases compromises are reached, but as my earlier examples suggested, official designation is not sufficient; without a constituency it has little clout.

Unfortunately, many types of historic resources fall through the cracks of the existing inventory system. Structures in isolated locations, utilitarian structures, and rare property types for which there is no constituency or sympathetic owner fall out of reach of the program despite any intrinsic historic value of the resource. For example, the early concrete bridges that were the state of the art when built in the teens now stand abandoned on bypassed highways. Coal supply towers along the Southern Pacific Railroad built in the 1920s but outmoded by the mid-forties are without advocates. They may not seem significant or of high priority, but if these structures are out of reach of the organized survey process their very existence may never be recorded. The preservation community and historical groups ranging from railroad historians to tourist clubs must go beyond existing programs in order to inventory the structures related to their particular interests.

There is also a need to inventory rural areas that conventional programs have neglected. Towns such as Snowflake, Taylor, and Shumway, where nineteenth-century Mormon immigration is clearly illustrated by the architecture, have received little attention from existing public programs. The same is true for isolated structures in towns along the old Route 66—communities like Seligman or Oatman that have been bypassed now that I-40 has replaced both the railroad and the highway. It is important not to overlook places such as these which may not be major areas today but are integral to the heritage of the state.

There has been very little scholarly research into Arizona architecture or prominent architects. Someday we will acknowledge that Frank Lloyd Wright was not the only architect to come to Arizona and start some serious inquiry into other influential designers. With examples of architects' work disappearing almost within the lifetime of the architects themselves, the need is urgent to do research before the buildings are gone and the legacy disappears. We also need an architectural archive for the drawings that remain. Architecture and architectural drawings must be recognized as artifacts that deserve curation in the same way we treat historic documents, maps, photographs, and other memorabilia.

Arizona architecture has always been closely tied to California and to the importation of styles from the East and Midwest. Yet there has been little effort to correlate Arizona buildings with their counterparts in other states, which would be one way to develop a clear picture of Arizona's immigration patterns. As an example, people from Peoria, Illinois, brought the design of their community church with them to construct in Peoria, Arizona. There is no better illustration than Peoria of the desire of early Arizona settlers to establish familiar imagery in the West. Yet these connections are seldom analyzed, and no clear relationship has been established between historic themes in Arizona and their concurrent architecture.

The universities can help develop such knowledge by expanding history and preservation-related programs. All three state universities are introducing preservation programs dealing with architecture, planning, and public history. These programs should be nurtured so that sufficient training is available in the state to establish a network of people qualified in the various disciplines to carry out preservation efforts ranging from sound historical research to appropriate architectural conservation practices.

In high schools and elementary schools, history teachers and art teachers should begin to incorporate buildings and sites into the educational process. Buildings can be the focus of local history classes and subjects for all levels of drawing students. And in Arizona, where local materials were readily utilized in construction, a building can be a lesson in local geology and regional geography. It is no accident that the Northern Arizona University campus is the largest collection of Flagstaff red sandstone in Arizona or that a primary material for buildings in Globe is locally quarried dacite—two revealing cases of the relationship of architecture to environment. Use of buildings in the educational process should begin no later than secondary levels so that from the beginning students are in touch with history rather than believing that history is merely the memorization of dates.

We must continue to update and expand the perception of what is "historic." The pace of change in Arizona's built environment is so fast that recent history is disappearing before our eyes. Although it may seem absurd, the best illustration is the roadside strip—the area at the fringe of the city limits where the motels and mom-and-pop resorts that are the origin of Arizona's tourist industry are located. These facilities document both the tourist industry and the corollary impact of the automobile on Arizona tourism. In retrospect, the birth of tourism in the twenties has probably had as substantial an influence on Arizona history as the discovery of copper and gold.

Now, while it is still possible to trace the tourist boom across the state—Route 66 across northern Arizona, or Route 60/89 connecting Safford, Globe, Mesa, Tempe, Phoenix, Glendale, and Wickenburg—we should take a look at what remains along these routes. Strip development has already eroded the traces of the boom, and because of the presently unpopular image and negative connotations of today's commercial strip we are ignoring the demise of properties from the resort era. It is here that the tangible evidence of a discernible historic era may be gone before we recognize it for what it is. This situation will only worsen along with the growth pressures and developments already on the horizon.

Essential to academic research is its publication. Articles in popular magazines, newspaper columns, and walking-tour brochures are all easy to prepare and are widely available in some areas of the country, but they are still rare in Arizona. Knowledge about Arizona history and architecture should not be confined to the minds of academic and professional historians. It should become an obligation to disseminate the information to the general public in readily accessible formats. Perhaps it is time for historians to challenge publishers and the media to pay more attention to history.

Although we can set an agenda to record and educate about the past, we need to remain aware that history is being created around us. We can readily acknowledge that water supply and distribution systems for either irrigation or urban land use have had, and are now having, a profound effect on the twentieth-century growth of Arizona. It probably sounds farfetched to think of the Central Arizona Project as historic, but fifty years from now the CAP will probably be recognized as pivotal in allowing Arizona to compete as a Sunbelt state. It will undoubtedly be seen as relating to the broad patterns of Arizona history, which would make it eligible for the National Register of Historic Places. Looking ahead, we must consider the historic impact of what is going on around us by looking at what is influencing the state now and what may ultimately be significant. As the pace of change accelerates we will no longer be able to consider history as a study of past events. Growth pressures will challenge us to initiate an almost "commentative" observation of what is happening, especially given the sheer magnitude of development in Arizona's immediate future.

It is the mission of preservation historians to educate and sensitize the public to the inherent value of historical resources and what they mean to society's sense of the past. If we act quickly, in the year 2012 we will be able to see what came before. If not, the next twenty-five years of explosive development and growth will leave the state without a constituency that understands or even knows the basic history of Arizona. The few historic resources that will remain will have little relevance to a population with no frame of reference to the past.

ARIZONA ARCHIVES AT SEVENTY-FIVE: OUR RECORD AND OUR FUTURE

David H. Hoober and John Irwin

A half-century ago, a former Arizonan apologized to the Arizona Pioneers' Historical Society that he could add nothing to its archives. J. F. Farish, a pioneer of the 1880s, assumed that he and his times were not a part of history. Responding to a request for memoirs, he wrote, "My life in Arizona in the 80's had nothing of the pioneer element about it, nothing even of the picturesque or romantic, being limited to the prosaic duties of attending rodeos, branding cattle and following the chuck wagon. . . . Of course I knew the Earps, the Clantons, old Geronimo, Apache Kid and even Billy the Kid . . . but what of it? They were common property and everyone knew them."

For many of our residents our history is claimed as a "common property," and yet few feel genuine identification with it. Arizona offers examples of a preoccupation with nostalgia in the most unlikely places. Lake Havasu City is a curious spot for the rebirth of London Bridge, stone by stone. Contemporary culture, exemplified by *Arizona Highways,* is composed of a whole network of images associated with Arizona and the West: the cowboy, the romance of the Spanish borderlands, the myths of Anglo frontier life, and our Native American heritage. From Old Tucson come movies and television programs depicting this West—and dollars and jobs for today's economy.

It is a melancholy fact that on a more mundane level, historical matters are considered expendable, insignificant curiosities easily left alone. Actual records of our past are ignored. Many in Arizona would not know archives from endive. Even people who understand movements to preserve old buildings and museum collections of historical artifacts are indifferent to the fate of historical documents. These records exist in abundance—our lives are surrounded by paper, tape, disk, and film—in a myriad of different forms and functions, from the commonplace to the exotic. But they are often inaccessible and unusable. Moreover, they are extremely fragile, vulnerable to fire, water, sunlight, and neglect.

What are historical records? They are yellowed nineteenth-century diaries, filled with antique handwriting; they are letters sent home to a soldier's mother during the Korean War; they are petitions and statutes documenting the formation of La Paz County in 1983. The files in the governor's office and the Arizona Corporation Commission are historical records.

Who uses these records? All of us—students, scholars, buffs, family historians, folklorists, attorneys, musicians, film makers—in short, everybody. What is their importance to Arizona? Our state epitomizes the good and bad of the Sunbelt. It has grown 22 percent since the 1980 census, and 79 percent of the population lives in urban Maricopa and Pima counties. For some, Arizona may evoke images of the Old West, but for others it signifies a sprawling megalopolis, unending construction, and constant change. Although this growth may have brought with it new economic resources available for historical programs, at the same time it may have brought about a devaluation of historical concerns. The many people who have moved here have no roots in this land or in its past. Historical values often suffer if response is made only to immediate growth. Old buildings are destroyed because they are in the way; old records are thrown out because they take up too much space.

A recent report revealed that preservation of government historical records is a disgrace at the local, state, and national levels. This lack of care for our historical records is hardly news to local archivists, though it may be to other Arizonans. Historical records are not discussed at cocktail parties; the subject does not keep people on the edges of their chairs.

For many years Arizona was known as the "Baby State," the last of the contiguous forty-eight states. It remains in archival adolescence. In fact, it is archivally barely out of diapers. Why is this true? It is not for lack of trying. Quite the opposite. Six institutions in the state have made substantial progress toward building programs over the past twenty-five years.

A centralized historical agency, often a state historical society, has been the vehicle for strong archival programs elsewhere; Arizona's development has been in an opposite direction. No single agency has provided adequate leadership. Instead, responsibility for historical record keeping has been dispersed to many institutions, and no centralized leadership has emerged. There has been no common consensus, no shared goals. To the contrary, institutions compete for financial resources and often for collections. Arizona's institutions resemble isolated territorial outposts on the edge of archival civilization. The result has been a splintered effort, to say the least. For example, the University of Arizona Library is only a few blocks from the Arizona Historical Society. Both collect similar historical records, yet they have never developed an archival strategy or a cooperative program. Similar examples may be cited throughout the state. Often, the left hand does not know what the right hand is doing.

The Arizona Historical Society, organized in 1884, is the oldest of these six state institutions. Its archival program did not get off the ground until the 1960s, when it finally occupied a new building. This building received a new addition in the mid-1970s, making the society the largest archival site in the state, but there is still only a lone archivist with no staff.

Archival collections at Arizona's three universities were created relatively recently, even though they now have the largest budgets and staff. The University of Arizona Library had been collecting small quantities of original records for many years, but it was not until 1958 that its Special Collections Division was organized and manuscripts became an established priority. Similarly, the Arizona Historical Foundation was organized in 1959, and in 1967 it became housed at the Arizona State University Library, alongside ASU's own Arizona Collection. Up in Coconino County, the Northern Arizona University Library's historical collections and Northern Arizona Pioneers' Historical Society were jointly established in the early 1960s, but only in 1972 was an archivist hired, with collections made available to the public on a regular basis.

Sharlot Hall, Arizona's preeminent territorial historian from 1904 to 1911, founded the Sharlot Hall Museum in Prescott in 1928. During the first half of this century she collected valuable early records of Arizona, yet it has been only ten years since an archivist was hired and a new library/archives area was built for those records at the Prescott Historical Society, making these treasures more readily available to the public.

Finally, there is the State Archives, a division of the Department of Library, Archives and Public Records established in 1937. The struggle to create the Archives and to build a new addition to the State Capitol for it and the State Library is a fascinating study of perseverance in the midst of the Depression. The State Archives moved into its present quarters in 1939. This facility, planned for a state with a population of 500,000 which now has 3.5 million, ranks near the bottom of the heap of similar state institutions in the nation.

In addition to these six institutions there are of course many smaller historical records collections throughout the state in local museums, libraries, and businesses. These include the Century House Museum in Yuma, the local history collection at the Fredonia Public Library, and the Salt River Project Archives. At least 130 such collections were reported in 1983. They are often overlooked, but they contain significant historical data. All in all, a vast quantity of material has been saved, often through the quiet, heroic efforts of crusading individuals. We can applaud ourselves for what has

been accomplished over the last twenty-five years, but these accomplishments are meager in view of what faces us.

Some encouraging signs indicate an acceleration of interest in
historical records. Recent events in Arizona reflect national developments in the archival community. One of these is the positive local
impact of the National Historical Publications and Records Commission, a division of the National Archives and Records Administration.
For example, the formation of the City of Tucson archives was
initiated and nurtured by the NHPRC grant program. For more
than ten years the commission has been giving money to develop
such pilot projects and to organize and preserve collections throughout the states. A half-dozen projects in Arizona have been funded.
Another positive contribution by the NHPRC is the creation of the
Arizona Historical Records Advisory Board. This board is administered by the Arizona Department of Library, Archives and Public
Records. Composed of archivists, government officials, and interested citizens, it reviews Arizona's grant proposals and makes recommendations to the commission. A main benefit of this group's activities is that for the first time people from different sections of
Arizona have come together to examine records problems and to
work together toward their solutions. Since 1981, the NHPRC has
made it possible for more than forty states to study the conditions
of their historical records. *Preserving Arizona's Historical Records,* published in 1983, was the first study ever to examine the state of our
state's records.

Another organization of growing importance is the Coordinating Committee for History in Arizona, affiliated with the National
Coordinating Committee for the Promotion of History. Founded
in 1983, CCHA serves as an advocacy group for public history
matters, and it is becoming a forum for issues relating to the preservation of historical records.

Still another attempt at coordination is the State Archives' spon-
sorship of a series of meetings, "Planning for Arizona's Historical
Records" (PAHR). Representatives of historical collections at the
state's universities, the Arizona Historical Society, the Prescott Historical Society, and the Archives meet quarterly, and soon this group
will expand to include other institutions and agencies. These meet-

ings are laying the groundwork for a much-needed comprehensive statewide archival plan that the State Archives will develop. Such discussions of public policy are encouraging signs.

Just as encouraging is the impetus for the construction of a new state archives building. A legislative appropriation in 1986 for a feasibility study, it is hoped, will soon be followed by support for design and construction of a new building. When Arizona's archives has a suitable home, it will be able to provide a model for Arizona. Other institutions are also planning new buildings or additions: the new Flagstaff City–Coconino County Library includes a records vault, and the Arizona Historical Society continues to plan a major building in Tempe. These are encouraging signs, indeed.

What Should We Do in the Future?

The agenda for Arizona's archives and records interests can be summarized in three points: planning, education, and promotion. These functions, fostered by an environment of cooperation, can help us reach our goals. Planning will enable Arizona to establish criteria and mechanisms to identify and retain records of enduring value, and archival programs to ensure the preservation, availability, and use of those records.

What are our priorities for identification and retention of records? The first is the formation of appraisal strategies. Appraisal is the archivist's most difficult task. How can we anticipate which records will be sought by researchers twenty-five years or more from now? How can we support collection, storage, and reference programs for them? Clearly defined appraisal guidelines and collecting policies are needed for us to be able to select appropriate collections and care for only the most useful materials within them. A second need is for cooperation in collecting. We can achieve this by developing documentation strategies. A documentation strategy has two parts: First, it requires a study of what records are now being kept permanently. Second, it involves the development of a plan to ensure efficient and economical collection of the right records. These two strategies will be indispensable planning tools.

Archivists often compete for the same materials. Nowhere in the country, certainly not in Arizona, can we afford to continue this. We need to make some difficult choices about who should do what. Should Arizona State University be our state's repository for congressional collections? Should the Historical Society dominate the collection of photographic materials? Should the State Archives be concerned only with the public records of Arizona government? Should collecting interests be established along lines of geography, subject matter, or chronology? The wish to establish such jurisdictional or subject documentation strategies may appear naive, but those decisions are necessary if we are to do our best to preserve the historical record. Who will take the lead? The PAHR discussions and a statewide archival plan are excellent beginnings if administrative support for their recommendations is forthcoming.

Another question we must answer relates to the kinds of materials to be collected. We can no longer restrict ourselves to collecting traditional paper records. Few people keep diaries today; much communication occurs over the telephone rather than through letters. We need to shift our attention to how we communicate so that we can capture information about us.

TV newsfilm and videotape should be collected. Such an undertaking is expensive, but it will provide us with historical information not available from the printed page. Oral history materials should be gathered and preserved to fill the gap in the written historical record. Success will require the same level of commitment to oral history as to other programs of our institutions. Oral history is as valid as museum exhibits, publications programs, and library purchases. We must be willing to bear the cost.

Native American records are increasingly important. Can and should we help in the development of tribal archives? Could agreements be made for non-Indian institutions to care for tribal records? Hispanic-American records are important to the history of Arizona. How well are they being preserved?

We must collect materials of the twentieth century. Business records, documentation of protest movements, anything relating to environmental concerns, and evidence of the impact of urbanization on Arizona are collecting areas for which we should plan. Mining, the military, and the Indian wars are important and interesting parts of our past. But we cannot risk ignoring other events, themes, and groups.

In addition, we are confronted with a proliferation of records of different media. The kinds of materials and topics just described would be difficult to identify and preserve if we dealt only with traditional paper material. Information stored on disks and tapes may not be kept or may not be accessible. Individuals who write using word processors may not keep early drafts. Technology changes hardware and software. Incompatibility between them can deprive us of access to the information they contain. Who will lead in mastering the implications of automation?

A final need for identification of appropriate materials relates to records creators. This is most difficult in dealing with producers of private materials, such as letters, diaries, and memoirs. The principal obstacle here, as all children of the late twentieth century realize, is that people *write* less and less. That makes attention to oral history even more critical.

Planning and cooperation must be extended to government officials, who also need help in caring for records. In the next quarter-century we must continue to build on the excellent records management program we have in Arizona. Records management is the orderly control of the complete life-cycle of records from their creation to their eventual disposition. A unit of the Department of Library, Archives and Public Records, the Records Management Division, has been operating in a state-of-the-art building since 1980. It successfully promotes the development of records schedules in state and local governments and provides storage for noncurrent, nonpermanent records. In 1986, there were more than fifty thousand boxes in its warehouse near the Capitol; an expansion of its building is planned. Records management is an integral part of historical records preservation. Archivists need to work closely with records managers to develop appraisal standards that isolate the small quantity of valuable records that should be preserved from the mountains of paper churned out each year. The growth of programs in both government and business is slowly ushering in a new age of records administration. This is a bright spot in Arizona.

Records programs on the local level have not fared well. Vast quantities of valuable government records molder and disintegrate in substandard storage areas. Local records have been dumped down mine shafts, lost in floods, and ferreted away in the night. Stories about the chaotic state of record keeping in the past have almost become folklore. Take an incident which occurred in December 1986 in Tombstone, as reported in the *Arizona Republic*. A Benson man returned to Tombstone officials a priceless city council minute book from the early 1880s which he had purchased for $25.00. Events documented in the volume included the city's incorporation and the gunfight at the OK Corral. The book had been missing for fifteen years. For his trouble, the man was made an honorary marshal and given a key to the city.

The cause of local records preservation requires assistance in several areas. First, professional assistance must come from records managers and archivists for agencies and institutions establishing records programs. Second, the Department of Library, Archives and Public Records and organizations such as the League of Arizona Cities and Towns and the Arizona Association of Counties should sponsor seminars and other training programs on records appraisal, organization, and storage. Decision makers such as city councils and county boards and administrators should be apprised of the importance of establishing responsibility and authority in a records office. Third, local support from historical societies, genealogy groups, and teachers organizations must be a part of any strategy for drawing attention to concerns about local government records. They will benefit from the availability of historical materials, and so they should become true "friends."

A State Archives system that has resolved the apparent conflict between centralization and decentralization is a fourth and compelling result of planning. Economy dictates the need for a central repository and a well-trained staff. But how can we ensure convenient access to materials for people who live far from the capital? We should consider some kind of regional cooperative effort in which approved local repositories could be used in a network system. Regardless of how the conflict is resolved, two points must be recognized: (1) there must be regular assistance from major professional institutions such as the Department of Library, Archives and Public Records and the Arizona Historical Society for local organizations and government offices, and (2) we must ensure a commitment to the best care and use of the records rather than insistence on local control under inappropriate and unsafe conditions. Promotion of local history, with all its benefits, is poorly served by provincialism. All people interested in records must insist on establishment of standards and adherence to them by all of us. A fifth need for local records programs, closely linked to this, is preservation microfilming and microfilming of frequently requested materials for use in local communities. It is not necessary or cost effective to microfilm everything, but microfilm is one of several tools we can use to ease our burdens. Central and local historical repositories can benefit from having original documents cared for safely in one place, with convenient copies available in another.

Public awareness of the need to provide better care for our records is one of the brightest spots for the future. Nothing lasts forever, but long-term care is the goal of conservation. This is accomplished by proper storage and handling of materials. Disaster, both natural and manmade, poses an obvious threat. Not so obvious is the fact that paper and other recording media carry within their chemical structures the seeds of their own destruction. Through the efforts of the State Archives Conservation Section, as well as the excellent educational programs offered by the Arizona Paper and Photograph Conservation Group, the message of conservation is being spread. For example, most people in Arizona who work with old photographs are now aware of the hazard of nitrate negatives. Most people are probably aware of the disadvantages of plastic lamination of documents. The dismal news, according to a recent national study, is that "more than 80 percent of records accessioned into state archives each year, and in some states a much higher percentage, will never receive preservation attention." Massive work in the future will be required. And yet, Arizona's conservation effort stands out among other states. As one local historian from Springerville said at a conservation workshop, "Hell, before I came here I didn't even know I had problems!"

Frank G. Burke, acting archivist of the United States, recently said, "Our memory is at risk. We've preserved wetland, we've preserved wildlife, we've preserved downtown areas, we've preserved prehistoric sites and we've preserved buildings. Downtown areas and buildings are indications of what we've done in the past. Documents tell us who did it and why they did it."

The author of a recent study of the conditions of our records found that a large percentage of 2.5 billion pages of historical records held in state archives are deteriorating. State archives will need $471 million over the next ten years to preserve their holdings properly. There is a risk of having a documentation gap in the nation. Some material can be restored at great expense and with considerable expertise, but the best preservation step one can take is to provide adequate facilities, adequate housing, and proper storage. The study concluded that our goal is to manage the risk and to curb the accelerated deterioration.

As important as planning is another goal which has been ignored: education. The development of archival programs has been seriously crippled by a lack of formal educational opportunities. Arizona has many historical records programs, but only a handful of archivists. Custodians of our records need to master numerous techniques and concepts, yet there are few training programs in the United States and none in Arizona. This occupation has, at best, a quasi-professional status. National standards are uncoordinated, and there is no certification requirement. The Society of American Archivists is currently attempting to establish national certification standards. Although the state has elaborate procedures for the certification of medical personnel, attorneys—even hairdressers—none exist for the curators of our permanent and valuable records.

In the past the Arizona Historical Foundation has offered some basic archival workshops. An occasional archives class has also been offered at Arizona State University. However, for the situation to improve, a graduate-level program of instruction needs to be established as part of the curriculum at one of our universities. When this finally occurs, historical records programs should improve, as libraries did after the establishment of the Graduate Library School at the University of Arizona in 1968.

The goals and objectives described here can be achieved most

effectively if we remember that we need to *promote* archives if they
are to be valued and used. We have not been very good evangelists.
Outreach programs are required to demonstrate the importance
of historical records. Further, we need to be more assertive with
resource allocators, whether they be elected government officials,
executive or legislative, members of boards of trustees, or institution
directors.

Twenty-five years from now, an Arizona archivist will write to
some of our contemporaries to solicit memoirs and personal papers.
It would be tragic and ironic if they reacted as our pioneer of the
1880s, J. F. Farish, did. "Of course I knew the land developers, the
politicians, the business leaders, the athletes, and some of the crooks
in those groups, but what of it? They were common property and
everyone knew them," he or she might respond. "By the way, what
are the letters and diaries you requested? I had some computer
disks and optical disks that my grandfather used several years ago,
but surely you aren't interested in them. I just deleted a tape full
of family photographs. What would you ever do with those things,
anyway?"

MEMORIES FOR THE FUTURE: THE ROLE OF ORAL HISTORY

Reba N. Wells

As the forty-eighth state of the Union, Arizona has just completed its first seventy-five years. In the minds of many citizens who lived through them, the period was exciting and colorful and is still fresh and clear. Scores of older Arizonans remember the day statehood was achieved—February 14, 1912—and the rousing celebrations all over the territory: they were there. Those citizens are the links that connect us and the present with Arizona's earlier people—Indian, Hispanic, Anglo—and are thus able to push back history another generation to parents and grandparents who were living in the Southwest in the nineteenth century. Through that generational chain or through their own participation, that older generation remembers the significant events and traditions of territorial and early statehood days. Its members recall details of fact and feelings about the development (or decline, in some cases) of communities, towns, cities, businesses, governments, and historic sites. Unfortunately, most of what they know has never been written down, and they will not be here when Arizona observes its hundredth birthday in 2012. This historical knowledge will be irretrievably lost unless we act now.

Similarly, we have seventy-five years of statehood about which we know very little. Few writers have taken more than a descriptive look at the period after 1912. Our efforts to preserve a broad knowledge of these seventy-five years remain small. We are in grave danger of losing the memories of this period because it seems near to us and therefore unhistorical. Although most people appreciate the urgent need to capture the late territorial and early statehood past before those who remember it are gone, the opportunity likewise to capture years since 1912 is of major importance as well. For instance, do we have any real sense, based on the memories of our citizens, of how twentieth-century urban growth has occurred and what it has meant in their lives, or what has happened in our rural areas on the twentieth-century ranch or farm? Politically, we have very limited knowledge of how we came to particular decisions or enacted our laws. What we do have are lists of events, legislation, and people. We do not know what Arizonans thought or felt—how they as individuals responded to their situation. Arizona's political history, its business history, its social history, and its labor history is more than a straightforward, simple record of events. We need to understand how those events took shape, how they came to unfold as they did, how people came to make specific decisions (for example, to pass particular laws), and how they responded to events and decisions. That recent history is at this moment beyond our grasp.

Yet there is a practical way to tap those living memories, through the modern research technique known as "oral history." Oral history has the potential of "freezing and extending the living memory into the infinite future."[1]

Oral History

The term *oral history* was apparently coined in 1942 by a Greenwich Villager, Joe Gould, who claimed, according to a *New York Times* article, that he was compiling "an oral History of our Time." Over the years, other terms have been suggested—oral documentation, living history, life review, and life history—but none of them has caught on. Similarly, varied definitions can be found in different disciplines, but most practitioners agree that oral history has these characteristics: "the process of collecting, usually by means of a tape-recorded interview, reminiscences, accounts, and interpretation of events from the recent past which are of historical significance."[2] The Oral History Association puts its simply: "a method of gathering and preserving historical information in spoken form."[3]

History in its broadest definition is our collective memory of the past. Since the days of the Greek Herodotus, historians have quizzed knowledgeable persons about their firsthand understanding of events. An eyewitness account of an event is still one of the most interesting forms of journalism. In 1558, Bernardino de Sahagún, a Franciscan missionary to Mexico, brought together several Indians reputed to have the best knowledge of Aztec lore so that he and his assistants could interview them at length and record their memories. That may have been the first set of oral history interviews in North America. Since then, many reminiscences have been collected. Some of the most successful were the federal government's efforts in the Great Depression to record the memories of rural folk in the South, both former slaves and poor whites. However, the oral history movement as we know it today began in 1948, when Professor Allan Nevins launched his Oral History Project at Columbia University.

Nevins, known as "the Father of Oral History," had long been concerned that valuable historical information was slipping away because no one was systematically interviewing people who had made an impact on politics, business, the professions, and other fields. In 1948, Frederic Bancroft, a friend of Nevins and one of Columbia University's earliest Ph.D.'s, gave his alma mater $1.5 million to acquire new materials in American history; of that, $3,000 was earmarked for Nevins's pet project, oral history. Initially notes were taken in longhand, but Nevins soon began to work with a wire recorder. Soon, tape replaced wire, portable recorders the bulky heavier ones, and cassettes the reels.

Nevins continued his interviewing with a series of special projects at Columbia University. In 1950–52, he and Ernest Hill produced four thousand pages of memoirs of radio's early announcers, program directors, technicians, and executives. A few months later, at the Ford Archives in Dearborn, Michigan, a large industrial oral history project about Henry Ford and his automobile empire generated twenty-six thousand pages of material and a three-volume history of the Ford Motor Company. In 1951, Nevins started a special project on oil wildcatting in Texas, and a year later William Owens began the University of Texas's history of the oil industry. About the same time, the Forest History Society began its program. In 1954, the University of California, Berkeley, established the first regional oral history office, followed in 1959 by a program at the University of California, Los Angeles. Programs in New York, Texas, and California remain in the forefront of oral history, but offices, projects, and programs in many other states have followed their lead.

At first, oral history was seen primarily as a means of collecting nontraditional source materials for future historians to use. Little emphasis was placed on dissemination of information. Access to tapes and transcripts was often heavily restricted or closed until the death of the informant. By the 1960s, however, this had changed. In 1961, the Columbia Oral History Project published its first catalogue and published its first report. In addition to greatly increasing the collection's usefulness, this widely circulated document helped publicize the value of oral interviews as tools for the collection and preservation of history.

By the 1970s, oral history also became a tool for "new social history." Educators, feminists, and activists used the tape-recorded interview to "describe and empower the nonliterate and historically disenfranchised."[4] The 1976 Bicentennial celebrations sparked further interest in interviewing for family, ethnic, local, and regional history. Dozens of groups, from libraries and historical societies to corporations and labor unions, began their own programs. In 1965, 90 projects were underway in the United States. A decade later that number had almost quadrupled with an additional 165 projects in progress outside the United States, representing every continent.

In the 1980s, the collection, preserving, and processing of interviews continued, but the emphasis had turned to wider accessibility and use. Innovative projects for drama, multimedia exhibits, popular publications, radio, and television are being funded by public and private agencies. Gerontologists are exploring the therapeutic value for senior citizens. There is increased concern that high standards be met in the quality of tapes produced, both in sound and in content, and that ethical practices be stringently observed. In 1980, the Wingspread Conference sponsored by the Johnson Foundation in Racine, Wisconsin, produced evaluation guidelines for oral history work, providing standards "for the evaluation of existing efforts and guidance in the establishment of new programs."[5]

New technology has made possible microforms and computerized finding aids, and good software for the word processing of transcripts, catalogues, and guides. Full-length books, dramas, and movies have been produced based on oral history. Oral history collections are now a respected and valued part of many university and institutional libraries, with subject files in just about every topic of study (for example, immigration, economic development, political history, folklore, social history, working-class history, agriculture, arts, aviation, industry, finance, education, housing, urban affairs, international affairs, diplomacy, journalism, publishing, literature, labor, law, medicine, science, military affairs, politics, public affairs, the popular arts, religion, social activism, civil rights, women, and pioneers).

Since its foundation in 1967, the Oral History Association has provided invaluable service to all those interested in any aspect of the movement, producing newsletters, directories, workshops, the annual *Oral History Review*, and other publications. Several state and three regional associations (including the Southwest Oral History Association) have been created, as well as an international association, each with its own program and publications. Today there is a broad awareness that the systematic recording of memories is as vital a source for history as written documents, if the record is produced and used with all the circumspection that historical methodology demands. Oral history has come of age. As Louis Starr, Nevins's successor at the Columbia Oral History Project, observed, oral history "draws vigor from a lively sense of mission, a strong professional association, and a future that excites imaginations in half a dozen disciplines."[6]

Oral History in Arizona

Serious attempts at collecting Arizona memories began in the 1920s and early 1930s and were directed primarily at territorial pioneers, those Anglo settlers who had arrived in Arizona before statehood was achieved in 1912. For example, Edith Stratton Kitt, the energetic longtime secretary of the Arizona Pioneers' Historical Society in Tucson, began in the late 1920s to interview the "survivors of pioneer times," whom she encouraged to drop into the Historical Society office and sit for an interview.[7] In addition, Mrs. Kitt herself made trips to outlying parts of the state just to collect reminiscences. Many of those interviews were converted to biographical sketches, although some handwritten original notes do remain. Others, too, did monumental duty in preserving early biographical memories: the first territorial historian Sharlot Hall and her successors, Senator Carl Hayden, the Daughters of the American Revolution, the federally funded W.P.A. writing projects, and some archaeologists and ethnologists concerned with preserving Indian lore.

In 1949, the year after Nevins began his project at Columbia, Odd S. Halseth, the first director of the Pueblo Grande Museum in Phoenix, interviewed eminent archaeologist-ethnologist Frederick Webb Hodge while he was director of the Southwest Museum in Los Angeles. In the early 1950s, there were a few other individual interviews, but mostly those early tapes, a mere handful, were of Indian dances or interpretive talks at some of the national parks and monuments. A large collection at the University of Arizona Library is the LARITA Collection (Lewis Audio Visual Research Institute and Teaching Archive) with more than seven hundred and fifty tapes, each fifteen to thirty minutes. The format is not actually that of an oral history interview but more like a radio talk show with Charles Lewis recording an unstructured interview with various well-known personalities who were visiting in Tucson or elsewhere in Arizona. Most of the celebrities are not Arizonans.

During the 1970s, the sponsoring organizations doing oral history became more varied, ranging from the National Park Service, historical societies, and history and anthropology professors to city and county libraries, the Lowell Observatory, Pima Air Museum, and the Verde Valley Horseman's Club. One large collection produced in the 1970s is some four hundred and fifty video tapes for the Center for Creative Photography at the University of Arizona. In the 1980s, few organized special projects are concentrating on a specific topic. Most interviews are still the "salvage" type, taping the old-timers. Some of the better-known special projects of the 1980s include Women in Arizona, Women and Work, the Peoria School District, the Tucson Railroad Project, and a History of the Legal Profession in Arizona.

Despite these efforts, oral history in Arizona has developed slowly and sporadically, and the collections are beset with problems. Only a few tapes were created in the 1950s, and a few more in the 1960s. Even now, in 1987, there are fewer than six thousand known reels and cassettes. Of that total, many are not oral history, but simply recordings on tape of lectures, speeches, or radio talk shows and programs. Many are duplicates of tapes created and deposited elsewhere such as those of the Doris Duke Indian Collection (copies at the Arizona State Museum in Tucson) and the University of New Mexico's Louis Blachly Pioneer Tapes (copies in Special Collections at the University of Arizona).

Each of the state's three major universities, Northern Arizona University, Arizona State University, and the University of Arizona, has an oral history collection, consisting of a combination of wire recordings, records, and cassette tapes. Collections at the four branch museums of the Arizona Historical Society—Tucson, Phoenix, Yuma, and Flagstaff—were created through projects sponsored by each division. Only a few collections have been created by trained professionals. Most interviews have been conducted by volunteers, by researchers for their own work, or by students for classroom projects.

It is fortunate that some good early information about Arizona has been preserved in this manner. However, there are major problems. The tape collections are of uneven quality both in content and technique. Some are clear, static-free, well-conducted interviews, but others are of very poor quality. The techniques used are often unrefined, especially in the earlier decades of gathering; most collections are only partially transcribed; and many do not have adequate finding aids for public access. A major obstacle is the lack of a guide or catalogue to the various collections of oral history tapes dealing with Arizona's history. Consequently, the tapes are practically never used. One step in the right direction is the inclusion of approximately a dozen collections in Arizona in a directory published in 1986 by the Southwest Oral History Association, *Guide to Oral History Collections in the Southwest Region.* However, the major repositories, such as the three universities, are not represented.

Oral history has not had a high priority for any of the major historical and educational institutions in the state, and many of the existing collections have not been properly stored or processed. In too many cases, the tapes have been stuck into a file cabinet and forgotten. However, within the last three years several repositories have made a sincere effort to conserve and process their collections.

Toward the Centennial

As Arizona enters the last decade of the twentieth century and moves toward its hundredth birthday in 2012, why should we be concerned with preserving the memories of the nineteenth and twentieth centuries? Even if we recognize the value of history in our lives, are there not more than enough written materials in this age of paper proliferation to document any writing about our national life? What new dimensions can oral history provide? Oral history, properly used, supplements in a number of ways the goal of all historical knowledge—helping us lead richer lives.

As primary source material, oral history tapes can, first of all, fill the informational gaps left by the increasing dearth of private letters, diaries, and other personal documents. Information can be gathered about tangible cultural artifacts (buildings, equipment and tools, furniture and decorative items, and clothing) and about the processes that created those items. As such information is collected from a wide segment of our population, the objects or material culture take on added meaning and offer glimpses into life in the past which provide us with a greater sense of continuity and worth.

Arizona's population will grow to over 6.2 million by 2012, partly through continued emigration from other states and from Mexico. These new arrivals will undoubtedly introduce changes in the existing political power structures, and in the size and cultural character of Arizona's towns and cities. Oral history helps us understand the human behavior associated with such demographic and social changes. Individuals from these groups can give us their individual firsthand accounts of what happened and share their feelings. This record of our feelings is as important as the simple facts that outline a situation.

Arizona's sizable Native American and Hispanic populations enjoy rich, lengthy historical heritages. It is vital that we understand how these groups as well as the state's other ethnic minorities (such as Asian Americans and Blacks) have either solved or failed to solve their problems in the past, how they have reckoned with change, how they are endeavoring to make better lives for themselves and their children, and how they compare their past experiences to their present situations. Oral history makes possible a better understanding of the largely unrecorded views of our citizens.

Oral history, in order to be a useful tool, must be a high priority. We must begin now to correct the deficiencies. It is not enough to create tapes. To be useful the tapes must be accessible. Guides must be produced, preferably annotated ones that will give researchers and other users enough information to determine which tapes to listen to. Ideally, all significant usable tapes will be transcribed completely. An interim, less costly, step would be abstracting each tape, giving concise chronological information so that its significant contents can be quickly determined and made available.

We need an organization to pull together the many groups and individuals who have collections or who are now creating collections. A clearing house is needed to disseminate information, encourage cooperation, and open communication.

Key Arizona leaders need to be convinced that oral history is valuable. They should give it high priority. Perhaps the governor could establish an Oral History Commission to promote and assist the development of oral history programs throughout the state. In this way, hundreds of oral history interviews could be collected, not just with older people, but with active business and civic leaders who have observed and participated in recent changes in communities and in the state. Every county could have an organization that would coordinate projects to reach a cross-section of the population.

Adequate funding and systematic training are two requirements for such a program. A grant program could provide financial assistance to qualified institutions and individuals. A state commission could give guidance in the choice and planning of special projects particularly significant to Arizonans. An organized program, facilitated through city and county libraries as well as our major educational institutions, could train and equip volunteer interviewers. A newsletter could be published, and statewide conferences could be sponsored. These continuing activities could educate and provide an ongoing opportunity for oral history practitioners to discuss common concerns.

Oral history would then capture the rich variety of memories now being irretrievably lost. We need that personal and individual history to understand better what our past is; how fact and folklore have mixed; how Arizonans came to make certain choices about their families, their lifestyles, and their communities' growth and development that are affecting us now; who we twentieth-century Arizonans are; and ultimately why we are approaching our centennial in the ways we are.

Notes

1. Waddy W. Moore, "The Wingspread Criteria and the Arkansas Nurses Project," *Oral History Review* 14 (1986): 51.
2. Alice Hoffman, "Reliability and Validity in Oral History," in *Oral History: An Interdisciplinary Anthology,* ed. David K. Dunaway and Willa K. Baum (Nashville: AASLH, 1984), 68.
3. "Goals, Guidelines, and Evaluation Criteria of the Oral History Association," in *Oral History: An Interdisciplinary Anthology,* ed. Dunaway and Baum, 415.
4. David K. Dunaway and Willa K. Baum, eds., *Oral History: An Interdisciplinary Anthology* (Nashville: AASLH, 1984), xiii.
5. William W. Moss, *Oral History: Evaluation Guidelines* (Oral History Associaton, Inc., 1980), foreword.
6. Louis Starr, "Oral History," in *Oral History: An Interdisciplinary Anthology,* ed. Dunaway and Baum, 21.
7. C. L. Sonnichsen, *Pioneer Heritage* (Tucson: Arizona Historical Society, 1984), 92.

ABOUT THE
CONTRIBUTORS

ROGER ALAN BREVOORT is the Architectural Historian with the Arizona State Historic Preservation Office. He has worked as a historic preservation consultant for the Rockingham Planning Commission, Exeter, N.H.; the New Hampshire State Historic Preservation Office; and the University of New Hampshire.

RICHARD W. ETULAIN is Professor of History at the University of New Mexico. His major publications include *Owen Wister; The Popular Western; The Frontier and American West; Jack London on the Road;* and *The American Literary West.* His most recent books are *Fifty Western Writers; Conversations with Wallace Stegner on Western History and Literature; Faith and Imagination: Essays on Evangelicals and Literature;* and *Western Films: A Brief History.* He has served as editor of the *New Mexico Historical Review.*

DAVID HOOBER has been Arizona's State Archivist since November 1985. Before taking that post, he was archivist and curator of manuscripts for the Nebraska Historical Society and for the Arizona Historical Society. He is a member of the national council of the American Association for State and Local History and a member of the board of the National Historical Publications and Records Commission.

JOHN IRWIN is Associate Director for Public Services at the Flagstaff City–Coconino County Public Library, where he is currently developing a records management program and archives for the City of Flagstaff. He has worked in the archives of the Nebraska Historical Society and was the Special Collections Librarian and Archivist at Northern Arizona University. In 1982–83 he served as consultant to the Arizona Department of Library, Archives and Public Records and prepared the publication *Preserving Arizona's Historical Records: The Final Report of the Arizona Historical Needs and Assessment Project.*

PETER IVERSON is Coordinator, Social and Behavioral Sciences, Arizona State University West. Until 1986, he taught history at the University of Wyoming, where he was professor and chair of the History Department. He has also taught at Arizona State University and at Navajo Community College. His books include *The Plains Indians of the 20th Century; Carlos Montezuma and the Changing World of American Indians; The Navajo Nation;* and *The Navajos: A Critical Bibliography.* He is now working on *The Plains Indians: A History* and *Cowboys and Indians in the Modern West.* In 1984 the Navajo Nation presented him with the Chief Manuelito Appreciation Award for Contributions to Navajo Education.

BETH LUEY is Senior Lecturer and Co-Director of the Public History Program at Arizona State University. She is the author of *Handbook for Academic Authors* and of several articles on scholarly publishing. Her current projects include an annotated bibliography on scholarly editing to be published by the Association for Documentary Editing and, with Noel Stowe, a history of the accounting profession in Arizona.

OSCAR J. MARTÍNEZ is Professor of History and Director of the Center for Inter-American and Border Studies at the University of Texas at El Paso. His publications include *Border Boom Town: Ciudad Juárez Since 1848; Fragments of the Mexican Revolution; The Chicanos of El Paso; Across Boundaries: Transborder Interaction in Comparative Perspective;* and *Troublesome Border: U.S.-Mexico Borderlands Issues Through Time.* He is president of the Association of Borderlands Scholars.

GERALD D. NASH is Presidential Professor of History at the University of New Mexico, where he has served as chair of the History Department. His books include *Issues in American Economic History; U.S. Oil Policy, 1890–1964; Perspectives on Administration: History; The Great Transition: A History of 20th Century America; The American West in the 20th Century; The Great Depression and World War II;*

and *The American West Transformed: The Impact of the Second World War.* He was editor of *The Historian* for ten years.

KAREN L. SMITH is Manager of the Archives Department of the Salt River Project. She is the author of *The Magnificent Experiment: Building the Salt River Reclamation Project, 1890–1917* and of "The Campaign for Water in Central Arizona, 1890–1903," *Arizona and the West* 23 (Summer 1981). She was the research coordinator for the Phoenix History Project and director of Discovering Early Phoenix for the Phoenix Historical Society.

NOEL J. STOWE is Assistant Dean of the Graduate College of Arizona State University and Co-Director of the Public History Program. He has published research on the history of California and Mexico, and in public history. With G. Wesley Johnson, he is the editor of a special issue on public history curriculum development of *The Public Historian* and is writing a history of accounting in Arizona with Beth Luey. In 1985–86 he was chair of the National Council on Public History.

REBA N. WELLS is Assistant Director and Chief Curator of the Arizona Historical Society/Phoenix. She has worked as a historical consultant on preservation, archival, museum, and restoration projects in Phoenix, Yuma, Cochise County, Florence, and Sun City. She is working on a book on the San Bernardino Valley and on a monograph on Mary Velásquez Riley, matriarch of the White Mountain Apache Tribe.

INDEX